THIRD EDITION

Physical Best
Activity Guide

Elementary Level

Physical Best Activity Guide

Elementary Level

National Association for
Sport and Physical Education

*an association of the American Alliance for Health,
Physical Education, Recreation and Dance*

Human Kinetics

Library of Congress Cataloging-in-Publication Data

Physical Best (Program)
 Physical Best activity guide : elementary level / National Association for Sport and Physical Education. -- 3rd ed.
   p. cm.
 Includes bibliographical references.
 ISBN-13: 978-0-7360-8117-7 (soft cover)
 ISBN-10: 0-7360-8117-8 (soft cover)
 1. Physical education and training--Study and teaching (Elementary)--United States. I. National Association for Sport and Physical Education. II. Title.
 GV365.P5 2011
 372.86--dc22
                    2010034115

ISBN-10: 0-7360-8117-8
ISBN-13: 978-0-7360-8117-7

The Web addresses cited in this text were current as of October 2010, unless otherwise noted.

Acquisitions Editors: Scott Wikgren and Sarajane Quinn; **Developmental Editor:** Ragen E. Sanner; **Assistant Editor:** Anne Rumery; **Copyeditor:** Robert Replinger; **Permission Manager:** Dalene Reeder; **Graphic Designer:** Joe Buck; **Graphic Artist:** Dawn Sills; **Cover Designer:** Keith Blomberg; **CD Face Designer:** Susan Rothermel Allen; **Photographer (cover):** © Human Kinetics; **Photographer (interior):** © Human Kinetics, unless otherwise noted; **Art Manager:** Kelly Hendren; **Associate Art Manager:** Alan L. Wilborn; **Illustrator:** © Human Kinetics; **Printer:** Versa Press

Printed in the United States of America   10 9 8 7 6 5 4

The paper in this book is certified under a sustainable forestry program.

Human Kinetics
Web site: www.HumanKinetics.com

United States: Human Kinetics
P.O. Box 5076
Champaign, IL 61825-5076
800-747-4457
e-mail: humank@hkusa.com

Canada: Human Kinetics
475 Devonshire Road Unit 100
Windsor, ON N8Y 2L5
800-465-7301 (in Canada only)
e-mail: info@hkcanada.com

Europe: Human Kinetics
107 Bradford Road
Stanningley
Leeds LS28 6AT, United Kingdom
+44 (0) 113 255 5665
e-mail: hk@hkeurope.com

Australia: Human Kinetics
57A Price Avenue
Lower Mitcham, South Australia 5062
08 8372 0999
e-mail: info@hkaustralia.com

New Zealand: Human Kinetics
P.O. Box 80
Torrens Park, South Australia 5062
0800 222 062
e-mail: info@hknewzealand.com

E4737

CONTENTS

ACTIVITY AND REPRODUCIBLES FINDER

Activity number	Activity title	Activity page	Concept	Primary	Intermediate	Reproducibles (on CD-ROM)
3.1	Aerobic Movements	31	Aerobic fitness	•		Aerobic Cards
3.2	Frantic Ball	34	Aerobic fitness		•	Frantic Ball Worksheet
3.3	Artery Avengers	36	Physical activity	•		Artery Avenger Assessment Sheet
3.4	Endurance Matchup	38	Health benefits	•		Aerobic Benefit Card
						Aerobic Benefit Puzzle
						Endurance Minutes Take-Home Worksheet
3.5	Treasure Island	40	Health benefits		•	Healthy Money Bills
3.6	Powerball Hunt	42	Warm-up and cool-down	•		Locomotor Movement Cards
						Number Cards
3.7	You Should Be Dancing	45	Warm-up and cool-down		•	Dance Step Signs
						Dance Step Descriptions
3.8	Aerobic Activity Picture Chart	47	Frequency	•		Aerobic Activity Picture Chart
3.9	Fing Fang Fooey	49	Frequency		•	Aerobic Activity Fitness Log
3.10	Animal Locomotion	51	Intensity	•		Animal Locomotion Task Signs
3.11	Jumping Frenzy	54	Intensity		•	Jumping Frenzy Instruction Cards
						Am I Giving My Heart a Workout? Chart
3.12	Around the Block	57	Time	•	•	Around the Block Timed Activity
						Around the Block Home Worksheet
						Am I Giving My Heart a Workout? Chart
3.13	Musical Sport Sequence	60	Time	•		Time Your Activity Worksheet
3.14	Six-Minute Jog	63	Time		•	Six-Minute Jogging Record Sheet
						Aerobic: Yes or No?
3.15	Aerobic Scooters	66	Type	•		Scooter Station Signs
						Am I Giving My Heart a Workout? Chart
						Aerobic: Yes or No?
3.16	Aerobic Sports	69	Type		•	Aerobic Sport Station Signs
						Physical Activity Pyramid for Children
3.17	Aerobic FITT Log	71	Overload principle		•	FITT Log
						FITT Log Worksheet

(continued)

Activity Finder *(continued)*

Activity number	Activity title	Activity page	Concept	Primary	Intermediate	Reproducibles (on CD-ROM)
4.1	Hit the Deck	80	Muscular strength and endurance	•		Hit the Deck Exercise Cards
4.2	Muscle Hustle	82	Muscular strength and endurance		•	Muscle Hustle Station Signs
						Muscle Hustle Scoresheet
4.3	Super Hero Muscles	85	Health benefits		•	Muscular Strength and Endurance Benefit Sheet
						Super Hero Muscles Puzzle Pieces
						Super Hero Cards
4.4	Sport Roundup	88	Health benefits		•	Sport Roundup Station Cards
						Muscular Strength and Endurance Health Benefit Cards
						Sport Roundup Task Sheet
4.5	Opposing Force	92	Frequency	•		Exercise Picture Chart for Runner
						Exercise Picture Chart for Sitter
4.6	Muscular Strength and Endurance Activity Log	95	Frequency		•	Muscular Strength and Endurance Activity Log
4.7	Animal Tag	97	Intensity	•		Animal Cards
						You Are It! Cards
4.8	Survivor Course	100	Intensity		•	Survivor Course Station Signs
						My Intensity Training
4.9	Time Your Workout	102	Repetition and time	•		Practicing Sets and Reps and Learning About Time
						Set and Reps Chart
4.10	Clean the Beach	105	Specificity	•		None
4.11	Shuffle and Hustle	107	Specificity		•	Shuffle and Hustle Suit Posters
4.12	Push-Up Curl-Up Challenge	109	Progression		•	Push-Up Challenge Poster
						Curl-Up Challenge Poster
						Push-Up Curl-Up Challenge Log
4.13	Stability Progression	112	Progression		•	Push-Up Progression With a Stability Ball
						Curl-Up Progression With a Stability Ball
						Push-Up and Curl-Up Challenge Handout
4.14	Lower-Body Challenge	115	Specificity	•	•	Lower-Body Challenge: Teacher's Guide for Station Setup and Utilization
						Lower-Body Challenge Station Level 1 Signs
						Lower-Body Challenge Station Level 2 Signs

Activity number	Activity title	Activity page	Concept	Primary	Intermediate	Reproducibles (on CD-ROM)
4.15	Upper-Body Challenge	119	Specificity	•	•	Upper-Body Challenge: Teacher's Guide for Station Setup and Utilization
						Upper-Body Challenge Station Level 1 Signs
						Upper-Body Challenge Station Level 2 Signs
4.16	Muscular Strength and Endurance FITT Log	123	Progression		•	FITT Log
						FITT Log Worksheet
5.1	You Can Bend	132	Flexibility	•		You Can Bend Pictures
						You Can Bend Homework Worksheet
5.2	Flexible Fun	135	Flexibility		•	Definition Cards
5.3	Beginning Yoga Poses	138	Health benefits	•		Beginning Yoga Pose Signs
						Flexibility Health Benefits Poster
5.4	Intermediate Yoga Poses	140	Health benefits		•	Intermediate Yoga Pose Signs
						Flexibility Health Benefits Poster
5.5	Stability Ball With Flexibility	142	Warm-up	•		Stability Ball Exercise Pictures
5.6	Stretching Out Tag	145	Warm-up and cool-down		•	Warm-Up Wall Chart
						Warm-Up Station Signs
						Static Stretching Exercise Signs
						Cool-Down Wall Chart
5.7	Flexibility Activity Picture Chart	149	Frequency	•		Flexibility Activity Picture Chart
5.8	Towel Stretching for Flexibility	151	Frequency		•	Towel Stretching for Flexibility Sign
						Towel Stretches for the Day Homework
						Towel Stretching for Flexibility Log
5.9	Caterpillar Stretch	154	Intensity	•		Human Caterpillar Picture
5.10	At Least 10 Leopard Cats	157	Time	•		Stretching Reminders
						At Least 10 Leopard Cats Sign
						At Least 10 Leopard Cats Stretch Signs
5.11	Roll the Stretch	159	Specificity, or type	•	•	Stretching Picture Sign (Primary)
						Stretching Picture Sign (Intermediate)
						Roll the Stretch Assessment Rubric
5.12	Stretch Marks the Spot	161	Specificity, or type		•	Stretch Activity Station Signs
						Stretch Activity Worksheet
						Stretch Evaluation Sheet

(continued)

Activity Finder   *(continued)*

Activity number	Activity title	Activity page	Concept	Primary	Intermediate	Reproducibles (on CD-ROM)
5.13	Flexibility FITT Log	163	Progression		•	FITT Log
						FITT Log Worksheet
6.1	Maintaining Balance	171	Body composition	•		Body Composition Benefit Signs
6.2	Disc Golf and Body Composition	173	Body composition		•	Body Composition Fact Cards
6.3	Activity Time	175	Health benefits	•		Clock Illustration
6.4	Activity Pyramid Circuit	177	Health benefits		•	Physical Activity Pyramid for Children
						Activity Pyramid Cards
						Activity Pyramid Match Cards
						Check Your Activity Pyramid Worksheet
6.5	Brown Bag Dinner	180	MyPyramid	•		MyPyramid Poster
						Food Pictures
6.6	Getting Nutrients	183	Nutrients		•	Nutrient Wall Signs
						Fuel Up the Body Homework Sheet
6.7	Hoop It Up With Food	186	Nutrition	•		Hoop It Up With Food Pictures
						MyPyramid Poster
						Hoop Cards
						Fill Your Plate Homework Sheet
6.8	A Variety of Protein	189	Nutrition		•	Protein Food Pictures
						Select Your Protein Homework Sheet
6.9	Calorie Burn-Up	191	Metabolism	•		None
6.10	Metabolism Medley	194	Metabolism		•	Physical Activity Pyramid for Children
6.11	Bowl a Snack	196	Body composition and nutrition	•		Paper Food
7.1	Fitness Tag	201	Fitness components	•		Fitness Tag Exercise Posters
						Health-Related Fitness Definition Posters
7.2	Fitness Four-Square	204	Specificity		•	Fitness Four-Square Exercise Cards
7.3	Mixing Fitness and Nutrition	207	Nutrition		•	Mixing Fitness and Nutrition Stretching Exercises Signs
						Nutrient Wall Signs
						Mixing Fitness and Nutrition Home Activity Sheet
7.4	Making Muscles	210	Specificity		•	Making Muscles Signs
						Muscle Muscles Signs (Labeled)
						Making Muscles Station Signs
						Making Muscles Home Extension Worksheet

Activity number	Activity title	Activity page	Concept	Primary	Intermediate	Reproducibles (on CD-ROM)
7.5	Total-Body Workout	213	FITT principle		•	Total-Body Challenge Extension
7.6	Roll the Dice Fitness Routine	217	Balanced workout		•	Roll the Dice Signs
						At Work and at Play Handout
7.7	Mini Triathlon	220	Pacing		•	Pacing Your Mini Triathlon Record Sheet
						Am I Giving My Heart a Workout? Chart
7.8	Blackout Fitness Bingo	223	Total fitness workout		•	Blackout Fitness Bingo Card
8.1	World Fitness	228	Developing fitness areas		•	World Fitness Station Signs
8.2	Rake the Leaves	230	Benefits of fitness	•		Aerobic Fitness Health Benefits Poster
8.3	Family Fun Night Circuit	233	Benefits of activity and risk factors of inactivity	•	•	Letter Home to Guardians
						Family Fun Night Circuit Station Signs
						Risk Factor Cards
						Family Fun Night Circuit Questionnaire
8.4	Fitness Frenzy With Partners	236	Specificity of exercises		•	Fitness Frenzy With Partners Signs
						Fitness Frenzy With Partners Worksheet
8.5	Risk Factor Mania	238	Aerobic fitness		•	Heart Health Risk Factor Cards
						Am I Giving My Heart a Workout? Chart
8.6	Up and Down With Jump Ropes	242	Aerobic fitness and flexibility	•	•	Exercise Cards
8.7	Heart Smart Orienteering	244	Aerobic fitness and FITT		•	Orienteering Master Sheet
						Heart Smart Orienteering Questions Cards
						FITT Homework Assignment
8.8	March Into Fitness	247	FITT principles		•	March Into Fitness Station Signs
						Am I Giving My Heart a Workout? Chart
8.9	Exercise Your Rights Day	250	Schoolwide exercise	•	•	Exercise Your Rights Cards
						Health Benefits Signs
						Exercise Your Rights Letter to Guardians
8.10	Energize With Exercise	253	Cooperative learning	•	•	Energize With Exercise Routine
8.11	Marvelous Muscles for Summer	256	Specificity		•	Marvelous Muscles for Summer Station Signs
						Muscle Diagrams
8.12	Dash for Cash	258	Health-related fitness components	•	•	Dash for Cash Fitness Station Signs
8.13	Summer Fun–Summer Shape-Up Challenge	261	FITT principles	•	•	Summer Fun–Summer Shape-Up Challenge Activity Sheet

Additional Handouts

Chapter	Page	Concept	Reproducibles (on CD-ROM)
2	13	Total fitness	Building Physical Fitness
2	14	Principles of training	Principles of Training Poster
2	17	FITT guidelines	FITT Guidelines
2	20	Goals	Goal-Setting Worksheet
3	29	Aerobic fitness	Becoming Your Physical Best: Aerobic Fitness Newsletter
4	78	Muscular strength and endurance	Becoming Your Physical Best: Muscular Strength and Endurance Newsletter
5	130	Flexibility	Becoming Your Physical Best: Flexibility Newsletter
6	169	Body composition	Becoming Your Physical Best: Body Composition Newsletter
6	170	Body composition	Physical Activity Pyramid
6	170	Body composition	MyPyramid
8	226	Building blocks of fitness	ABCs of Fitness

PREFACE

This guide contains information that you need to help kindergarten through fifth grade students gain the knowledge, skills, appreciation, and confidence to lead physically active, healthy lives. The easy-to-use instructional activities have been developed and used successfully by physical educators across the United States. You will find competitive and noncompetitive activities, demanding and less demanding activities, and activities that allow maximum time on task.

ABOUT PHYSICAL BEST

Physical Best is a comprehensive health-related fitness education program developed by physical educators for physical educators. Physical Best was designed to educate, challenge, and encourage all children in the knowledge, skills, and attitudes that they need for a healthy and fit life. The goal of the program is to help students move from dependence to independence and responsibility for their own health and fitness by promoting regular, enjoyable physical activity. The purpose of Physical Best is to educate *all* children, regardless of athletic talent and physical and mental abilities. Physical Best implements this goal through quality resources and professional development workshops for physical educators. Physical Best is a program of the National Association for Sport and Physical Education (NASPE), a nonprofit membership organization of over 15,000 professionals in the sport and physical education fields. NASPE, an association of the American Alliance for Health, Physical Education, Recreation and Dance, is dedicated to strengthening basic knowledge about healthy lifestyles among professionals and the public. Putting that knowledge into action in schools and communities across the nation is critical to improved academic performance, social reform, and the health of individuals.

OVERVIEW OF PHYSICAL BEST RESOURCES

New to this edition will be suggestions found within various activities for incorporating special types of equipment such as heart rate monitors, stability balls, and stretch bands. A new chapter titled "Combined-Component Training" has been added to help you integrate all aspects of fitness in activities. Also new to this edition is an appendix which lists Internet resources to use when developing special fitness events.

Above all, the activities are designed to be educational and fun! Packaged with the book is a CD-ROM that contains reproducible charts, posters, and handouts that accompany the activities of the third edition. Editable versions of some of the worksheets have been included.

This book has two companion resources:

▶ *Physical Education for Lifelong Fitness: The Physical Best Teacher's Guide, Third Edition* is a comprehensive guide to incorporating health-related fitness and lifetime physical activity into physical education programs. The guide provides a conceptual framework based on recent research, covering topics such as behavior, motivation and goal setting, health-related fitness curriculum development and teaching methods, components and principles of fitness, and inclusion in health-related fitness and health-related fitness assessment. The guide also contains a wealth of practical information and examples from experienced physical educators. The third edition has streamlined and reorganized many of the chapters; added practical information, a glossary, and resources for physical educators; and updated information and references throughout the text.

▶ *Physical Best Activity Guide: Middle and High School Levels, Third Edition* is similar in scope to the elementary guide but is geared toward 6th- through 12th-grade students. The information is more in-depth and allows a deeper and richer understanding of the importance of daily physical activity. The middle school and high school level guide contains an additional section focused on personal health and fitness planning. This section provides students with an introduction to the skills needed to be physically active for life after they graduate from high school. Other features for the third edition include the addition of a CD-ROM containing printable materials that supplement the activities, many new activities in each chapter, and the continued inclusion of the activity chapter, titled "Combined-Component Training," that incorporates multiple health-related fitness components.

RELATED RESOURCES

During a typical school year, many educators use more than one program and a variety of teaching resources, overlapping different approaches on a day-to-day basis. With this in mind, it may be reassuring to know that although Physical Best is designed to be used independently for teaching health-related fitness, the following resources can be used in conjunction with the Physical Best program. *Fitnessgram/Activitygram*, *Fitness for Life*, and the NASPE products listed in this section are suggested resources to complement Physical Best.

Fitnessgram/Activitygram

Fitnessgram/Activitygram (developed by the Cooper Institute) is a comprehensive health-related fitness and activity assessment as well as a computerized reporting system. All elements within *Fitnessgram/Activitygram* are designed to assist teachers in accomplishing the primary objective of youth fitness programs, which is to help students establish physical activity as a part of their daily lives.

Fitnessgram/Activitygram is based on a belief that extremely high levels of physical fitness, while admirable, are not necessary to accomplish objectives associated with good health and improved

function. All children need to have adequate levels of activity and fitness. *Fitnessgram/Activitygram* is designed to help all children and youth achieve a level of activity and fitness associated with good health, growth, and function.

Fitnessgram/Activitygram resources are published and available through Human Kinetics, as are the materials for the Brockport Physical Fitness Test, a health-related fitness assessment for students with disabilities.

Fitness for Life

Fitness for Life is a comprehensive K through 12 program designed to promote lifelong healthy lifestyles and associated health-related physical fitness, wellness, and other health benefits. The high school text, *Fitness for Life* (updated 5th ed.), was the first text for secondary personal fitness classes and earned a Texty Award for excellence. *Fitness for Life* has been shown to be effective in promoting physically active behavior after students finish school. *Fitness for Life: Middle School*, also a Texty Award winner, helps middle school students learn concepts of physical activity, fitness, nutrition, and wellness. Both texts are based on NASPE standards and have extensive ancillary packages to make teaching and learning easy and effective.

Fitness for Life: Elementary School, designed to be a significant part of the total school wellness program, features plug-and-play video activity routines for use in the classroom and in physical education classes. Guides for classroom teachers and school coordinators, as well as lesson plans for physical educators, are included along with DVD and CD resources. Students are active while learning important physical activity, fitness, and nutrition concepts. More than 28 activity routines and 160 videos containing grade-appropriate activities with nutrition and physical activity messages are included in the Fitness for Life: Elementary School program.

Both *Fitness for Life* and *Physical Best* are based on the HELP philosophy, which promotes **H**ealth for **E**veryone with a focus on **L**ifetime activity of a **P**ersonal nature. The two programs complement one another effectively, because the *Physical Best Activity Guides* (all levels) can be used before and after a *Fitness for Life* program, as well as during the program to provide supplemental activities. In fact, the two programs are so compatible that

Physical Best offers teacher training for *Fitness for Life* course instructors.

NASPE Resources

NASPE publishes many additional useful and related resources that are available by calling 800-321-0789 or online through the AAHPERD store at www.aahperd.org.

Quality Physical Education Resources

- ▶ *Moving Into the Future: National Standards for Physical Education, Second Edition* (2004). Stock No. 304-10275.
- ▶ *PE Metrics: Assessing the National Standards* (2008). Stock No. 304-10458.
- ▶ *Beyond Activities: Learning Experiences to Support the National Physical Education Standards: Elementary Volume* (2003). Stock No. 304-10265.
- ▶ *Beyond Activities: Learning Experiences to Support the National Physical Education Standards: Secondary Volume* (2003). Stock No. 304-10268.
- ▶ *Physical Activity for Children: A Statement of Guidelines for Children Ages 5–12* (2003). Stock No. 204-10276.
- ▶ *Active Start: A Statement of Physical Activity Guidelines for Children from Birth to Five Years* (2009). Stock No. 304-10488.
- ▶ *Active Kids and Academic Performance* (2010). Stock No. 304-10502.

Appropriate Practice Documents

- ▶ *Appropriate Practices in Movement Programs for Children Ages 3–5* (2009). Stock No. 304-10487.
- ▶ *Appropriate Instructional Practice Guidelines for Elementary School Physical Education* (2009). Stock No. 304-10465.
- ▶ *Appropriate Instructional Practice Guidelines for Middle School Physical Education* (2009). Stock No. 304-10464.
- ▶ *Appropriate Instructional Practice Guidelines for High School Physical Education* (2009). Stock No. 304-10471.
- ▶ *Appropriate Instructional Practice Guidelines for High Education Physical Activity Programs* (2009). Stock No. 304-10489.

Opportunity to Learn Documents

- ▶ *Opportunity to Learn Standards for Elementary Physical Education* (2009). Stock No. 304-10484.
- ▶ *Opportunity to Learn Standards for Middle Physical Education* (2009). Stock No. 304-10485.
- ▶ *Opportunity to Learn Standards for High School Physical Education* (2009). Stock No. 304-10486.

Assessment Series

Assorted titles relating to fitness and heart rate.

PHYSICAL BEST CERTIFICATION

Physical Best provides accurate, up-to-date information and training to help today's physical educators create a conceptual and integrated format for health-related fitness education within their programs. NASPE–AAHPERD offers a certification program that allows physical education teachers to become Physical Best Health–Fitness Specialists. The Physical Best certification has been created specifically for the purpose of updating physical educators on the most effective strategies for helping their students gain the knowledge, skills, appreciation, and confidence needed to lead physically active, healthy lives. It focuses on application—how to teach fitness concepts through developmentally and age-appropriate activities.

To earn certification through NASPE–AAHPERD as a Physical Best Health–Fitness Specialist, you will need to do the following:

- ▶ Attend the one-day Physical Best Health–Fitness Specialist Workshop.
- ▶ Read this book, as well as *Physical Education for Lifelong Fitness: The Physical Best Teacher's Guide, Third Edition,* and the *Fitnessgram/Activitygram Test Administration Manual.*
- ▶ Use the required resources mentioned earlier to complete an online examination.

For more information, call Physical Best at 800-213-7193.

ACKNOWLEDGMENTS

Many physical educators contributed their time and expertise to this project. Besides being grateful for the overall guidance of the Physical Best Steering Committee, NASPE would like to thank editors Laura Borsdorf and Lois A. Boeyink for their willingness to take on the challenge, for their creativity in writing, and for their perseverance which helped make this edition a reality; Sarajane Quinn for her continued guidance on the direction of this book and support in soliciting and providing ideas and experiences; Susan Schoenberg, NASPE's senior manager for professional services, for her in-house coordination, facilitation, editing, and support of the third edition, and Mary Ellen Aull for her tremendous assistance in organizing and assisting with the book development process for NASPE.

The following individuals contributed new activities or significant editorial input:

Second Edition Contributors

Ellen Abbadessa, Arizona

Brenda Belote, Virginia

Michael Bishoff, Maryland

Bill Brady, Virginia

Renee Butler, Missouri

Denise Chenoweth, Maryland

Susan Forman, Arizona

Jennie Gilbert, Illinois

Krista Gillette, New York

Linda Hatchett, Alabama

Colleen Porter Hearn, Virginia

Jill Humann, New Jersey

Melody Kyzer, North Carolina

Lauren Lieberman, New York

Michael Mason, Maryland

Carolyn Masterson, New Jersey

Joan Morrison, Maryland

Sally Nazelrod, Maryland

Carolyn Nelson, Ohio

Angie Odom, Missouri

Janice O'Donnell, New Hampshire

John Perna Jr., Maryland

Anthony Santillan, Arizona

Kim Sinkhorn, Ohio

Diane Tunnell, Washington

Lisa Weiland-Foster, Hawaii

Jeanine Wert, New York

Debbie Wilkinson, Arizona

Third Edition Contributors

Deborah Ballinger, Pennsylvania

Baltimore County Public Schools, Maryland

G. Bert, Washington

Lois Boeyink, Iowa

Laura Borsdorf, Pennsylvania

Mary Buddemeier, Maryland

Cathy Caldwell, Indiana

Charles Corbin, Arizona

Hal Cramer, Maryland

Charlene Darst, Arizona

Paul Darst, Arizona

Steffanie Engle, Maryland

Del Engstrom, Pennsylvania

Lorri Engstrom, Pennsylvania

Joanna Faerber, Louisianna

Bob Fitzpatrick

Catherine Galvin-Muti, New York

Jill Goldman, New Jersey

Linda Holloway, Florida

Carol Irwin, Tennessee

Connie Jander, Missouri

Pat Jones, Pennsylvania

Jane Keily, Wisconsin

Libby Leventry, Maryland

Louisiana AAHPERD

Maria Macarle, New York

Beth Marchione, Pennsylvania

Ray Martinez, Wisconsin

Gail Meyer, Iowa

Sally Nazelrod, Maryland

Kevin O'Brien, Ohio

Joel Paisley, Pennsylvania

Kristin Paisley, Pennsylvania

John Perna, Pennsylvania

Sara Jane Quinn, Maryland

Peter Rattigan, New Jersey

Jennifer Reeves, Arizona

Kelly Schattall, Maryland

Roberta Sipe, Indiana

Ellen Smith, Florida

Eric Vander Velden, Iowa

Kathy Wagner, Kansas

Gary Wojton

Susan Wunder, Maryland

We would also like to thank the many anonymous contributors who gave their time, creative ideas, and effort to this work.

PART 1

Introduction

OVERVIEW OF THE PRESIDENTIAL YOUTH FITNESS PROGRAM

The Presidential Youth Fitness Program (PYFP) is a voluntary program that includes a health-related assessment, as well as educational and motivational tools, to support educators and empower students to adopt an active lifestyle.

Launched in September 2012, PYFP offers a comprehensive school-based program that promotes physical activity and fitness for improving the health of America's young people.

PYFP is built around three pillars:

1. Professional development and education
2. Assessment
3. Recognition and awards

Although seemingly separate in nature, these pillars are linked by the expertise and contributions of the program's partners and their collective interest in equipping physical educators with the materials and information they need to deliver a high-quality, beneficial health-related fitness education experience to their students.

PYFP is built from a partnership of five organizations: American Alliance for Health, Physical Education, Recreation and Dance; Amateur Athletic Union; Centers for Disease Control and Prevention; The Cooper Institute; and President's Council on Fitness, Sports and Nutrition. These organizations came together with a goal to provide one national youth fitness test that focuses on health and equips educators with the resources and knowledge necessary for helping their students lead active lives.

The Three Pillars

Here is a closer look at the program's three pillars.

1. Professional development. PYFP will equip educators with the knowledge and tools required for implementing a high-quality fitness education experience for students and for promoting and engaging them in physical activity regardless of a school's physical education budget. That includes integrating elements of the Physical Best program, with access to resources to support the successful teaching of health-related fitness. Online and in-person training opportunities are available at www. presidentialyouthfitnessprogram.org.

2. Assessment. FITNESSGRAM® is the adopted assessment of PYFP. Developed in the early 1980s by The Cooper Institute, Fitnessgram includes a variety of health-related physical fitness assessments of aerobic capacity, muscle strength, muscle endurance and flexibility, and body composition. Scores from these assessments are compared to Healthy Fitness Zone® standards to determine students' overall physical fitness and to suggest areas for improvement when appropriate. Using Fitnessgram keeps the focus of fitness assessment on promoting and improving personal health rather than performance and athletic ability.

3. Recognition and awards. Providing an opportunity to recognize students for reaching personal fitness goals and physical activity behaviors is the final pillar of the Presidential Youth Fitness Program. Students who reach the Healthy Fitness Zone on at least five test items are eligible for the Presidential Youth Fitness Award. Understanding how to use recognition in a responsible manner that includes all students is a key part of the professional-development package. In addition, schools have the opportunity to be recognized for creating an environment that supports PYFP and physical activity, in general, as described through the development of comprehensive school physical activity plans (visit www.aahperd.org/cspap).

The three areas around which the program is built come together to provide a robust experience for teachers and their students.

Physical Best and the PYFP

Physical Best, including the teacher's guide and activity guides, complements PYFP's mission by providing the how and why of teaching health-related physical activity and fitness-enhancing skills and behaviors. The program's partners seek to provide a fun and beneficial experience for *all* youths, regardless of ability or health status.

This activity guide includes a variety of activities that can count toward a student's daily physical activity and, therefore, set him or her on a path to earning a Presidential Active Lifestyle Award (PALA+), one of the awards that make up the PYFP recognition pillar. *The Physical Best Teacher's Guide* provides more guidance and information on using the Presidential Youth Fitness Award.

For the latest resources and information on the Presidential Youth Fitness Program, visit www.presidentialyouthfitnessprogram.org.

Teaching Health-Related Fitness to Elementary School Students

Chapter Contents

To build a foundation in teaching health-related fitness activities, we look first to national standards. Many of the national standards that have been developed for physical education, health, and dance can be applied to teaching health-related fitness activities. In the first part of this chapter, we list the national standards from these areas and emphasize the standards that are addressed most often when teaching health-related fitness.

The chapter ends with a brief summary of how Physical Best can be incorporated in a physical education curriculum and a detailed look at the Physical Best activity template. All the activities in this book follow this template, and the explanations provided in this chapter will help you choose the right activity for a particular group of students. You can also use this template as a guide for developing your own activities.

NATIONAL STANDARDS FOR PHYSICAL EDUCATION

The national standards for physical education are based on the definition of the physically educated person as defined by *NASPE Outcomes of Quality Physical Education Programs* (NASPE, 1992). According to this document, a physically educated person

► has learned skills necessary to perform a variety of physical activities,

► is physically fit,

► participates regularly in physical activity,

► knows the implications of and the benefits from involvement in physical activities, and

► values physical activity and its contributions to a healthful lifestyle.

NASPE intended all five parts of the definition "not to be separated from each other" (NASPE, 1992). The definition was further delineated into 20 outcome statements. The definition and outcome statements were used as the basis for the development of the national standards for physical education, originally published by NASPE in 1995 and revised in 2004 (see the sidebar "National Standards for Physical Education"). The standards define what a student should know

NATIONAL STANDARDS FOR PHYSICAL EDUCATION

Physical activity is critical to the development and maintenance of good health. The goal of physical education is to develop physically educated individuals who have the knowledge, skills, and confidence to enjoy a lifetime of healthful physical activity. A physically educated person:

- **Standard 1**: Demonstrates competency in motor skills and movement patterns needed to perform a variety of physical activities.
- **Standard 2**: Demonstrates understanding of movement concepts, principles, strategies, and tactics as they apply to the learning and performance of physical activities.
- **Standard 3**: Participates regularly in physical activity.
- **Standard 4**: Achieves and maintains a health-enhancing level of physical fitness.
- **Standard 5**: Exhibits responsible personal and social behavior that respects self and others in physical activity settings.
- **Standard 6**: Values physical activity for health, enjoyment, challenge, self-expression, and/or social interaction.

From *Moving into the future: National standards for physical education* (2004) from the National Association for Sport and Physical Education (NASPE), 1900 Association Drive, Reston, VA 20191-1599.

and be able to do as a result of a quality physical education program. Although all standards are taught to some extent through and during health-related fitness education, two standards are emphasized:

► **Standard 3**: Participates regularly in physical activity.

► **Standard 4**: Achieves and maintains a health-enhancing level of physical fitness.

Integrating the national standards in physical education, health, and dance provides an important way to promote the effects of physical activity on health and an individual's personal choice to be physically active. None of these disciplines stands alone. Few student groups are focused on just one purpose, whether in health, competition, or aesthetics. Although some students have a greater interest in or a more facile learning style for one of these areas, all youngsters benefit from learning and applying these standards. The recognition of these interdisciplinary links helps us maximize our energies for teaching and learning essential content of all three disciplines

NATIONAL HEALTH EDUCATION STANDARDS

The national health education standards published in *Achieving Health Literacy* (Joint Committee on National Health Education Standards, 1995) are linked to the physical education standards. Health education affords unique knowledge about maintaining health, preventing disease, and reducing risk factors in all situations and settings—and it helps to influence behaviors that promote these aims. These goals relate not only to physical activity but also to other areas of personal, family, and community life.

Health standards 1, 3, and 6 are most closely related to fitness education.

> ▶ **Standard 1**: Students will comprehend concepts related to health promotion and disease prevention.
> ▶ **Standard 3**: Students will demonstrate the ability to practice health-enhancing behaviors and reduce health risks.
> ▶ **Standard 6**: Students will demonstrate the ability to use goal-setting and decision-making skills to enhance health.

NATIONAL HEALTH EDUCATION STANDARDS

- **Standard 1**: Students will comprehend concepts related to health promotion and disease prevention.
- **Standard 2**: Students will demonstrate the ability to access valid health information and health-promoting products and services.
- **Standard 3**: Students will demonstrate the ability to practice health-enhancing behaviors and reduce health risks.
- **Standard 4**: Students will analyze the influence of culture, media, technology, and other factors on health.
- **Standard 5**: Students will demonstrate the ability to use interpersonal communication skills to enhance health.
- **Standard 6**: Students will demonstrate the ability to use goal-setting and decision-making skills to enhance health.
- **Standard 7**: Students will demonstrate the ability to advocate for personal, family, and community health.

From *Achieving health literacy: National health education standards* (1995) from the American Alliance for Health, Physical Education, Recreation and Dance (AAHPERD), 1900 Association Drive, Reston, VA 20191-1599.

NATIONAL STANDARDS FOR DANCE EDUCATION

The national standards for dance education (see page 6; NDA, 1996) are also linked to physical education. Dance is both a movement form (as are sports, aquatics, fitness activities, and outdoor recreational activities) and a physical activity that provides health and fitness benefits. As a physical activity, however, dance is unique in that it is also an art form, affording opportunities to create, communicate meaning, and interpret cultural issues and historical periods. Standard 6 (making connections between dance and healthful living) is of primary importance in health-related fitness education.

INTEGRATING PHYSICAL BEST INTO THE ELEMENTARY PHYSICAL EDUCATION CURRICULUM

Physical Best Activity Guide: Elementary Level, Third Edition is more than a compilation of elementary activities that children participate in during their physical education classes. The guide provides instruction for physical education teachers to

NATIONAL STANDARDS FOR DANCE EDUCATION

What every young American should know and be able to do in dance:

- **Standard 1**: Identifies and demonstrates movement elements and skills in performing dance.
- **Standard 2**: Understands choreographic principles, processes, and structures.
- **Standard 3**: Understands dance as a way to create and communicate meaning.
- **Standard 4**: Applies and demonstrates critical and creative thinking skills in dance.
- **Standard 5**: Demonstrates and understands dance in various cultures and historical periods.
- **Standard 6**: Makes connections between dance and healthful living.
- **Standard 7**: Makes connections between dance and other disciplines.

From the National Standards for Arts Education and the National Dance Association (NDA), an association of the American Alliance for Health, Physical Education, Recreation and Dance. The source of the National Dance Standards (*National Standards for Dance Education: What Every Young American Should Know and Be Able to Do in Dance*) may be purchased from the National Dance Association, 1900 Association Drive, Reston, VA 20191-1599, or 703-476-3421.

help children learn about physical fitness and understand the importance of being healthy and leading physically active lives. Physical fitness concepts are taught through the described activities in the book. Therefore, *Physical Best Activity Guide: Elementary Level, Third Edition* is an integral part of an elementary health and physical education curriculum.

Physical Best activities vary in length of time required to complete and may further vary based on class size, classroom environment, and other factors. Because the activities vary in length, a combination of activities can serve as an entire lesson or individual activities can be infused into other lesson plans. The activities provide ideas and resources for teachers to use during their health and physical education lessons, for homework assignments, and through extracurricular activities and special events. Reproduc-

ibles found on the CD-ROM provide visual aids and extensions of the activities to help children better understand the concepts taught within the activities.

An important part of each Physical Best activity is the section titled "Sample Inclusion Tips." All children desire to be active and move, but for many teachers it is often difficult to know what adaptations to make to integrate some class members into an activity or even into the curriculum. Providing inclusive programs requires gaining the necessary knowledge and skills to include individuals with and without disabilities, being accountable for a positive attitude, ensuring equal treatment across all lines of diversity, and effectively communicating, both verbally and nonverbally. As the professional conducting the program, you are responsible for successfully including all participants. Modifications and accommodations should be made based on students' needs and ability. Addressing the needs of all students can be challenging. Motivating students of varying levels of ability, enhancing skill development, and enabling all students to participate and maintain similar levels of activity is a common goal for teachers. Modifying the equipment, boundaries, rules, and instructions are things that you can do to help and support students with disabilities. To ensure a successful educational environment, teachers look for simple, quick solutions that can help a diverse student population. Making accommodations as well as practicing the activity ensures such success. Refer to the Tips for Inclusion sidebar for information on modifications.

Physical Best activities instruct children about principles of training and the importance of being physically active and fit. The activities teach children the concepts of warm-ups and cool-downs, frequency, intensity, time, type, progression, and overload. Furthermore, the activities are fun and challenging. Physical Best emphasizes individuality, encourages students to participate to the best of their ability, and accentuates the importance of participation in regular physical activity on all or most days of the week. Competition is kept to a minimum and is often introduced only as part of the child's inherent motivation to do his or her best when participating in playful activity.

Through Physical Best, you will be able to instruct children about health-related fitness while

TIPS FOR INCLUSION

- Review the activity and determine the student's needs.
- Focus on the student's abilities, not the disability.
- Adapt the game to the individual, not the individual to the game.
- Allow all students to move freely with minimal assistance.
- Equipment—Modify equipment according to the student's abilities:
  - Vary the ball size, texture, and color according to the student's needs.
  - Attach a cord to balls and other objects so that students with mobility problems and coordination issues can retrieve these objects independently.
  - Use larger striking implements that have a broader contact surface.
  - Use lower goals, targets, and platforms.
  - Use a larger target space or larger goals.
  - Attach Velcro to an extension so that students in wheelchairs can reach independently for objects located on the floor.
  - Place objects—balls, cards, and so on—at a height so that students can reach them if they have difficulty bending over (poor balance) or if they are in wheelchairs.
  - Jump ropes—Jump ropes can be used individually or in groups of threes. Cut or fold jump ropes in half for students with ambulatory concerns.
  - Scooter activities—Use long scooters for students who are not ambulatory and need to be placed on their abdomens. To create a long scooter, tie two scooters together to make a larger scooter surface. You can also use some type of trunk support attachment for students who need help using a seated position.
  - During parachute activities, attach an elastic cord from a wheelchair to a parachute so that the student in the wheelchair is attached to the activity but can move freely.
  - Attach some type of carrier (backpack or bag) to a wheelchair for students to place objects in so that their hands are free to manipulate the wheelchair for movement.
  - Hula hoops—Cut hula hoops in half so that students in wheelchairs and students using walkers can move into hula hoops when asked to do so during movement activities.
- Boundaries
  - Mark the boundaries of the area and adjust when necessary by decreasing distance or simplifying patterns within the area.
  - Use some type of beeper to mark the boundaries for students with visual impairments so that they can move freely through space during activities.
- Remove obstacles from the area.
- Rules—Adapt the rules so that the game or activity is challenging but still allows the student an opportunity for success:
  - Allow the ball to stay stationary.
  - Don't set time limits.
  - Provide partner assistance.
  - Adjust distance as needed.
  - Allow students extra turns to accomplish the task.
- Prompts
  - Use picture communication symbols (PCS) to set up a schedule of the class activities in the gym. This method will help students transition from one activity to another.
  - Try to avoid overloading your students with too much challenge or too much language.
  - Use picture communication symbols (PCS) to support verbal directions.
  - Demonstrate or model the activity when giving verbal directions.
  - Use visual, verbal, and physical prompts together if needed.
  - Try to use one- or two-step directions. Keep it simple!

also teaching about motor skills and the skill-related components of fitness. Therefore, children learn to travel using different locomotor patterns, moving their bodies in different levels and pathways. They learn that movement increases their heart rates and makes their muscles stronger. Children practice manipulative skills such as throwing, catching, and kicking and at the same time learn several sport-related stretches and muscular endurance activities. Integrating the concepts and sport skills enables children to discover the benefits of being strong and flexible.

Finally, teachers who regularly work with children can instruct them to self-assess health-related fitness levels. Practicing the Fitnessgram assessments and the Physical Best activities throughout the year enables youth to learn about health-related physical fitness levels and what it takes to become healthier. Moreover, the Physical Best program helps to involve children in physical activity outside school as noted by the home extension ideas provided with each activity lesson in this book.

PHYSICAL BEST ACTIVITY TEMPLATE

Activities that help students learn while doing are the most successful for teaching lifelong fitness. The *Physical Best Activity Guides* provide a wealth of activities designed specifically to help students learn through doing.

These activities provide a great start to developing an excellent program, but you'll want to add more activities especially suited for your students. Following is a step-by-step explanation of the Physical Best activity template that can serve as a guide for developing your own activities.

▶ **Level**—Carefully consider the level of the students for whom you are developing the activity. Although you will note that all the activities in this text were developed for primary grades (K–2) or intermediate grades (3–5), you can easily modify many activities up or down for students of varying ages and abilities.

▶ **Concept**—The activity teaches one or more concepts, written in language appropriate to the level of the students. Physical Best includes activi-

ties for defining the component of fitness and teaching the health benefits for that component, for warm-ups and cool-downs, the FITT guidelines, progression, and overload. (The chapters "Body Composition" and "Special Events" follow a different format but still list the concept or concepts taught.) See figure 2.1 in chapter 2 for further clarification of how the components, principles of fitness, FITT guidelines, and health- and skill-related areas all interrelate with each other. Remember, teaching with a concepts approach helps students learn about all the various factors that affect their physical fitness and how they can manipulate these areas to enhance their fitness now and for a lifetime.

▶ **Purpose**—This component of the template states the student-centered objectives, describing what you want the students to learn.

▶ **Relationship to National Standards**—This component explains which of the national standards in physical education, health education, and dance education the activity addresses.

▶ **Equipment**—This component lists everything needed to conduct the activity. You need to stay informed regarding new types of equipment and technology and should incorporate these items into classroom and home extension ideas to keep activities fresh.

▶ **Reproducibles**—This component lists what can be found on the accompanying CD-ROM to support the activity. These include charts, signs, task cards, student worksheets, home extension worksheets, and other resources. You are encouraged to print the reproducibles that appear on the CD-ROM. They are created for letter-sized paper but can be enlarged according to your needs. Each is labeled by activity number and reproducible title to help you keep them organized.

▶ **Procedure**—This component lists steps to conduct the activity, including an introduction (often called a set-induction), activity steps and directions, and closure.

▶ **Teaching Hints**—This part of the template offers ideas for variations, extensions, and increases or decreases in level (for example, notes about intensity, ability groupings, and challenges), as well as safety tips and other ideas for effectively teaching the activity.

▶ **Sample Inclusion Tips**—One or more tips for adapting the activity to meet the needs of students with varying abilities and health concerns are found in this component. Note that a tip for one activity may be useful for other activities as well. Consider modifying your environment, equipment, rules, boundaries, and instructional cues when developing a lesson plan. Refer to the Tips for Inclusion sidebar on page 7 for help with making appropriate modifications.

▶ **Variations**—Variations provide additional ways to modify the activity or equipment to increase and vary participation challenges and enhance the learning of the concept being taught.

▶ **Home Extension**—Extension of the lesson provides students with information that will help them continue the activity at home and in other nonschool environments.

▶ **Assessment**—This component explains how you or the students will know that they have learned the information stated in the purpose. If you make sure that students understand what concept is being taught and what the educational purpose of the activity is, then the type of assessment used should examine what was stated in the purpose and concept. Assessment may include teacher discussion, student feedback, and review and homework assignments. The activities can be short and do not have to be written.

SUMMARY

When you use Physical Best, you are teaching the applicable standards through activity in an age-appropriate and sequential manner. Using the activity template will ensure that your activities are educational, easy to administer, and can be easily assessed. Choose activities that fit into your lesson plans, and you will teach and reinforce important fitness concepts throughout the year. Most important, these activities have been developed by physical educators for physical educators and have been tested in the real world to ensure that they not only teach the concepts but also allow students to have fun while performing physical activity.

Introduction to Health-Related Fitness Concepts

Chapter Contents

This chapter introduces the principles of health-related fitness education. An introduction to the components of health-related fitness can be found at the beginning of each corresponding chapter in part II and can be used as a quick reference when teaching the activities in that chapter. For more in-depth study and explanation of these concepts, refer to *Physical Education for Lifelong Fitness: The Physical Best Teacher's Guide, Third Edition* (2011), which contains several new concepts that differ from those of the previous edition, especially in the aerobic fitness chapter.

HEALTH-RELATED FITNESS VERSUS SKILL-RELATED FITNESS

Health-related fitness includes the components of aerobic fitness, flexibility, muscular strength, muscular endurance, and body composition and nutrition. Health-related fitness is the focus of the Physical Best program because these five components are directly tied to levels of everyday health, can be enhanced fairly easily, and help prevent or lessen the effects of hypokinetic diseases and conditions initiated or made worse by lack of physical activity (Hoeger & Hoeger, 2011). Examples of hypokinetic diseases and conditions include obesity, diabetes, and hypertension.

Skill-related fitness includes the components of coordination, agility, reaction time, speed, power, and balance. Although people must have adequate amounts of these components to live a healthy life, large amounts of the skill-related components are primarily necessary to participate well in recreational activities. Many skill-related components of fitness rely heavily on one or more health-related components. For example, speed, power, and balance all depend on the presence of muscular strength and muscular endurance, which are health-related components. In addition, the skill-related components are often more difficult to change significantly, and indeed large increases in these components are usually not necessary for most children unless they are heavily involved in specific highly competitive sports or recreational pursuits. Although participation in skill-related activities contributes to overall fitness, it is important to remember that when

emphasizing general overall health and wellness, the main focus of physical fitness programs will be on the health-related components (Hoeger & Hoeger, 2011). Figure 2.1 illustrates the relationship between the health- and skill-related components of fitness as well as the various actions that can be taken to enhance each of these components. Through Physical Best activities, students will gain in-depth knowledge about the various health- and skill-related components of fitness and ways in which to enhance these areas through hands-on experiences that emphasize the use of the various fitness principles.

PHYSICAL FITNESS

In teaching health-related fitness, we should not lose sight of the importance of physical activity and the development of fun activities that encourage children to be active (Graham et al., 2010). Physical Best has consistently emphasized the development of physical fitness as a lifelong process of active lifestyles, rather than the product of actually being physically fit or the outcome of exercise performed on a regular basis. The focus of our lessons should not be on developing physically fit children, but on teaching children basic concepts, skills, and the value of physical activity so that they will be competent to participate in activities now and in the future.

As you use the Physical Best materials, keep the following definitions in mind to assist you in motivating your students to become physically active, thereby initiating the long path to lifetime fitness and associated health benefits. *Physical fitness* is defined as a set of attributes that people have or achieve relating to their ability to perform physical activity (USDHHS, 1996), whereas *physical activity* is defined as any bodily movement produced by muscle contraction that increases energy expenditure (USDHHS, 1996; NASPE, 2004b). *Physical fitness* is also defined as "the ability to meet the demands of daily life safely and effectively without being overly fatigued and still have energy left for leisure and recreational activities" (Hoeger & Hoeger, 2011, p. 19). Motivation to be physically active does not come solely from knowing and appreciating the health benefits of increased activity. Children should be taught that being physically active enables them to play longer

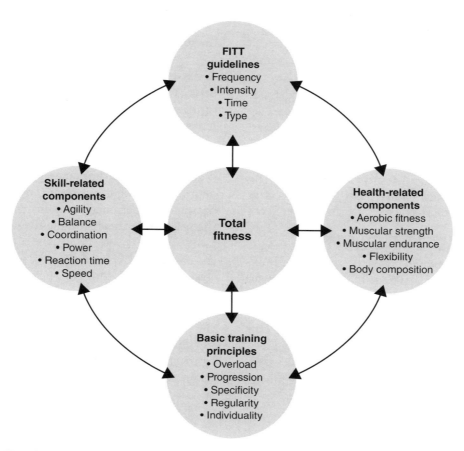

Figure 2.1   This figure shows how the components and principles of physical fitness work together. It is also available as a reproducible, Building Physical Fitness, on the CD-ROM.

without getting tired and that they will have more energy for leisure activities—all of which yield health benefits unbeknownst to children unless you make the relationship clear.

INCLUSION IN PHYSICAL EDUCATION

Including all your students should be an important part of your planning and teaching process, not an afterthought. Ensuring that every student receives physical activity experiences and programs to enhance fitness needs is the trademark of the caring and creative teacher. Many students with disabilities require a structured program of fitness to reduce secondary conditions, to maintain functional independence, to provide an opportunity for leisure and enjoyment, and to enhance the overall quality of life by reducing

environmental barriers to good health. Although not every student can equally benefit from, or even participate in, every activity, including everyone in your health-related fitness program isn't just a good idea; it's the law.

Research points to three main reasons that children participate in leisure-time activity and sports (Weiss, 2000; Meredith & Welk, 2005):

▶ The development and demonstration of physical competence (athletic skills, fitness, physical appearance)

▶ Social acceptance and support from friends, peers, and significant adults

▶ Participation in fun activities promoting positive experiences

The Tips for Inclusion sidebar on page 7 provides some considerations for including all students in activities.

PRINCIPLES OF TRAINING

The principles of training are important to know and utilize when developing movement programs. They include principles of individuality, overload, progression, specificity, and regularity. You can use them to help guide your students as they learn to develop sound movement programs and to gain higher levels of fitness and movement skills safely and effectively. A reproducible sign of the principles is available on the CD-ROM and can be displayed to remind students of these principles (see figure 2.2).

The *individuality principle* takes into account that each person begins at a different level of fitness, has personal goals and objectives for physical activity and fitness, and different genetic potential for change. Although changes in children's physiological responses to training and conditioning are often difficult to measure because of confounding problems with changes associated with the normal growth and maturation process, recognize that students in your classes will respond differently to the activities that you prepare for class. Some will improve, some will not; some will enjoy the activities, others will not. Your job is to provide plenty of opportunities for choice in your classroom, taking into account each student's initial fitness level and personal goals.

The *overload principle* states that a body system must perform at a level beyond normal in order to adapt and improve physiological function and fitness. You can increase the overload by manipulating the frequency, intensity, or duration (time) of an activity. To explain overload to children, let them experience it firsthand. For younger children you can talk about the length of time that they are participating in an activity. With older children you can keep track of the number of minutes they can sustain an activity or how many repetitions they can perform. You can also use a backpack with books or weights and monitor heart rate without the backpack and then with the backpack, explaining how the body will adapt to the heavy load and later be able to do the same load with less effort.

Progression refers to how people should increase the overload. Progression is a gradual increase in the level of exercise that can be manipulated by increasing the frequency, intensity, time, or a combination of all three components. Children should understand that improving their level of fitness is an ongoing process. All progression must be gradual to be safe. If the overload is applied too soon, the body does not have time to adapt and the benefits may be delayed or an injury may occur, either of which can discourage or prevent a child from participating. For example, young children may progress from performing a reverse curl-up, in which they focus on lowering the body, and work toward performing a regular curl-up. You can use the same strategy with push-ups, first focusing on the lowering phase. As the children progress they will gain enough strength to perform the complete push-up. The objective is to challenge students but also create opportunities for success.

To help students better understand progression and see that they are improving, give them opportunities to track their progress (keep a log or journal). You can also effectively help them achieve this understanding by using pretests and posttests.

Specificity, or type of exercise, states that explicit activities targeting a particular body system must be performed to bring about fitness changes in that area. For example, you must perform activities that have an aerobic component to them in order to stress the cardiorespiratory system if you

Principles of Training

Individuality
Overload
Progression
Specificity
Regularity

Principles of Training
From NASPE, 2011, *Physical Best activity guide: Elementary level, 3rd edition* (Champaign, IL: Human Kinetics).

Figure 2.2 Principles of Training.

want to improve aerobic fitness. This principle applies to all areas of health- and skill-related fitness and can apply within a single area of fitness. For example, performing a biceps curl will increase the strength of the biceps muscle but has no effect on the leg muscles.

The premise behind the *regularity principle* is based on the old adage "Use it or lose it." Any fitness gains attained through physical activity are lost if we do not continue to be active. Recognize that the body needs a limited amount of recovery time between bouts of exercise. Too little recovery time may lead to injury or overtraining, and too much time between activity sessions can lead to detraining, or loss of the acquired benefits of physical activity and fitness. The time of recovery also varies by the area of health-related fitness. For example, the American College of Sports Medicine (ACSM, 2000) recommends three alternate days per week for strength and endurance activities of a vigorous nature, whereas daily activity is best for improving flexibility. Likewise, the minimum frequency for aerobic improvement is three days per week, and five to seven days is optimal. You should emphasize consistency in activity and not training and conditioning unless you are coaching athletes. Alternatively, remember that recommendations for children's physical activity include daily activity versus the traditional ACSM adult model for fitness training.

Physical Activity Guidelines for Americans, published by the U.S. Department of Health and Human Services (2008), contains additional recommendations for children and youth. Although these guidelines also emphasize the need to focus on the process of performing physical activity on most days of the week, they give specific guidelines that you can use when preparing their programs.

KEY PHYSICAL ACTIVITY GUIDELINES FOR CHILDREN AND ADOLESCENTS

The U.S. Department of Health and Human Services' *2008 Physical Activity Guidelines for Americans* can be found at www.health.gov/paguidelines/guidelines/chapter3.aspx. These guidelines include specific physical activity guidelines for children and adolescents, which are as follows:

▶ Children and adolescents should do 60 minutes or more of physical activity daily. This physical activity time should focus on three types of activity: aerobic activity, muscle-strengthening activity, and bone-strengthening activity. These three fitness components were chosen because each type has important health benefits.

- Aerobic—Most of the 60 or more minutes per day should be either moderate- or vigorous-intensity aerobic physical activity and should include vigorous-intensity physical activity on at least three days a week. Examples of aerobic activities include tag activities, running, hopping, skipping, jumping rope, dancing, biking, swimming, and sport activities such as soccer and basketball.

- Muscle strengthening: As part of their 60 or more minutes of daily physical activity, children and adolescents should include muscle-strengthening physical activity on at least three days of the week. Muscle-strengthening activities might include unstructured activities such as playing on playground equipment, climbing trees, rope climbing, or tug-of-war, as well as more structured activities such as curl-ups, lifting weights, or working with resistance bands.

- Bone strengthening—As part of their 60 or more minutes of daily physical activity, children and adolescents should include bone-strengthening physical activity on at least three days of the week. Bone-strengthening activities, according to the Health.gov document, are those that "produce a force on the bones and promote bone growth and strength." This force is commonly produced by impact with the ground. Examples are running, jumping rope, hopscotch, and sports activities such as gymnastics, basketball, and volleyball.

▶ It is important to encourage young people to participate in physical activities that are appropriate for their age, that are enjoyable, and that offer variety.

From www.health.gov/paguidelines/guidelines/chapter3.aspx.

Additional ideas regarding appropriate fitness activities for children can be noted from examining the Physical Activity Pyramid for Children (see figure 2.3). Several Physical Best activities incorporate the use of the Physical Activity Pyramid for Children to aid children in learning about different types of physical activity and how various activities belong in a balanced fitness program.

FITT GUIDELINES

Physical Best activities apply the FITT guidelines to improve health and fitness and help students learn fitness guidelines that they can apply for a lifetime (see figure 2.4). The acronym *FITT* describes the frequency (how often), the intensity (how hard), the time (how long), and the type (what kind) of activity necessary for improving and maintaining fitness. It also pro-

vides the recipe for safely applying the previously described principles of training. As you apply these guidelines to children, remember they are not miniature adults and that the adult exercise prescription model should not be applied until the child is at the secondary level. Refer to the third edition of the *Physical Best Teacher's Guide* for detailed explanations of the FITT guidelines and new recommendations concerning the use of these guidelines with children. The U.S. Department of Health and Human Services also stresses the importance of using age-appropriate physical activities. Young children often play hard but in an intermittent type of work and rest format. Even older children and adolescents often participate in activities that require alternating moderate or vigorous activity with short rest periods. All activity of this type counts towards performing 60 minutes per day of physical activity.

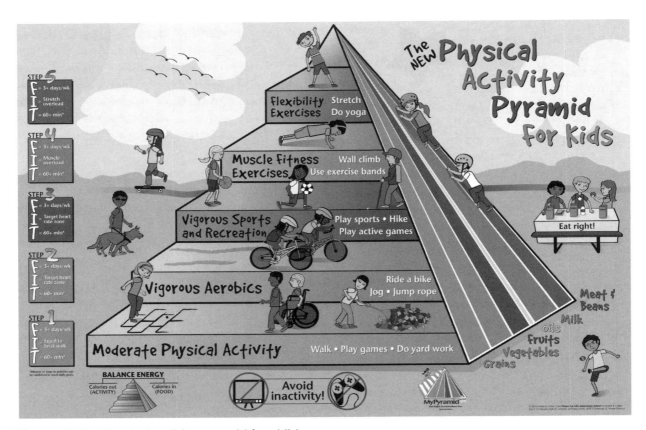

Figure 2.3 Physical activity pyramid for children.

Reprinted, by permission, from D. Lambdin et al., 2010, *Fitness for life: Elementary school classroom guide kindergarten* (Champaign, IL: Human Kinetics), 11.

FITT Guidelines

Frequency
Intensity
Time
Type

Figure 2.4 FITT Guidelines. A reproducible version of the FITT guidelines is available on the CD-ROM.

THE ACTIVITY SESSION

Whether you are teaching kindergartners or high school seniors, you should share the purpose of the lesson and state how the day's activity will help students reach class goals or personal goals. Every activity should incorporate a systematic approach not only to ensure safety but also to prepare the body for the rigors of the workout. The main physical activity must be developmentally appropriate so that students can feel and understand, through participation, the importance of being physically active. Cool-down time should also be incorporated, and it can be used as time to review and assess learning.

The following tips will help you integrate these concepts into your activity sessions:

Tips for Teaching Fitness

- Be aware of varied abilities of students.
- Tell purpose and key points of the lesson to students.
- Review key points during the lesson.
- Check for understanding. Give students time to think and respond. The teaching hints, sample inclusion tips, and assessment ideas given with each activity lesson will help you with this.

- Use hands-on experiences to supplement presentations.
- Challenge students to encourage regular participation in activities.
- Relate fitness concepts to experiences in their lives. You will find ideas to help with this under the home extension part of each activity lesson.

Reprinted, by permission, from C. Corbin and R. Pangrazi, 1997, *Teaching strategies for improving youth fitness,* 2nd ed. (Reston, VA: AAHPERD).

More information on teaching strategies for health-related fitness can be found in *Physical Education for Lifelong Fitness: The Physical Best Teacher's Guide, Third Edition.*

MOTIVATING STUDENTS

The goal of Physical Best is to motivate youth to be lifelong participants in physical activity. Most young children love to move and be active. But as they become more involved in the many activities and experiences of life, they often move away from physical activity and into more sedentary lifestyles. Such actions significantly compromise their present and future health and quality of life. Therefore, youth must learn about the importance of, and begin focusing on, lifelong habits of physical activity.

Many factors influence participation in physical activity by children. Chapter 2 of *Physical Education for Lifelong Fitness: The Physical Best Teacher's Guide, Third Edition* (2011) says that most of these factors can be placed in one of four categories: biological or physical, psychological, social, and environmental. Biological or physical influences include gender, age, weight, physical ability, and physical environment (e.g., a safe place to play or space to play). Psychological factors include self-efficacy, internal self-control, value placed on the experience, global self-esteem and self-worth, and satisfaction. Social factors include guardians, siblings, family, peers, teachers, physicians, and others important in our lives. Environmental factors include day of the week, seasons, setting, organization, and competing opportunities.

The Cooper Institute's third edition of *Fitnessgram/Activitygram Test Administration Manual*

(Meredith & Welk, eds., 2007, pp. 18-20) gives several actions that physical educators can incorporate into their programs to enhance physical activity and fitness levels in children. These suggestions are paraphrased here:

► Help children enhance their physical fitness and skill levels through a variety of appropriate physical activities.

► Provide children with relevant reasons why they should participate in regular physical activity (e.g., looking good and having fun).

► Help students identify times and places to perform daily physical activity.

► Help students identify their support groups and ways to use them.

► Have students develop specific goals and sign contracts that they will participate in the activity required to achieve a goal. Be sure that the list of activities is specific and the student has identified the time, place, and other needed details necessary for success.

► Encourage students to track their physical activity participation by using logs and calendars.

► Show interest in the fitness activities of students by asking questions about their endeavors.

► Discuss progress and problems and remind students that being active is not always easy. Have students discuss with others ideas about how to stay active and how to meet activity goals. Praise effort and the reaching of even small accomplishments because positive feedback helps enhance competence and intrinsic motivation.

► Recommend primarily low- to moderate-intensity activities such as walking or biking because students are more likely to maintain these activities than some team sport activities.

► Be a role model for your students. Be physically active and share with your students the benefits that you receive from being active.

► Encourage guardian participation in physical activity whenever possible.

Adapted, by permission, from The Cooper Institute, 2004, *Fitnessgram/Activitygram test administration manual*, 3rd ed. (Champaign, IL: Human Kinetics), 18-20.

Additional suggestions for motivating students include the following:

► Award the process of participation rather than the product of fitness.

► Emphasize self-testing programs. Do not base grades on fitness test results.

► Use music whenever possible.

Keeping the various motivational factors described in mind as well as the recommendations for how best to use them should be of tremendous value to physical educators who are attempting to motivate youth to initiate and continue movement experiences.

Tying Motivation to Physical Best

The Physical Best program emphasizes the teaching of health-related fitness activities in ways that help children answer the two important questions that Welk (1999) identified as important in motivating children to be active: "Is physical activity worth it?" and "Am I able?" Physical Best resources are developmentally appropriate, standards-based, and emphasize learning through doing. The Physical Best program focuses on each child's individual preferences and capabilities, and it emphasizes personal improvement rather than comparing children with each other or with unrealistic performance-based standards (The Cooper Institute, 2004).

Each Physical Best activity also helps you to motivate children through use of a standardized Physical Best activity template. The components of the template are briefly identified in chapter 1. When you use the information given within each component of the template to teach an activity, all students have the opportunity to enhance their understanding of the worth of physical activity, enhance their time on task, gain in fitness, and increase confidence in their own abilities.

SETTING GOALS

Goals provide direction. Just as teachers regularly use standards and objectives to guide their teaching, students need to learn to use goals to guide their learning and manage their lives. The focus of the *Physical Best Activity Guides* is on lifetime fitness education through interesting activities that enhance the teaching of important concepts that lead toward active, healthy lifestyles. All teachers are responsible for helping students learn about the goal-setting process and for providing opportunities for students to refine their goal-setting skills.

The research on goal setting is extensive, and specific information on the motivational aspects of using goals can be found in chapter 2, "Physical Activity Behavior and Motivation," of *Physical Education for Lifelong Fitness: The Physical Best Teacher's Guide* (NASPE, 2011). Ideally, teachers should encourage students to set goals in every lesson. Because student-set goals create intrinsic motivation and self-determination, they provide students with a sense of ownership over their learning, which in turn directs their attention toward the task at hand, makes the activity more personally meaningful (relevant) for them, and provides regular opportunities for them to monitor their own progress. A sister program to Physical Best, the Fitnessgram program has been designed with goal setting and self-management in mind—allowing students to self-assess, enter their own scores, print out and review their results, and compare current performance scores with previously recorded ones (Ernst et al., 2006; Plowman et al., 2006). For you to take full advantage of these processes, however, you must understand the different types of goals and then teach students about goals.

Types of Goals

Just about any activity can include goal setting, as long as you understand the general principles of setting goals. These principles include using a multiple goal-setting strategy, which includes the setting of immediate (today), intermediate (for example, two to six weeks), and long-term goals (for example, semester, annual, lifetime), as well as using process (technique related), performance (personal best), and product (outcome or winning) goals. Students need to be taught that long-range goals are best achieved by setting immediate and intermediate goals and that goals focused on process and personal performance will often lead to achieving group and outcome goals.

Cox (2007) describes outcome, performance, and process goals as follows:

▸ Outcome goals—Focus on the outcomes of events, such as winning, outperforming others, and so on, and involve interpersonal comparison (winning versus losing, place in finish order, winning record).

▸ Performance goals—Specify an end-product that will be reached by the student independently of other performers and the physical education class (achieving the healthy fitness zone, strike outs by a pitcher, goals saved by a keeper, shooting percentage by a player, free throw percentage, achieving a personal best time, and so on).

▸ Process goals—Specify behavior throughout a performance (keeping the head down, being the first to get to the ball, using correct form in curl-ups, attending to technique cues during activities, and so on).

Determining the Focus of Goals

Our goals, as teachers, should be to increase student participation in moderate to vigorous physical activity to more than 60 minutes per day. Therefore, the focus of goals should be to

▸ increase knowledge needed to engage in lifelong physical activity,

▸ increase attitudes needed to engage in lifelong physical activity,

▸ increase skills needed to engage in lifelong physical activity,

▸ increase activity time in physical education to 50%,

▸ increase the number of students participating 50% of the time in physical education.

Some of these lend themselves to teacher goals for more effective teaching. Others should involve students in setting personal goals.

All activities in the *Physical Best Activity Guides* can and should be considered goal-setting activities. You are encouraged to teach concepts and then guide students toward self-management and personal goal setting. To help you get started, use the activities that provide logs to assist in goal setting. Later, branch out and use the objectives for each activity as the starting point to encourage students to accept personal responsibility for their learning.

Good Goals

Helping students set good goals and committing to their achievement is the final aspect of teaching about goal setting (see the Goal Setting sidebar). Good goals are specific, measureable, optimally challenging (neither too difficult nor too easily achieved), relevant to the child's needs and interests, and achievable within a specific period. Students will need oral and written feedback to assist them in writing good goals. But with regular practice and an emphasis on personal responsibility through commitment to goals, students will easily adopt the practice. You should revisit the goals with students and hold them accountable to expending effort toward achievement of their goals, if the process is to become an integral part of physical education and lifetime fitness and activity. Good goals are set by students with teacher feedback and with commitment from both the student and the teacher to allow time to assess progress toward the goals. *Physical Best*, *Fitnessgram*, and *Fitness for Life* all include logs and activities that can help students monitor progress toward important goals leading to lifelong physical activity and health.

In addition, a standalone goal-setting worksheet to use with young children is provided on the CD-ROM (see figure 2.5).

Here are some strategies to help students set good goals:

- ▶ Involve students in identifying and setting goals.

Figure 2.5 Goal-Setting Worksheet.

- ▶ Start small and progress.
- ▶ Focus on improvements relative to a student's past behavior.
- ▶ Set specific and measureable goals.
- ▶ Set challenging and realistic goals.
- ▶ Write down the goals.
- ▶ Provide students with strategies or options to meet their goals; let other students help with ideas, too.
- ▶ Support and give feedback about progress toward goals.
- ▶ Create goal stations.
- ▶ Provide opportunities for periodic evaluation by the teacher and through student self-evaluation.

GOAL SETTING

What?

Goal setting is a mechanism that helps students understand their limits and helps them feel satisfied with their accomplishments. . . . They can be our Wishes. . . . They might be our Dreams for the Future.

Why?

- Goals are motivating!
- Goals create feelings of self-control.
- Achievement promotes feelings of self-satisfaction, esteem, and efficacy.
- Using goals created from personal assessment establishes ownership and fosters pride in the fitness process.

When?

- From the beginning
- Throughout the year
- Daily
- In school and out of school

How?

Learn the strategies for goal setting

- Learn to make them personal
- Learn to use them to empower others

Reprinted, by permission, from D. Ballinger, L. Borsdorf, and J. Bishop, 2008.

SUMMARY

For the prepubescent child, the emphasis should be placed on increasing physical activity, developing skills, and providing access to a variety of sports and activities that can serve as a primer or foundation for conditioning programs during puberty and beyond. Keep in mind that fitness is a journey, not a destination, and that the goal is to progress toward self-assessment and self-delivery of health-related fitness activities. Are you and your students ready for the fun of leading a physically active life? If so, progress to the activities that follow.

Activities

Aerobic Fitness

Chapter Contents

As we examine the concept of aerobic fitness in children, we should recognize that research in this area is limited. We should not rely on aerobic fitness assessment to indicate endurance performance in children, nor should we develop aerobic training programs that parallel the adult exercise prescription model. Although the relationship between physical activity and aerobic fitness is weak in children (Rowland, 1996, p. 112), the goal of the Physical Best program is to enhance the quality and productivity of every child's life through physical education and help establish lifelong activity habits. Refer to *Physical Education for Lifelong Fitness: The Physical Best Teacher's Guide, Third Edition* (2011), and *Developmental Exercise Physiology* (Rowland, 1996) for more information concerning the relationship of physical activity and aerobic fitness in children.

DEFINING AEROBIC FITNESS

Aerobic fitness is the "ability to perform large muscle, dynamic, moderate to high intensity exercise for prolonged periods" (ACSM, 2000, p. 68). To a child this definition may mean the ability to play longer without becoming tired. Many field tests are available to assess aerobic fitness. Physical Best endorses Fitnessgram by the Cooper Institute. The Brockport Test by Winnick and Short may be used with students with disabilities.

Many health benefits are associated with physical activity (Hoeger & Hoeger, 2011). A report by the California Department of Education (2002) indicated that higher levels of fitness in children were associated with higher academic performance on standardized testing. A study by Bass et al. (2010) also substantiated a correlation between physical fitness levels and academic achievement in youth. Additional information regarding how physical activity may help academic performance is given in NASPE's *Active Kid and Academic Performance* brochure (2010). Remember that children are concrete learners and that the benefits of health-related fitness may not mean much to them at this level. To enhance understanding, you must connect the benefits to something that they can relate to and experience personally and immediately, for example, "Can you run around the playground without stopping?" Potential health benefits include the following:

▶ Strengthens the heart (lower resting and working heart rate, faster recovery)
▶ Decreases blood pressure
▶ Strengthens muscles and bones
▶ Increases energy (to play longer)
▶ Allows performance of more work with less effort (carry toys without becoming tired or needing help)
▶ Reduces stress and tension (get along better with others)
▶ Enhances appearance and feeling of well-being; improves quality of life
▶ Improves ability to learn (get homework done faster)
▶ Promotes healthy body composition
▶ Increases self-confidence and self-esteem (greater social opportunities)
▶ Enhances sleep
▶ Improves lipid profile (increases HDL [good cholesterol], decreases triglycerides)
▶ Helps control weight

Our health and well-being change constantly throughout our lives, including the years during childhood. Most children have little interest in the health benefits that they may later recognize in adulthood. At the elementary level, you should select activities that develop and encourage active lifestyles, ultimately leading to improved quality of life. Introduce health-related benefits in a language that children understand, and repeat those benefits in activities across the curriculum.

TEACHING GUIDELINES FOR AEROBIC FITNESS

Teach fitness concepts through physical activity, minimizing classroom lessons in which students are inactive. Primary grade students should focus on locomotor skills—moving in personal space, exploring fast and slow movement and high and low movement, and learning to work together, including reacting to each other. Circuits or station activities provide excellent opportunities to challenge students independently, develop motor skills, and develop health-related fitness. Keep your groups small, no larger than five at a station. Activities for grades 3 through 5 should include manipulating objects in and through space, gradually increasing speed and accuracy, and incorporating cooperative learning activities. It is important for you to emphasize the importance of pacing, that the heart is a muscle and benefits from movement just like other muscles, and that it is not recommended that elementary age children participate in continuous aerobic activities for long durations (Graham et al., 2010).

In selecting and performing activities, follow the training principles outlined in chapter 5 of *Physical Education for Lifelong Fitness: The Physical Best Teacher's Guide, Third Edition* to develop aerobic fitness. This section contains new material, and you will notice that planning a lesson around attaining a specified target heart rate is not appropriate for elementary or middle school children. Children in primary grades can monitor intensity levels by monitoring their breathing rate and body heat and by placing a hand over the heart. Terms like *slow* (turtle) or *fast* (race car) can be used to describe heart rate. Intermediate-level students (grades 3 through 5) can begin to locate the carotid and radial arteries, but do not use target heart rate zones at this level. You should not expect most students in elementary school to calculate target heart rate values. This task is more appropriate for middle and high school students. In any case, avoid the use of target heart rate zones as requirements for participation in physical activity. Table 3.1 provides information on how to apply the FITT guidelines for elementary (5- to 12-year-old) youth.

Remember that alternating cycles of vigorous activity followed by a recovery period characterize the level and tempo of children's play activity (Bailey et al., 1995; Corbin & Pangrazi, 2002). Plan multiple activities with rest periods to provide variety and simulate children's natural play pattern. To regulate intensity, engage children in moderate to vigorous activity instead of using target heart rates. Provide adequate rest periods as intensity increases. Do not underestimate the importance of skill development, especially at the elementary level. Physical Best activities provide many opportunities to address motor skills during aerobic fitness activities.

NASPE (2004a, p. 5) offers this definition of moderate physical activity: "Activities of moderate intensity can be performed for relatively long periods of time without fatigue." The authors suggest that moderate physical activity includes games like hopscotch and four-square, low-activity positions such as goalie or outfield in softball, brisk walking, bike riding, and some chores and housework. They define vigorous physical activity as "movement that expends more energy or is performed at a higher intensity than brisk walking. Some forms of vigorous activity, such as running, can be done for relatively long periods of time while others may be so vigorous (e.g., sprinting) that frequent rests are necessary" (p. 5). Refer to *Physical Education for Lifelong Fitness: The Physical Best Teacher's Guide, Third Edition*, chapter 5, "Aerobic Fitness," for more information about intensity.

Table 3.1 FITT Guidelines Applied to Aerobic Fitness: Children (5–12 years)

Frequency	• Developmentally appropriate physical activity on all or most days of the week • Several bouts of physical activity lasting 15 minutes or more daily
Intensity	• Mixture of moderate and vigorous intermittent activity • Moderate = low-intensity games (hopscotch, four square), low activity positions (goalie, outfielders), some chores, yard work • Vigorous = games involving running, chasing, playing sports (levels 2 and 3 of activity pyramid)
Time	• Accumulation of at least 60 minutes and up to several hours of activity • Up to 50% of accumulated minutes should be accumulated in bouts of 15 minutes or more
Type	• Variety of activities • Activities should be selected from the activity pyramid • Continuous activity should not be expected for most children

TRAINING METHODS FOR AEROBIC FITNESS

The three main training methods for developing and maintaining aerobic fitness are continuous training, interval training, and circuit training.

- ▶ Continuous training is the same activity performed over an extended period. Rarely is this type of activity observed in children. Fartlek, a modification of continuous training, intersperses periods of increased intensity with continuous activity over varying natural terrain. This type of activity can be modified and used at all grade levels. Fartlek is especially good in exploratory activities at the primary grades and in station or circuit training.

- ▶ Interval training involves alternating short bursts of activity with rest periods. Young children naturally engage in this type of activity.

- ▶ Circuit training involves several different activities, allowing you to vary the intensity or type of activity as children move from station to station. Circuit training is an excellent method for creating variety and stimulating student motivation.

SAFETY AND AEROBIC FITNESS

Use caution with children during activity periods, because children respond to exercise differently than adults do (Bar-Or, 1993, 1994; Zwiren, 1988; Rowland, 1996). You should give special consideration when manipulating the principles of training and the FITT guidelines. Include frequent rest periods, use rates of perceived exertion scales, and be aware of hot, humid weather. Many elementary children are not aware of the signs that the body gives when becoming overheated such as "decreased perspiration, weakness, flushed skin, throbbing head, nausea/vomiting, diarrhea, numbness in the extremities, blurred vision, unsteadiness, disorientation, and incoherency" (Hoeger & Hoeger, 2011, p. 300). If any such symptoms occur, the child should stop play-

ing, move to shade, and drink fluids (Hoeger & Hoeger, 2011).

As children become more active you will want to provide information to reduce the risk of injury or illness that may lead to periods of inactivity. The information will be especially valuable when children leave your physical education program and continue to be active after school or in the community. Observe the following safety guidelines:

- ▶ Supervise the program closely and individualize the activity.

- ▶ Explain rules clearly and insist that students follow them.

- ▶ Have students wear protective clothing and gear appropriate for the sport, including
  - proper shoes for the activity,
  - helmets for cycling and other sports, and
  - light clothing in the heat.

- ▶ Obtain medical information concerning preexisting conditions.

- ▶ Minimize exposure to the sun and heat by using shaded space or by having children wear sunscreen and hats.

- ▶ Recognize that exercise or activity on very hot and humid days or very cold days may increase health risks. Children have low tolerance to exercise under these conditions (Bar-Or & Malina, 1995) because they
  - have a large surface area per unit of mass,
  - sweat at a lower rate,
  - have high metabolic heat production, and
  - take longer to acclimate to hot environments.

- ▶ Recognize signs and symptoms of heat illness or cold injury and do what you can to lessen the health risk.
  - Provide plenty of cool water, shade, and rest periods, and reduce intensity of activity.
  - Have students wear layered clothing and limit exposure to cold.
  - When necessary, conduct class indoors to limit exposure to air pollution.

Physical Best provides you and your students with the knowledge, skills, values, and confidence to engage in physical activity now and in the future through enjoyable activities.

AEROBIC FITNESS NEWSLETTER

Use the Aerobic Fitness Newsletter (located on the CD-ROM) to introduce, reinforce, and extend the concepts behind developing and maintaining good aerobic fitness (see figure 3.1).

Figure 3.1 Becoming Your Physical Best: Aerobic Fitness Newsletter.

The following are ways that you might use this tool:

- ▶ Send the newsletter home as a guardian-involvement tool during a mini unit focusing on aerobic fitness.

- ▶ Use the newsletter to help you feature aerobic fitness as the "Health-Related Fitness Component of the Month."

- ▶ Introduce the activity ideas as a whole-group task. Ask students to choose one activity to perform outside class in the next week. They should report their progress through a log, journal, a guardian's signature on the newsletter, or other means.

- ▶ Validate and promote student involvement in physical activity outside class time and the school setting.

- ▶ Among students who can read, promote reading to learn across your curriculum, further supporting the mission of elementary school.

- ▶ Use the newsletter as a model or springboard to create your own newsletter, tailored specifically to your students' needs.

Feel free to use the Aerobic Fitness Newsletter in a way that helps you teach more effectively to the specific needs of your students and their guardians. See table 3.2 on page 30 for a grid of activities in this chapter.

Table 3.2 Chapter 3 Activities Grid

Activity number	Activity title	Activity page	Concept	Primary	Intermediate	Reproducibles (on CD-ROM)
3.1	Aerobic Movements	31	Aerobic fitness	•		Aerobic Cards
3.2	Frantic Ball	34	Aerobic fitness		•	Frantic Ball Worksheet
3.3	Artery Avengers	36	Physical activity	•		Artery Avenger Assessment Sheet
3.4	Endurance Matchup	38	Health benefits	•		Aerobic Benefit Card
						Aerobic Benefit Puzzle
						Endurance Minutes Take-Home Worksheet
3.5	Treasure Island	40	Health benefits		•	Healthy Money Bills
3.6	Powerball Hunt	42	Warm-up and cool-down	•		Locomotor Movement Cards
						Number Cards
3.7	You Should Be Dancing	45	Warm-up and cool-down		•	Dance Step Cards
						Dance Step Descriptions
3.8	Aerobic Activity Picture Chart	47	Frequency	•		Aerobic Activity Picture Chart
3.9	Fing Fang Fooey	49	Frequency		•	Aerobic Activity Fitness Log
3.10	Animal Locomotion	51	Intensity	•		Animal Locomotion Task Signs
3.11	Jumping Frenzy	54	Intensity		•	Jumping Frenzy Instruction Cards
						Am I Giving My Heart a Workout? Chart
3.12	Around the Block	57	Time	•	•	Around the Block Timed Activity
						Around the Block Home Worksheet
						Am I Giving My Heart a Workout? Chart
3.13	Musical Sport Sequence	60	Time	•		Time Your Activity Worksheet
3.14	Six-Minute Jog	63	Time		•	Six-Minute Jogging Record Sheet
						Aerobic: Yes or No?
3.15	Aerobic Scooters	66	Type	•		Scooter Station Signs
						Am I Giving My Heart a Workout? Chart
						Aerobic: Yes or No?
3.16	Aerobic Sports	69	Type		•	Aerobic Sport Station Signs
						Physical Activity Pyramid for Children
3.17	Aerobic FITT Log	71	Overload principle		•	FITT Log
						FITT Log Worksheet

PRIMARY

Aerobic fitness—*Aerobic* means "with oxygen." Aerobic fitness occurs when your heart, lungs, and muscles work together over an extended period. Doing physical activity encourages your heart to beat harder, your lungs to breathe better, and your muscles to get more oxygen.

Purpose

▶ Students will engage in sustained physical activity that causes an increase in heart rate and breathing rate.

▶ Students will define aerobic fitness.

▶ Students will state the changes in the body when doing aerobic activities.

Relationship to National Standards

▶ Physical education standard 3: Participates regularly in physical activity.

▶ Health education standard 3: Students will demonstrate the ability to practice health-enhancing behaviors and reduce health risks.

Equipment

▶ Fast, upbeat music and music player

▶ Pedometer to track steps if desired

Procedure

1. Place the Aerobic Cards in the center of the gym. Have the face of the cards turned up so that students can make sure that they get all three cards. A star is on the back side of three cards.

2. Students jog or walk briskly in a circular formation, going clockwise around the perimeter of the gym when the music starts. Remind students that they will be going for one minute and encourage them to find a pace that will allow them to keep moving during that time—not too fast and not too slow.

3. You should stand in a position to monitor the students or walk in the opposite direction, using positive eye contact.

4. When the music stops, each student goes to the middle circle, takes an Aerobic Card, and looks at the picture. If a student draws a star card, have her or him explain the picture to the class.

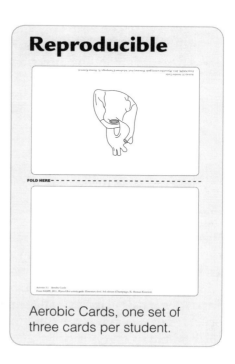

Aerobic Cards, one set of three cards per student.

5. Repeat with a different locomotor movement. Students stop and pick up a different card. Continue until students have all three cards.

6. At the end of the activity have the students without the stars explain the picture on the front in relation to the definition of aerobic fitness.

Teaching Hints

▶ Review the definition of aerobic fitness.

▶ Have students put movement into the definition: Aerobic fitness develops when the heart (make a fist and place over heart), lungs (place hands on lungs), and muscles (make muscles with both arms) all work together over an extended period.

▶ Point out to students what is happening to their bodies as they perform the activity. The heart is beating faster, breathing is faster, muscles may be getting tired, sweat is occurring, the face is getting red, and thirst may develop.

▶ A pedometer can keep track of a student's steps. Students can note the number of steps that they take each minute and be encouraged to increase that number. Have them think about the changes that are taking place in the body as they increase the number of steps taken.

▶ Have students start out moving slowly and then increase speed.

Sample Inclusion Tip

Students who move at a slower pace should keep to the perimeter of the room when going in a circle. This allows for a better traffic pattern with faster children on the inside. Speed does not matter, but students should be encouraged to keep moving at their original pace.

Variations

▶ Vary the length of time that music plays with different grade levels.

▶ Print cards on red paper to represent aerobic fitness activities.

▶ After moving in one direction for a while, you can say, "Carefully turn around on the balls of your feet and go the other way." Teaching children how to pivot helps with this direction.

▶ Have students move around the gym in a scattered formation or circle.

Home Extension

Have students see whether they can continue doing aerobic activity by walking around the block at home without stopping. Check for participation by a show of hands in the next class. Ask what changes occurred in the body when they finished the workout.

The Aerobic Movements activity gives students a workout using their hearts, lungs, and muscles while they learn to define aerobic fitness.

Assessment

- ▶ Have students use the cards to state the definition.
- ▶ Have students do the arm movements as they state the definition.
- ▶ Listen to a student give the definition to a partner.
- ▶ Check the distance that students moved with pedometers to see how hard they worked during the lesson.
- ▶ A class discussion can have students describe the changes that occur in the body during aerobic activity: heart beating faster, breathing harder, using many muscles, sweating.

FRANTIC BALL

INTERMEDIATE

Aerobic fitness—*Aerobic* means "with oxygen." Aerobic fitness is the ability of the heart, lungs, and muscles to perform activity over a sustained period. The heart rate represents how fast the heart pumps blood (which carries oxygen) through the body. When the body requires more oxygen to be transported to the muscles, the heart beats faster and the person breathes harder.

Purpose

▶ Students will evaluate how physical activity increases the heart rate.

▶ Students will examine the effects of how moving and participating in activity will increase the heart rate.

Relationship to National Standards

▶ Physical education standard 2: Demonstrates understanding of movement concepts principles, strategies, and tactics as they apply to the learning and performance of physical activities.

▶ Physical education standard 4: Achieves and maintains a health-enhancing level of physical fitness.

Equipment

▶ Three balls for each group of five students; 6- to 8-inch (15 to 20 cm) foam balls recommended

▶ Upbeat, fast music and music player

▶ Heart rate monitors (optional) for students to see the various heart rate changes that occur during the different activities

Procedure

1. Students take their heart rate while standing. Explain that a resting heart rate is slow because the body is not active.

2. Place students in groups of five. They will learn a star passing pattern (see figure 3.2). A student can't pass to an adjacent person. They should say the name of the person to whom they are passing. Add at least three balls to each group. Have students stop and take their heart rates.

3. They are now ready to move freely throughout the space and pass one ball. Students need to travel safely by staying on their feet, watching where they are going, and following directions. Students should move freely through the activity area but stay as a group so that they can continue the star passing pattern. Try to move from one end of the gym to the other.

Reproducible

FRANTIC BALL WORKSHEET

Name _____ Date _____

Write down three physical activities or sports that you did at home and describe your heartbeat and your breathing.

Example:
Activity: I played soccer with my friend. We were shooting goals.
My heartbeat: fast when I was dribbling to the goal to shoot.
I was breathing: OK and not very hard.
Activity: I walked the mall with my grandmother.
My heartbeat: good at first and then fast just before we stopped.
I was breathing: fast because she walked far and fast.

Activity 1: _____

My heartbeat:

I was breathing:

Activity 2: _____

My heartbeat:

I was breathing:

Activity 3: _____

My heartbeat:

I was breathing:

Activity 3.2 Frantic Ball Worksheet
From NASPE, 2011, *Physical Best activity guide: Elementary level*, 3rd edition (Champaign, IL: Human Kinetics).

Frantic Ball Worksheet, one per student.

4. When the music starts, each group of students continues to move around the gym. Remind them to watch the person who will be passing them the ball. They are to move constantly anywhere around the area and watch the group member who will be passing them the ball. The star passing pattern continues as the students move.

5. When the music stops, students stop and take their heart rates.

6. Compare the number of beats per minute to their resting heart rates and to the heart rate that results from other activities and various durations of exercise. Talk about how movement helps define aerobic fitness.

7. Talk about what they can do to increase the heart rate in this activity.

8. Repeat the activity and see whether they accomplished the task of increasing the heart rate. Were they successful? Why or why not?

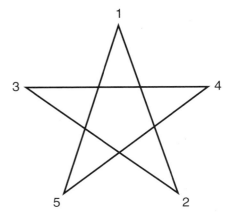

Figure 3.2   Star passing pattern.

Teaching Hints

▶ Define aerobic fitness before beginning the activity.

▶ Tell students that this activity will help them understand what aerobic fitness means.

▶ Taking the heart rate helps students see the effects of movement in developing aerobic fitness.

Sample Inclusion Tips

▶ Students who are unable to move a lot will be required to move a short distance after they have passed the ball.

▶ Use larger foam balls.

Variations

▶ Have students stand and pass a ball and then do a push-up after the pass.

▶ Have students move and dribble a ball five times before passing. Discuss how different sports will affect the heart rate.

▶ Go to the assessment questions and compare how heart rate changes with different sports.

Home Extension

Have students try out three physical activities or sports at home and check how fast their hearts are beating while they are playing. Remind them that physical activities include home chores like making their beds, picking up their rooms, emptying the trash, and raking leaves. They should use the Frantic Ball Worksheet to report their findings.

Assessment

Ask these questions in a classroom discussion:

▶ Did you notice a difference in your heart rate when you came to class, stood and passed, and moved and passed?

▶ What does a fast heart rate do for the body?

▶ How does a fast heart rate help the body?

▶ What did you do to increase your heart rate?

PRIMARY

Physical activity—Physical activity helps clear fat from arteries (tubes through which blood flows), which helps keep your heart healthy.

Purpose

▸ Students will be able to identify and discuss that too much fat will clog the arteries.

▸ Students will be able to discuss how to use moderate physical activity to help keep the heart and blood vessels healthy.

Relationship to National Standards

▸ Physical education standard 4: Achieves and maintains a health-enhancing level of physical fitness.

▸ Health education standard 1: Students will comprehend concepts related to health promotion and disease prevention.

Equipment

▸ Soft balls (fats) (e.g., yarn balls, paper balls)

▸ Hula hoops (arteries)

▸ Cones

▸ Frisbees (shields)

Procedure

1. Explain how blood flows through our arteries (hoops) and how too much fat (yarn balls) in our foods, over the long term, can cause the arteries to clog. Remind students that activity can reduce the amount of fat in the arteries. Explain that the more active they are in the game, the less fat (yarn balls) will collect in their team's arteries (hoops).

2. Divide the students into two groups.

3. Line up cones in the middle of a room to divide the room into two halves. Tell students not to cross over the line. Place the hula hoops (arteries) in the back of each half. Place the yarn balls (fat) randomly around on the floor (see figure 3.3).

4. Students throw one yarn ball at a time across the room to the opposite hula hoops, trying to fill their opponents' hula hoops with fat balls.

5. After fat balls are in hoops, students cannot take them out. Fat balls that do not land in a hula hoop may be picked up and thrown again.

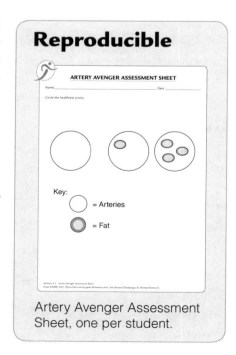

Artery Avenger Assessment Sheet, one per student.

6. The game continues until you have a good example of fat balls in hoops to have a discussion. Remember that they need some fat to be healthy!

7. Reset the activity.

8. For the second round, select students to act as artery avengers in a ratio of three avengers to six hoops. This ratio should provide some challenge and allow sufficient room for students to move safely about. Artery avengers can block yarn balls (fats) from entering the hoop with a Frisbee, which they should hold like a shield. Tell the students that the shields represent physical activity that helps keep fat from building in the arteries. The avengers may roll out balls that did not land in a hoop to their teammates so that they may throw them.

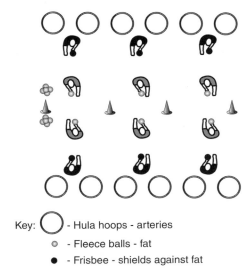

Key: ◯ - Hula hoops - arteries
    ○ - Fleece balls - fat
    ● - Frisbee - shields against fat

Figure 3.3 Setup for Artery Avengers.

Teaching Hints

▸ Students should be made aware of the fact that some fat is essential for a healthy body.

▸ If you have colored Frisbees, you could name them. For example, green represents vegetables, blue represents water, and red represents increased blood flow from exercise. This adaptation adds teaching the role of proper nutrition in maintaining heart health, in addition to physical activity.

▸ Demonstrate to students how arteries become clogged by drawing it on the board or overhead projector.

Sample Inclusion Tips

▸ For students with limited mobility, designate a peer helper to help pick up the balls.

▸ Place a hula hoop at the center line for those with difficulties throwing for distance or grasping and manipulating objects.

Variations

▸ Use balls of different colors and name each colored ball a different risk factor, such as stress, diabetes, poor diet, or smoking.

▸ Use the shield suggestions in "Teaching Hints."

Home Extension

Have students show their families this activity by placing items in something round. Students can explain to them how arteries become clogged and what causes the clogging. Also, they can explain that being physically active can help keep arteries healthy.

Assessment

▸ At the end of the activity have students stand by the healthiest artery (they should go to the artery with the fewest fat balls in it). They should identify hoops largely filled with fat as unhealthy.

▸ Have students fill out the Artery Avenger Assessment Sheet. Ask them to circle the healthiest artery. The correct answer is the artery with no fat buildup.

ENDURANCE MATCHUP

PRIMARY

Health benefits—Having aerobic fitness helps you learn better, enjoy life, and feel good. Physical activity encourages your heart to beat stronger, your lungs to breathe better, and your muscles to become stronger.

Purpose

Students will identify the health benefits of aerobic activities.

Relationship to National Standards

- ▶ Physical education standard 4: Achieves and maintain a health-enhancing level of physical fitness.
- ▶ Health education standard 3: Students will demonstrate the ability to practice health-enhancing behaviors and reduce health risks.

Equipment

- ▶ 32 domes or poly spots
- ▶ Different color jerseys for each team of three students (optional)

Procedure

1. Place dome cones in eight lines down the gym and have four domes in each row. Under the domes are puzzle pieces made from the Aerobic Benefit Puzzle.

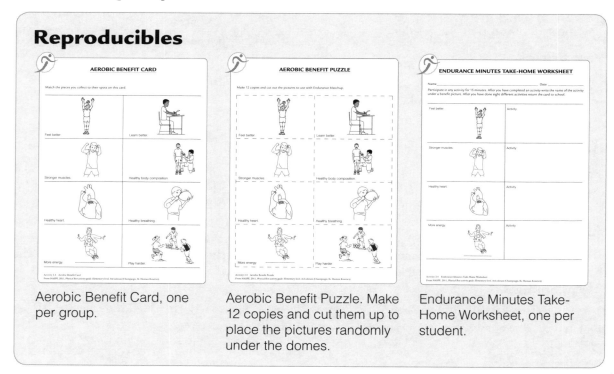

Reproducibles

Aerobic Benefit Card, one per group.

Aerobic Benefit Puzzle. Make 12 copies and cut them up to place the pictures randomly under the domes.

Endurance Minutes Take-Home Worksheet, one per student.

2. Place students in teams of four and give each team an Aerobic Benefit Card. If desired, have each team wear a different color jersey. For some groups, having teams of distinct colors helps students find their home teams faster and therefore makes the activity less confusing.

3. One student at a time runs to the other end, touches the wall, and then looks under any dome cone to find a puzzle piece to bring back. Students match the piece on the Aerobic Benefit Card. There will be more than one puzzle piece under each dome. Students are allowed to select the one that they need and leave the others.

4. After a student touches the wall the next person goes.

5. A team is finished when they have all eight pieces and no extras. They must name all eight benefits of aerobic fitness. Have students test each other.

Students run to find hidden puzzle pieces so that they can discover the health benefits of aerobic fitness.

Teaching Hints

▶ Ask students to study the Aerobic Benefit Card to learn why aerobic fitness is important.

▶ Tell students that they are going to be strengthening their hearts while learning additional ways aerobic fitness is important to their health.

Sample Inclusion Tip

Have students with motor problems go halfway down the gym before picking up a puzzle piece. They do not need to touch the wall. They may also go any time they are ready. Put puzzle pieces in a chair to make them easier to reach.

Variation

Make each team have a different color Aerobic Benefit Card. Make the puzzle pieces match the color of the Aerobic Benefit Card. Have students collect only the color of their Aerobic Benefit Card to make this simpler for younger students or students learning to read English.

Home Extension

Use the reproducible Endurance Minutes Take-Home Worksheet. Have each child discuss the sheet with her or his family. Guardians can use the comments part of the worksheet. This activity will enhance communication between yourself and guardians. After students complete the worksheet, they should return it to you.

Assessment

Check each team to see whether everyone can name the health benefits of aerobic fitness.

TREASURE ISLAND

INTERMEDIATE

Health benefits—Physical activity helps the body stay healthy. Activities performed often and over time will benefit the body in many ways.

Purpose

Students will be able to list the benefits of aerobic fitness.

Relationship to National Standards

- ▶ Physical education standard 3: Participates regularly in physical activity.
- ▶ Physical education standard 4: Achieves and maintains a health-enhancing level of physical fitness.
- ▶ Health education standard 3: Students will demonstrate the ability to practice health-enhancing behaviors and reduce health risks.

Equipment

- ▶ Four cones to represent Treasure Island in the middle of the room
- ▶ One hoop for each group of three students
- ▶ Upbeat music and music player
- ▶ Three jerseys, armbands, or objects to carry to identify pirates
- ▶ Pedometers (optional) to count steps

Procedure

1. Place the bills in the center of the floor, called Treasure Island. Each team has a hula hoop as home base. Bills go inside the hula hoop when students collect them.

2. Three students are taggers, or pirates. They are identified with a jersey or armband, or they can carry a object. Divide the rest of the class into groups of three. They take positions on the edge of the playing area with a hula hoop.

3. On your signal the first player from each line runs to Treasure Island, picks up one bill, and returns home without being tagged by a pirate.

4. If a runner is successful the bill goes in the hoop.

5. If a runner is tagged the bill (treasure) is returned to the pirate. The runner returns home, and the next player prepares to go.

6. Stop the activity and look to see how many different health benefits a team has gained.

7. After one minute, return the bills, and change pirates or taggers.

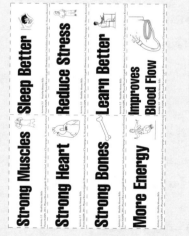

Reproducible

Healthy Money Bills with health benefits written on them are placed in the center of the playing area. Money can be copied on red paper to represent an activity dealing with heart benefits. Print 15 pages and cut into pieces to get 120 Healthy Money Bills.

Teaching Hint

Review all eight health benefits before beginning the activity. Doing aerobic activities produces benefits such as stronger muscles and bones, stronger heart, more energy, better sleep, relief from stress, ability to study better, and increased blood flow.

Inclusion Tip

Students with limited mobility cannot be tagged if they are standing still. These students do not have to wait a turn to go. They may continue to go at any time. You could have a closer starting line for these students. Bills can be placed on a box to make it easier for students to reach.

Variation

While students are waiting a turn to go, they can jump in place, jump rope, or jog in place to increase the number of steps on the pedometer and to be sure they are warmed up for their turn. Flexibility exercises can also be performed while waiting for a turn.

Treasure Island brings an element of fun to learning about the health benefits of aerobic fitness. Students run to avoid being tagged by pirates as they try to collect the most Healthy Money Bills.

Home Extension

Have students talk to their families about the many health benefits of aerobic fitness. They can invite their family and friends to take a walk with them or play an active game.

Assessment

- ▶ Direct the class in listing the health benefits of aerobic fitness either by recall or by picture recognition. Hold up a Healthy Money Bill to get an answer.
- ▶ Have students write down as many health benefits as they can remember.

POWERBALL HUNT

PRIMARY

Warm-up and cool-down—A warm-up prepares your heart, lungs, and muscles for activity by slowly increasing blood flow and raising your body temperature. Warming up will help keep you from injuring your muscles. A cool-down brings your body slowly back to normal temperature and returns blood flow to normal.

Purpose

▶ Students will explain the importance of warming up before and cooling down after an activity.

▶ Students will identify locomotor movements effective for warming up the body before other activity or cooling down the body after activity.

Relationship to National Standards

▶ Physical education standard 4: Achieves and maintains a health-enhancing level of physical fitness.

▶ Health education standard 3: Students will demonstrate the ability to practice health-enhancing behaviors and reduce health risks.

Equipment

None.

Procedure

1. Spread the numbered Locomotor Movement Cards out on the floor in the center of the activity room.

2. As students enter the room, hand each one a Number Card.

3. On a signal, students walk around the perimeter of the room. When they finish one lap, they find and collect a card with their number in the center of the room. When they flip their card over, they will dis-

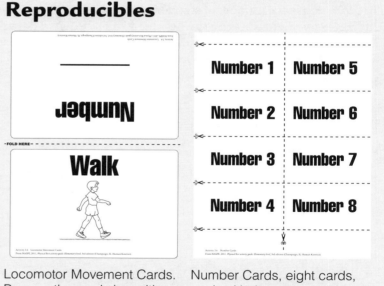

Reproducibles

Locomotor Movement Cards. Prepare the cards by writing a number on the back of each card, numbering one through eight. Print multiple sets of cards, mixing up the numbering order so that exercises are given different numbers. This arrangement will ensure that students find different types of movements to perform instead of always getting the same one.

Number Cards, eight cards, each with the same number per student.

cover a locomotor movement on the back. They perform this locomotor movement around the edge of the room for one lap.

4. After they complete the locomotor movement, they return the Locomotor Movement Card face down and look for another card with their number, then repeat moving around the gym.

Teaching Hints

▶ Talk to students about ways to warm up the body slowly. Warm-ups are used to get the blood flowing to warm up the muscles before using them. Students are less likely to hurt themselves if they loosen up the body slowly. They can begin by walking, skipping, or moving at a medium speed.

▶ Ask them whether they should run to warm up the body or go slower first.

▶ What else could they do to warm up the body besides doing locomotor movements?

▶ Why is the bear walk a good warm-up activity? (Answer: A bear walks with hands and feet on the floor, moves muscles slowly, and does not put a lot of weight on the hands and feet. This slow motion is good for warming up.)

▶ Can locomotor movements be used as a cool-down? Why? (Answer: Moving slowly gets the heart to slow down. Stretching exercises can help the muscle get back to normal.)

Sample Inclusion Tips

▶ Students can take turns partnering with a student in a wheelchair to assist with the card pickup. Alternatively, place cards on boxes to make picking them up easier.

▶ Use adaptations where necessary for locomotor movements; allow students to travel less distance before finding a card.

Students perform various locomotor movements while learning about the importance of warm-ups and cool-downs in Powerball Hunt.

Variations

▶ Add blank cards in the middle circle to make it harder for students to find their number.

▶ Use this game with flexibility activities as well. Teach students three flexibility exercises. After they have found their number, students perform one flexibility exercise before doing the locomotor movement. For example, students can do these stretches: sit and stretch, reaching for the legs; arm across the chest stretch; arms clasped above the head and gently stretched backward; stride step that is held in place. Active stretches can also be used, such as slow, high marching in place, slow jumping jacks, or grasshoppers (also called mountain climbers, in which students balance with hands and feet on the floor and bring the knee to the chest one foot at a time).

▶ Students can bounce a ball or jump rope around the gym instead of doing locomotor movements.

Home Extension

Review the locomotor movements and encourage students to practice them at home. Remind them to start with the easiest one and move to the one that makes them work harder. Have them report which locomotor movements they practiced when they come to class next time.

Assessment

▶ Check answers when you ask students why it is important to warm up the body slowly.

▶ Check answers when you ask student why it is important to cool down the body after exercise.

▶ Have students work together and rank the eight locomotor movements from slowest to fastest.

INTERMEDIATE

Warm-up and cool-down—A warm-up prepares your heart, lungs, and muscles for activity by slowly increasing blood flow and body temperature. Warming up will help keep you from injuring your muscles. A cool-down slowly brings your body back to normal temperature and the blood flow back to normal.

Purpose

Students will understand why a warm-up and cool-down are important in aerobic activity and how to do both properly.

Relationship to National Standards

▶ Physical education standard 6: Values physical activity for health, enjoyment, challenge, self-expression, and/or social interaction.

▶ Dance education standard 6: Makes connections between dance and healthful living.

Equipment

Appropriate music for each dance style and music player

Procedure

1. Review the importance of and rules for warming up and cooling down. Explain that dancing is an excellent way to increase the heart rate, thereby benefiting the heart and warming up the muscles.

2. Scatter the Dance Step Signs around the activity area. To emphasize the concept of warm-up and cool-down, place activity cards that describe dance steps of lower intensity on one side of the activity area and put cards for moves of higher intensity on the other side. For a warm-up, move through the lower-intensity dance steps first. Finish with the higher-intensity movements. Reverse the sequence for a cool-down.

3. Begin the activity by having the students first listen and then clap to the music, to get the beat.

4. Have students skip, jog, or use another locomotor action to travel to a

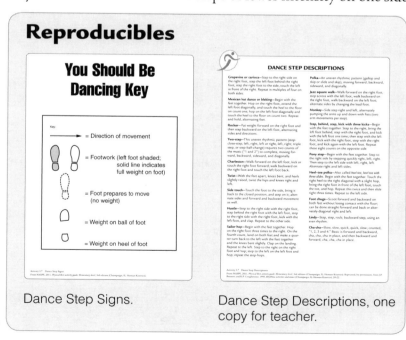

Dance Step Signs.

Dance Step Descriptions, one copy for teacher.

sign. Encourage students to perform the traveling actions to the beat of the music.

5. Direct them to perform the steps on the sign, sustaining the movement for a time, before they move to the next sign.

6. Help students cool down at the end of class by having them dance as a group using some of the easier steps. Use the Dance Step Descriptions to help you describe each dance for the students.

Teaching Hint

Make sure that students know the dance steps from previous lessons or introduce a few before beginning the activity. (For example, teach a new set of steps as a warm-up in lessons leading up to this activity.)

Sample Inclusion Tips

▶ For students who are hearing impaired, be sure to include the clapping mentioned in the procedure. Both you and the students can continue to clap as they move from card to card so that the student who is hearing impaired can maintain the tempo.

Dancing is a great way to increase the heart rate and warm up muscles.

▶ Students who are hearing impaired can also be helped by moving a dance ribbon fast or slow to describe the rhythm of the music.

▶ Have students who have difficulty with the dance steps dance to a slower beat.

Variation

As an alternative to using the Dance Step Signs provided on the CD-ROM, make a theme out of the steps to use with cross-curricular teaching (for example, coordinate with social studies by using all folk dance steps) or use all line dances, partner dances, all hip-hop steps, and so on to provide variety.

Home Extension

Have students listen to music at home with a friend and create their own dance steps for a warm-up or cool-down.

Assessment

▶ Have students explain the reasons why warming up and cooling down benefit the body.

▶ Discuss the differences between performing the lower-intensity steps and the higher-intensity steps. How did their heart rates feel (lower or higher)? How did their muscles feel (cooler or warmer)?

PRIMARY

Frequency—Frequency is how many days per week you do an aerobic activity. Being active three or four days a week is good, but doing some form of activity most days of the week is best.

Purpose

Students will understand and demonstrate how many days each week they should perform aerobic activity.

Relationship to National Standards

▶ Physical education standard 3: Participates regularly in physical activity.

▶ Health education standard 3: Students will demonstrate the ability to practice health-enhancing behaviors and reduce health risks.

Equipment

▶ Whatever equipment is necessary to perform an aerobic activity

▶ Pedometers, if available for checkout

Procedure

1. After students participate in a class activity that works on their aerobic fitness, explain that to have healthy hearts they need to engage in physical activity on all or most days of the week. Have the students brainstorm a list of activities that raise their heart rates. Encourage them to use examples from outside physical education class.

2. Pass out the Aerobic Activity Picture Chart, explain how to fill it out, and ask students to work with their guardians at home to fill it out for one to two weeks.

Teaching Hints

▶ Encourage students to find different ways to stay active. Give them examples that fit the opportunities in their community.

▶ Construct a bulletin board with hand-drawn or magazine pictures of the different activities that the students found to do.

▶ You may want to complete a chart as an example to show the students.

Sample Inclusion Tips

▶ Discuss with students individually what physical activities they participate in outside of school.

▶ Use this activity as an opportunity for diversity training. Have students with disabilities share or demonstrate the activities that they participate in outside of school.

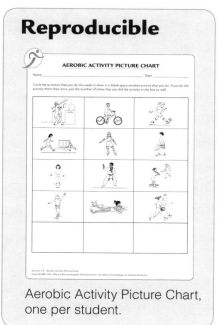

Aerobic Activity Picture Chart, one per student.

Variations

▶ Have students discuss their favorite aerobic activity with a friend or the class.

▶ Have a family day in physical education when family members join students in activities that the family can do at home to keep in shape.

Home Extension

To encourage participation in activity, have students fill out a chart for a week.

Assessment

▶ Have students tell you how many days per week they should give their hearts, lungs, and muscles a workout.

▶ Have students discuss their favorite aerobic activity with a partner in class and see whether they both agree that the activity is aerobic.

▶ Collect the homework sheet and lead a class discussion on the activities circled and added.

The Aerobic Activity Picture Chart helps students consider the activities that they do outside the classroom, such as martial arts, for their aerobic benefits.

FING FANG FOOEY

INTERMEDIATE

Frequency—Frequency is how many days per week you should perform aerobic activity to improve your heart rate, breathing rate, and muscle function. You should perform physical activity that you enjoy on all or most days of the week, and much of this activity should make you breathe harder and make your heart beat faster for long periods of time.

Purpose

Students will identify and demonstrate how many days a week they should perform aerobic activity.

Relationship to National Standards

► Physical education standard 4: Achieves and maintains a health-enhancing level of physical fitness.

► Physical education standard 5: Exhibits responsible personal and social behavior that respects self and others in physical activity settings.

► Health education standard 3: Students will demonstrate the ability to practice health-enhancing behaviors and reduce health risks.

Equipment

Pedometers or heart rate monitors (both optional) to keep track of a student's intensity level during the activity

Procedure

1. Divide the class into groups of three.

2. The activity is like rock, paper, scissors except that students use the words *fing, fang, fooey*.

3. After they say the words, each person holds out one, two, or three fingers.

4. They add the numbers of fingers exposed and use that number to count around the circle. Select one person to begin the counting; go around the circle and change leaders each time. The last person counted is the runner, and the other two chase the runner around the playing area until he or she is caught. When that happens, play begins again. Note: Two chasing one means that the chasing usually won't go long before the runner is caught and the game begins again.

Teaching Hints

► Discuss how the body feels during a workout.

► Discuss the number of minutes that students should be active daily along with how many days a week they should be active.

Reproducible

AEROBIC ACTIVITY FITNESS LOG

Name _____ Date _____

Date	Description of activity (what kind)	Time (how long)	Your initials

Activity 3.9   Aerobic Activity Fitness Log
From NASPE, 2011, *Physical Best activity guide: Elementary level, 3rd edition* (Champaign, IL: Human Kinetics).

Aerobic Activity Fitness Log, one per student.

▶ Remind the students that they had three people in their groups, which represents that they should have their hearts beating fast at least three days per week for 15 minutes or more, although doing so every day is even better!

▶ Discuss why vigorous activity is important and how are they going to fit it into their lives.

▶ Discuss that they have time to continue this activity at recess. If they play it, have them let you or their classroom teacher know. Encourage tag activities and other aerobic play at recess.

Students get the opportunity to add up their aerobic activity time during the chase portions of Fing Fang Fooey.

▶ Strive to give students activities that they can do on their own. After they learn tag activities, they can do them at recess and at home.

Sample Inclusion Tip

Give students a pool noodle to aid in tagging others.

Variations

▶ Have students dribble a ball while they are moving.

▶ Every time someone in their group runs, the group earns 1 point. At the end of the game the group adds up all the times the group ran. Here students can add up the aerobic activity time during the chase portion of the game.

Home Extension

Encourage students to learn how much activity each performs in a week by keeping track of their aerobic activities and the amount of time spent doing them. They can use the Aerobic Activity Fitness Log for tracking time spent and the type of activities done. Students should return the log at the end of the week.

Assessment

Ask students questions and have them respond by using a thumb motion. Yes answers are represented with a thumbs-up. No answers are represented with a thumbs-down. Ask these questions:

▶ Frequency is how many days per week you should perform aerobic activity to improve your heart rate, breathing rate, and muscle function. (Thumbs-up.)

▶ You should have your heart beating fast at least two days per week for 15 minutes or more. (Thumbs-down; the answer is three days per week.)

PRIMARY

Intensity—Intensity is how hard you work your heart during physical activity. As you work harder, your lungs breathe harder to bring in more oxygen. Your heart beats faster to move the blood through your body to deliver oxygen and nutrients to the muscles. As the blood flow increases, you get hotter and may begin to sweat. To replace the water that you lose through sweat, you should drink plenty of water before, during, and after activity.

Purpose

▶ Students will differentiate between movements that are more and less aerobically intense.

▶ Students will understand that the harder they work, the harder their hearts beat, the faster they breathe, and the hotter their bodies become.

▶ Students will understand that increasing the intensity of an aerobic activity will help strengthen the heart and lungs and move more blood throughout the body to feed muscles and other body parts.

Relationship to National Standards

▶ Physical education standard 4: Achieves and maintains a health-enhancing level of physical fitness.

▶ Health education standard 1: Students will comprehend concepts related to health promotion and disease prevention.

Equipment

▶ Tambourine or upbeat music and music player

▶ Pedometers, as variation

Procedure

1. Explain the concept of intensity. State that today students will be working harder and harder, checking their heart rates to see what their hearts do as they work harder. Ask students why it is important to increase the intensity of an activity (makes the heart stronger and improves the health of the lungs and blood vessels). Have students practice feeling their heart rates by placing one hand over the left side of the chest; this method will give a baseline heart rate to which they may compare their heart rates during the activity. Ask, "What else might your body do when it's working hard?"

2. Direct students to do the following:

   • Have them move to an open space of the activity area and move around in general space while being aware of others around them.

Reproducible

Walk Like a Dog

Activity 3.10 Animal Locomotion Task Signs
From *NASPE, 2011, Physical Best activity guide: Elementary level, 3rd edition (Champaign, IL: Human Kinetics).*

Animal Locomotion Task Signs.

Students have fun mimicking the actions and behaviors of animals while experiencing different levels of aerobic intensity.

- Ask them to check their heart rates by placing one hand over their hearts. They should simulate the pumping of the heart with the free hand whenever checking heart rate during this activity.
- When you hold up card 1 (walk like a dog), the students should walk for 30 seconds and then check their heart rates.

3. Hold up each of the Animal Locomotion Task Signs for 30 seconds and have students check their heart and breathing rates after each.

Teaching Hints

▶ Before beginning the activity, ensure that all students know how to feel their heart rates by placing a hand over the left side of the chest.

▶ Review signs that the body gives when you work harder: you get hotter, you begin to sweat, and your heart beats faster.

▶ Make sure that students know how to move safely in general space.

Sample Inclusion Tip

Consider allowing students who will require variations to the Animal Locomotion Task Signs the chance to review the signs before the lesson so that they can think about how they can best complete the tasks in class.

Variations

▶ After each 30 seconds of work have the students put their hands on their chests to feel their hearts beat. They should raise the other hand above the head and show how fast the heart is working by opening and closing the hand.

▶ Have students think of other animals that they would like to use in class.

▶ Students could use pedometers to see how many steps they take when performing the various animal walks. Ask students whether more steps would mean that the animal is working harder (more intensely) during the movement.

Home Extension

Have students watch animals and make up walks for them. They should think about how hard an animal works to move around. Have students tell a friend which animal that they saw did the most intense movement and see whether the friend agrees.

Assessment

▸ During the activity ask students to check their heart rates and breathing after each animal walk. Ask them to hold up one finger if the heart was beating slowly or not very fast and two fingers if the heart was beating very fast.

▸ After finishing, ask students what animal movements they thought were the hardest and why.

▸ Have students tell you how they can tell that one animal movement varies in intensity from another.

▸ Have students describe the body signs that they can use to know that they are working harder than normal.

▸ Ask students to tell you what type of activity makes the heart stronger and why.

JUMPING FRENZY

INTERMEDIATE

Intensity—Intensity is how hard you do your physical activity. As you work harder, your lungs work harder to bring in more oxygen. Your heart beats faster to move the blood through your body to deliver oxygen and nutrients to the muscles. As the blood flow increases, you get hotter and may begin to sweat. To replace the water that you lose through sweat, you should drink plenty of water before, during, and after activity.

Purpose

▶ Students will be able to state the benefits of good aerobic fitness.

▶ Students will demonstrate the principle of intensity by participating in a series of jumping activities that vary in intensity.

▶ Students will know how to check their heart rates to monitor the intensity of each activity.

Relationship to National Standards

Physical education standard 4: Achieves and maintains a health-enhancing level of physical fitness.

Equipment

▶ Cones, enough to designate a station for each three or four students

▶ Upbeat music and music player

▶ Jump ropes, one for each student

Procedure

1. Set up stations using Jumping Frenzy Instruction Cards or create your own. Have enough stations so that each station will have a maximum of four children if possible.

2. Make one or two of the stations rest or slow-down stops where students can stretch during the time that they are at this station. Place a copy of the Am I Giving My Heart a Workout? Chart there so that they can check how hard they have been working.

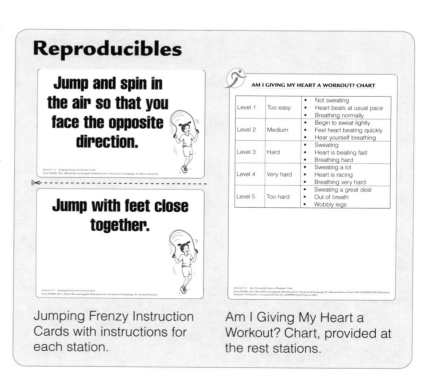

Jumping Frenzy Instruction Cards with instructions for each station.

Am I Giving My Heart a Workout? Chart, provided at the rest stations.

3. Remind students of the definition of aerobic fitness and define intensity as it relates to aerobic activity.

4. Have students warm up as a group.

5. Divide the class into groups of three or four. Have each group start at a different station and tell them to go clockwise or counterclockwise.

6. Have students work at each station for 15 seconds and then rotate to the next station.

7. Perform a group cool-down by walking around the activity space while conducting the oral assessment.

Teaching Hint

At the next class meeting, have the students increase the duration of the exercises by increasing the time at each jump station from 15 seconds to 20 seconds. This change will increase the intensity and reinforce the teaching of this concept.

Sample Inclusion Tips

Jumping activities help students explore varying intensity levels of aerobic fitness.

▸ Allow students who have trouble turning or jumping the rope to turn the rope at the side and just jump. Or split the rope in half so the student can hold a handle in each hand and have them turn the rope and continue to jump. This way they do not need to clear the rope.

▸ Students in wheelchairs can wheel their chairs back and forth over a line.

Variations

▸ Change the types of rest or slow down activities used at the rest stations, depending on the age of the group, students' fitness levels, and the duration that you perform the activity.

▸ Use double-dutch, elastic bands, or jump ropes and adjust the stations for a variation.

▸ Have small groups of students design a different set of stations using other locomotor activities. Have them name each station activity and describe how they can vary the intensity in the activity.

Home Extension

▸ Within a two-week period, see how many ideas the student can come up with for new jumping patterns.

▸ Suggest that they practice rope jumping with their friends at home and during recess.

Assessment

▶ After the activity, ask the group to rate their exertion level using the adjectives of light, medium, hard, and very hard, or use the Am I Giving My Heart a Workout? Chart. Have them tell you which one of the levels they think that they were using by holding up one through five fingers.

▶ Ask students which activities were most intense and why.

▶ Have students state or write a definition of intensity and give an example of how they could change the intensity of the activity (jump higher or lower, jump for a longer or shorter time, and so on).

AROUND THE BLOCK

PRIMARY AND INTERMEDIATE

Time—Time is how long you participate in an activity. Children should accumulate at least 60 minutes of physical activity on all or most days of the week and participate in several bouts of physical activity lasting 15 minutes or more each day.

Purpose

▶ Students will describe how time relates to aerobic fitness.

▶ Students will demonstrate how to pace themselves by participating in a cardiovascular activity for an extended period.

Relationship to National Standards

▶ Physical education standard 2: Demonstrates understanding of movement concepts, principles, strategies, and tactics as they apply to the learning and performance of physical activities.

▶ Physical education standard 4: Achieves and maintains a health-enhancing level of physical fitness.

Equipment

▶ 8 to 10 cones to define the sidewalk down the middle of the gym

▶ Four cones for the corners to define the running or walking pathway

Reproducibles

Around the Block Timed Activity for intermediate students, one per student.

Around the Block Home Worksheet for primary students, one per student.

Am I Giving My Heart a Workout? Chart, posted somewhere within the activity space for students to reference.

▶ Four hurdles with soft foam crossbars

▶ To support the hurdles use two low, four medium, and two high cones

▶ Four bases or poly spots

▶ Pedometers (optional) to keep track of steps

▶ Heart rate monitors (optional) to observe the difference in the heart rate during a workout

▶ Upbeat music and music player

Procedure

1. The sidewalk is defined with cones lengthwise down the middle of the gym and splitting at the end so that students can continue a path going left or right. Obstacles for leaping are placed in this lane, the sidewalk area (see figure 3.4).

2. Students walk around the block course for two minutes. Have them stop and discuss how their bodies feel different.

3. Students begin the path and move for two minutes by jogging around the course.

4. Students may choose to leap over obstacles or go around them.

5. At the conclusion of the workout, students check their heart rates and breathing rates. They should look for signs of the heart beating faster, sweaty and red faces, and breathing faster.

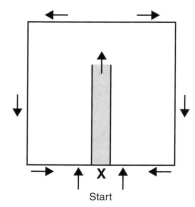

Figure 3.4 Floor diagram for Around the Block.

Teaching Hints

▶ Ask students questions to get them to think about the activity and how they feel after going for an extended period.

• As you work harder and longer, what happens to your lungs? (Answer: Your lungs work harder to bring in more oxygen.)

• Why does your heart beat faster? (Answer: To move the blood through your body to deliver oxygen and nutrients to the muscles.)

• As the blood flow increases, what happens to your body? (Answer: You get hotter and may begin to sweat. To replace the water you lose through sweat, you should drink plenty of water before, during, and after activity.)

▶ Have students place a hand on the heart and use the other hand to do opening and closing motions to demonstrate how fast the heart is beating. They can count the number of beats for six seconds and then add a zero to the end of the number to find the number of beats per minute. For young children, just use the feeling of the heart beating slow, fast, very fast, or racing, and breathing being slow or hard. Students can refer to the Am I Giving My Heart a Workout? Chart posted in the activity space to determine how hard they are working.

▶ Explain that to get a good workout for the heart, students must work for long periods; 15 minutes or more is preferred. Long workouts help keep the body strong and help it work better.

▶ Each student will show signs of a workout differently—face turning red, sweating, getting tired, becoming thirsty, breathing hard, or heart beating quickly.

▶ Discuss pacing as a way to sustain activity over a long period.

Sample Inclusion Tips

▶ Make the sidewalk wide enough for students using canes, walkers, or wheelchairs to use the course.

▶ Make a square inside the original square for students who participate at shorter distances.

▶ Leaping obstacles can be optional. You can set up speed bumps for wheelchairs with a small rope or a piece of cardboard taped in place, or by adding more obstacles to go around or through.

▶ Students may crawl or roll under hurdles when moving around the square. Refer to "Tips for Inclusion" in chapter 1.

Variations

▶ Include a variety of obstacles to leap or jump over to make the course challenging and interesting. Ideas include dome cones, jump ropes, tumbling mats, and animal beanbags.

▶ Record pedometer steps. Students can see how many steps they can get done in 10 minutes and compare that to the 10,000 steps needed daily. Repeat the activity at a later date so that students can see whether they are doing more.

▶ Have a group of students move the obstacles after a few minutes to keep the course interesting.

Home Extension

Have primary level students complete the Around the Block Home Worksheet with the help of their guardians and return it to class.

Have intermediate level students use the Around the Block Timed Activity to evaluate activities outside of the school.

Assessment

Ask these questions to check for understanding:

▶ How much time is needed to give the body an aerobic workout?

▶ How does pacing your speed affect your time in a workout?

▶ How did you pace yourself during the different periods? How did you do in the first one? In the second one?

MUSICAL SPORT SEQUENCE

PRIMARY

Time—Time is how long you participate in an activity. Children should accumulate at least 60 minutes of physical activity on all or most days of the week and participate in several bouts of physical activity lasting 15 minutes or more each day.

Purpose

▶ Students will create and perform an expressive dance movement sequence to music.

▶ Student will list different activities they can do after school that last 15 minutes or more to add up to 60 minutes of physical activity a day.

Relationship to National Standards

▶ Physical education standard 4: Achieves and maintains a health-enhancing level of physical fitness.

▶ Physical education standard 6: Values physical activity for health, enjoyment, challenge, self-expression, and/or social interaction.

▶ Health education standard 3: Students will demonstrate the ability to practice health-enhancing behaviors and reduce health risks.

▶ Dance education standard 3: Understands dance as a way to create and communicate meaning.

▶ Dance education standard 6: Makes connections between dance and healthful living.

Equipment

▶ Action pictures of popular athletes participating in their sports (from sport magazines, sport cards, sport section of the newspaper, and so on), at least five pictures for each student to choose from

▶ Pedometers (optional) to count steps and compare which routines took more steps

▶ Lively music and music player

Procedure

The amount of time that students are active is important to staying physically fit. Explain to students that if they are active 15 minutes at a time, four times a day, they will achieve the goal of being active for 60 minutes a day. For this activity, students look at pictures of various sport activities that they might like to do to stay active, but instead of just playing the sports, they will put the movements of the sports into a dance sequence. Dance is a fun way to get physical activity. By combining sports that students are already interested in with dance, you can get students thinking of unique ways that they can fulfill their 60 minutes of activity per day.

Time Your Activity Worksheet, one per student.

1. Have students stand in a large circle formation.
2. Scatter pictures in the middle of the circle.
3. On your signal, give the students a few minutes to browse through the photos and choose four photos that they like best.
4. After the students have collected their photos they return to their personal space and place the photos in front of them in their desired sequence.
5. After giving the students a few minutes to sequence their photos, instruct them to move their bodies like the athletes in their picture sequence after the music starts. Encourage the students to repeat the sequence several times while the music is playing.
6. You may give the students the freedom to rearrange their pictures to create a new sequence.
7. After five minutes of participating in their dance sequences, allow the class to return their photos to the general space and retrieve four different photos to sequence. They should create three sequences to equal 15 minutes of exercise.

Teaching Hints

▶ Collect pictures from magazines, newspapers, and other print media of popular athletes. Make certain to collect men and women athletes participating in a wide range of sports. You need to have at least four pictures available for each student in your class, but having more photos will allow greater creativity.

▶ Make your own photo gallery by using student drawings.

▶ Take pictures of students doing various sports and use them when you repeat this activity. Write captions under the photos so that others will know the activity.

Students use their creativity to put sport images into a dance sequence set to music. The music helps them learn to apply the concept of time to their aerobic fitness activities.

▶ Add household chores to the picture collection, such as vacuuming, dusting, cleaning, and raking leaves.

▶ Use a clock to show what 60 minutes and 15 minutes look like on a clock. Have students look at the clock when you begin and end the activity so that they will have a more accurate idea about time spent doing an activity.

▶ This activity is a good motivator for students who are hesitant to participate in dance activities. Using current photos of popular sport celebrities seems to increase student motivation. Including pictures of culturally determined (might need to explain what *culturally determined* means) forms of sport may also increase motivation levels.

▶ Have coworkers bring in pictures to use to collect photos faster.

Sample Inclusion Tip

Include photos of athletes with disabilities. If you have one, ask the county adapted physical education specialist for resources such as *Palaestra*, *Sports 'N Spokes*, or Web sites that have printable pictures of athletes from various disability sport associations (e.g., Disabled Sports USA—www.dsusa.org, Special Olympics International—www.specialolympics.org, and United States Quad Rugby Association—www.quadrugby.com) .

Variation

Students could work with a partner and create movements together or act out the activities or sports.

Home Extension

Distribute the Time Your Activity Worksheet and have students complete it at home. They should bring it back to class when they are done for a class discussion.

Assessment

- ► Ask, "Did you notice how you used all the muscles in your body?"
- ► Ask, "Did you notice how you kept yourself going during the whole time you were given?"
- ► Divide the students into small groups to share their sequences with their classmates. Ask the observing members to describe the sports that were demonstrated during the sequence.
- ► Have partners name three activities that they can do after school for 15 minutes or more. Observe their answers.
- ► Thumbs-Up or Thumbs-Down
  - • Can dancing or physical activities put together into a dance routine be considered physical activity? (Answer: thumbs-up)
  - • Should all your required minutes of physical activity each day be done all at once? (Answer: thumbs-down)
  - • Can you add 15 minutes at a time to your daily physical activity goal? (Answer: thumbs-up)

SIX-MINUTE JOG

INTERMEDIATE

Time—Time is how long you participate in an activity. Children should accumulate at least 60 minutes of physical activity on all or most days of the week and should participate in several bouts of physical activity lasting 15 minutes or more each day. Learning about pacing and knowing how to pace is important when performing aerobic activity. Without appropriate pacing a person will not be able to continue an activity for a long period.

Purpose

Students will be able to discuss the importance of pacing and length of time when doing aerobic activity.

Relationship to National Standards

▶ Physical education standard 2: Demonstrates understanding of movement concepts, principles, strategies, and tactics as they apply to the learning and performance of physical activities.

▶ Physical education standard 4: Achieves and maintains a health-enhancing level of physical fitness.

Equipment

▶ One pencil per student

▶ Approximately six straws per student to hand them each time they pass the starting point (depends on number of students in class and number of laps that they need to perform)

▶ 10 cones to mark the running area

▶ Pedometers and heart rate monitors (both optional) to check how fast the heart is beating at various times and how many steps are taken during the activity

Procedure

1. Set up a running track 1/10th of a mile long using 10 cones that are set 18 paces apart (or 100 m long using 10 cones set 10 m apart).

2. Explain that pacing is important to maintaining a steady aerobic pace for a longer period. This test uses

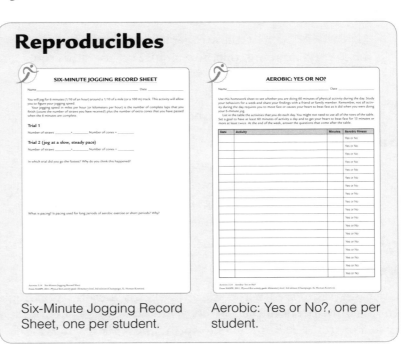

Reproducibles

Six-Minute Jogging Record Sheet, one per student.

Aerobic: Yes or No?, one per student.

a 1/10th-mile track (or a 100 m track) for 1/10th of an hour. At the end of six minutes, the students will know at what pace (how many miles per hour or kilometers per hour) they have jogged.

3. The students jog around the track while collecting a straw from you or their partners for each lap. After they hear the stop whistle, joggers calculate their miles per hour (or kilometers per hour) by counting the straws and the number of cones they have passed since passing their partners. For example, five straws and three cones past the partner equals 5.3 miles per hour. (On the shorter 100 m track, the same runner would have collected eight straws and passed five cones, indicating 8.5 kilometers per hour.)

4. The students record their scores and evaluate their pacing and level of aerobic fitness on their Six-Minute Jogging Record Sheets.

5. Perform the jog twice so that the students can adjust their pace and compare their two speeds.

Teaching Hints

Students learn how to pace themselves in Six-Minute Jog.

▶ Talk about finding a pace that they can maintain during the whole six minutes. Talk about how intense the pace feels. This will aid them in remembering the speed that helps them continue at a heart healthy pace.

▶ Explain the importance of time in an activity and the requirements for students their age.

▶ Let them know that many other activities count as physical activity, such as walking, riding a bike, and jumping rope, and require pacing skills too.

▶ Let them know that today they will be getting at least 12 minutes of good aerobic activity for the day.

▶ Talk to them about where they can make up the time difference.

Sample Inclusion Tips

▶ Everyone sets his or her own goal because personal goal setting is the most important point. Encourage students with mobility problems to work on finding the pace that allows them to go as far as possible during the activity and to use that pace during the second bout.

▶ Students with visual impairments may use a buddy to guide them around the course.

▶ Hand signals can help students with hearing impairments know when to start and stop.

Variation

Use two tests to see whether running the six minutes at various speeds gives students different ending miles per hour (kilometers per hour) results than does running the six minutes at a steady pace. For trial 1, ask students to sprint and walk in intervals. For trial 2, ask students to jog at a steady rate. Have them compare the two times.

Home Extension

Have the students complete the Aerobic: Yes or No? homework sheet at home and discuss the results with a friend or family member.

Assessment

Ask the students the following questions. Note that they will answer these questions again on their Aerobic: Yes or No? homework sheets. When the homework sheets are returned to you, have another brief discussion about the questions and answers.

▶ How does the amount of time that you spend in an activity affect your body?

▶ What is important about the time spent doing aerobic activities?

▶ How many minutes a day should you be doing aerobic activities?

AEROBIC SCOOTERS

PRIMARY

Type—Type means that certain activities use more oxygen, require you to breathe faster, and cause your heart to beat faster. You need to include aerobic activities in your life to help your heart and lungs grow stronger and work well.

Purpose

Students will identify heart-healthy activities.

Relationship to National Standards

▶ Physical education standard 4: Achieves and maintains a health-enhancing level of physical fitness.

▶ Physical education standard 6: Values physical activity for health, enjoyment, challenge, self-expression, and/or social interaction.

▶ Health education standard 3: Students will demonstrate the ability to practice health-enhancing behaviors and reduce health risks.

Equipment

▶ One scooter for each child

▶ Four beach balls

▶ Lively music and music player

Reproducibles

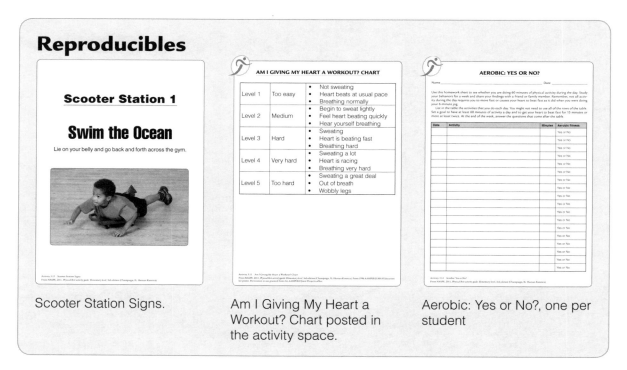

Scooter Station Signs.

Am I Giving My Heart a Workout? Chart posted in the activity space.

Aerobic: Yes or No?, one per student

Scooter activities are a fun way to help all students experience a new type of aerobic activity.

Procedure

1. Place the Scooter Station Signs around the gym with the equipment needed.
2. Explain to students that many types of activities can improve aerobic fitness.
3. Go through each station and demonstrate what students are expected to do.
4. Divide students into six groups.
5. Students begin the activity when the music begins. Students rotate to the next station when directed. Each student goes to all six stations.

Teaching Hints

▶ Go over the activity pyramid and explain the various areas.
▶ Review the definition of aerobic fitness; aerobic fitness develops when the heart, lungs, and muscles all work together over an extended period.
▶ Review the signs that the body gives when the heart is working hard from the Am I Giving My Heart a Workout? Chart, including breathing harder, heart beating faster, and becoming sweaty. Other signs include face turning red, muscles feeling that they are working hard, and getting tired.

Sample Inclusion Tips

▶ Connect two or more scooters together to make moving on a scooter easier.
▶ Have students take turns connecting with a partner and moving together.
▶ Students with disabilities can lie prone on a scooter to move more efficiently.
▶ Use some type of support mounted on the scooter for stability (for example, a milk crate with one side cut away mounted on the scooter gives the student trunk stability in a sitting position).

Variations

▶ Use a ball with some of the stations. Students can dribble and move, toss and catch, and shoot baskets. Using sport skills can help students relate to play and recreation time.
▶ Students can practice catching while moving.

Home Extension

Have students pay attention to their heart rates as they do activities at home and repeat activities which increased their heart rates.

Assessment

▶ Ask students to tell you which activity was aerobic and why or why not. Emphasize the signs of aerobic work to help them decide (heart working hard, breathing harder, face may be getting red, muscles are working longer than usual, and feeling tired). Students can refer to the Am I Giving My Heart a Workout? Chart.

▶ Have students list other activities that could be aerobic, such as swimming, jumping rope, jogging, and running in soccer or other sports.

AEROBIC SPORTS

INTERMEDIATE

Type—Type means that certain activities use more oxygen, require you to breathe faster, and cause your heart to beat faster. You must learn to choose activities that strengthen your heart.

Purpose

Students will identify heart-healthy activities.

Relationship to National Standards

▶ Physical education standard 4: Achieves and maintains a health-enhancing level of physical fitness.

▶ Physical education standard 6: Values physical activity for health, enjoyment, challenge, self-expression, and/or social interaction.

▶ Health education standard 3: Students will demonstrate the ability to practice health-enhancing behaviors and reduce health risks.

Equipment

▶ One basketball per student

▶ Six cones

▶ Four basketball hoops or use paper on the wall as a target

▶ Lively music and music player

▶ Pedometers (optional) to check how many steps are taken during the activity

▶ Heart rate monitors (optional) to compare the heart rates obtained in the various activities

Procedure

1. Place the Aerobic Sport Station Signs around the gym with the equipment needed.

2. Explain to students that many types of activities can improve aerobic fitness.

3. Go through each station and demonstrate what students are expected to do.

4. Divide students into six groups.

Reproducibles

Aerobic Sport Station Signs.

Physical Activity Pyramid for Children.

5. Students begin the activity when the music begins. Students rotate to the next station when directed. Each student goes to all six stations.

Teaching Hints

▶ Go over the Physical Activity Pyramid for Children and explain the various areas.

▶ Review the definition of aerobic fitness.

▶ Review the signs that the body gives when the heart is working hard, including breathing harder, heart beating faster, becoming sweaty, face turning red, muscles feeling that they are working hard, and getting tired.

▶ Remind students that some activities that they will be doing today with the basketball are aerobic and others are not. At the end of the workout they will have to decide which stations were aerobic.

Sample Inclusion Tips

▶ Have a lower basketball goal on the wall (or use a trashcan).

▶ Have a different peer helper at each station to help retrieve or pass the ball.

▶ Depending on students' levels of ability, several of these stations can be done at a low level (seated) or in a stationary position.

Aerobic Sports teaches students types of sport activities that they can do to stay aerobically fit outside of the classroom.

Variation

Use a soccer ball or other sport activities with the stations.

Home Extension

Have students list the types of activities that they have learned and what they do for the body. They may discuss their list with family members to see whether they agree with the answers. After revising their list if necessary, they should bring it back to you.

Assessment

▶ Ask students to tell you which activity was aerobic and why or why not.

▶ Have students list other activities that could be aerobic: swimming, jumping rope, jogging, and running in soccer or other sports.

▶ Use the Aerobic: Yes or No? assessment sheet.

INTERMEDIATE

Overload principle—The overload principle states that a body system (cardiorespiratory, muscular, or skeletal) must perform at a level beyond normal so that it can adapt and improve physiological function and fitness. Progression refers to *how* a person should increase overload. Proper progression involves a gradual increase in the level of exercise that is manipulated by increasing frequency, intensity, time, type, or a combination of more than one of these components.

Purpose

Students will learn and apply the training principles of progression and overload for aerobic fitness by completing a FITT Log and FITT Log Worksheet.

Relationship to National Standards

▶ Physical education standard 3: Participates regularly in physical activity.

▶ Physical education standard 4: Achieves and maintains a health-enhancing level of physical fitness.

▶ Health education standard 3: Student will demonstrate the ability to practice health-enhancing behaviors and reduce health risks.

Equipment

Pencils

Procedure

1. Briefly review the two-word definitions of the aspects of FITT—frequency (how often), intensity (how hard), time (how long), and type (what kind).

2. Ask students to offer brief examples of how they have applied the FITT guidelines to aerobic fitness in previous health-related fitness lessons.

3. Share descriptions of the concepts of progression and overload.

4. Distribute one blank FITT Log to each student. Review each category and how it

Reproducibles

FITT Log, one per student.

FITT Log Worksheet, one per student.

relates to FITT. Outline how students can apply progression and overload as they use this form.

5. Ask the class to share aerobic activities that they enjoy. Then tell them to choose one and write it on the log.

6. Have the students write their names on the log.

7. Assign students to log the aerobic fitness activity that they perform outside class for one week.

8. Have students fill in week 1 of the FITT Log Worksheet.

9. Guide students in setting goals for progression and overload and have them write the goal on the worksheet. They continue with the new goal for the next week.

10. At the end of each week meet with the class to discuss their progress and set new goals.

Teaching Tips

▶ Ask students at each class meeting how their logs are coming along.

▶ Require guardian initials if necessary to encourage participation.

Sample Inclusion Tip

Help students with special circumstances come up with alternative activities to suit their needs and abilities. You can modify activities suggested earlier in this chapter, provide suggestions for students who must stay indoors because of safety or space constraints, or otherwise help students develop activity ideas that will work for them.

Variations

▶ Ask the school's after-school care providers to provide space, time, and other support for students to add to their logs.

▶ Tie the Fitnessgram aerobic assessment to this activity.

▶ The activity is set up for one week and one month, but you can change it for specific circumstances to cover one day to two weeks to a month to several months. Select the period that works best for the specific needs of the students.

Home Extension

This activity is a home extension.

Students use the FITT Log to record their aerobic activities and set new goals.

Assessment

▶ Ask the students to tell you the two-word meanings for each of the FITT principles.

▶ After one week, review the logs with the students to ensure that they are participating safely. Make sure that they understand that maintaining the level at which they are working is appropriate for a period of a week.

▶ Continue monitoring the log with the students weekly to ensure that they understand how to maintain and increase their activity level safely by using the FITT principles wisely.

▶ After a certain period, a week or a month, have students review their logs with you and write about their experiences by answering questions such as the following:

- Were you able to build up to a higher level of intensity safely over the course of the month, do the activities more frequently each week, or spend more time doing each activity? Which changes did you make, if any?

- If you were able to make changes, how might the changes have affected your aerobic fitness?

- If you did not make changes, what might you be able to do differently in the future?

▶ Realize that many factors, such as the child's initial level of fitness and participation (if already high, the student may not progress for that reason), and other personal factors may affect the answers to these questions. Keeping this in mind, focus on the assessment as a means to teach and reinforce the concepts of progression and overload.

Muscular Strength and Endurance

Chapter Contents

© Felix Mizioznikov/fotolia.com

Although the literature does not offer a clear-cut conclusion about whether children attain health benefits from resistance training similar to those that adults achieve, children can safely improve muscular strength and endurance if they follow appropriate training guidelines. Sothern, Loftin, Suskind, Udall, and Becker (1999) reported findings that the prepubescent child is at increased risk for injury because of a reduction in joint flexibility caused by rapid growth of long bones. Their findings suggest that strength gains may reduce the risk of acute sport injuries and overuse injuries. For more information concerning the principles of training for muscular strength and endurance, refer to *Physical Education for Lifelong Fitness: The Physical Best Teacher's Guide, Third Edition*. This chapter includes several activities for developing muscular strength and endurance in elementary-level students.

DEFINING MUSCULAR STRENGTH AND ENDURANCE

Muscular strength is the ability of a muscle or muscle group to exert maximal force against a resistance one time through the full range of motion. A child perceives this as the ability to act independently, or to lift and carry objects without assistance. *Muscular endurance* is the ability of a muscle or muscle group to exert a submaximal force repeatedly over time. Frequently, the activities performed to develop muscular strength also develop some muscular endurance because many of the activities use the child's own body weight and involve several repetitions. Separating these two areas of health-related fitness is often difficult, so Physical Best suggests that at the elementary level you label your unit as muscular strength and endurance, or muscular fitness. Doing so will align your actions with the newest physical activity pyramid for kids (Corbin, 2010) in which the description of muscular fitness exercise is utilized for one of the pyramid levels.

Potential benefits of resistance training include the following:

- Increased muscular strength (I'm able to push or lift my bike.)

- Increased muscular endurance (I'm able to play a long time without my legs getting tired.)

- Improvement in aerobic fitness through muscular fitness circuit training (I'm able to play longer without getting tired.)

- Prevention of musculoskeletal injury (I will not get hurt as easily or often.)

- Improved sport performance (I can help my soccer team by being a better player.)

- Reduced risk of fractures in adulthood (builds stronger bones)

- Increased bone strength and bone growth through exercise during the skeletal growth period (builds stronger bones)

Activities found in this chapter will introduce and familiarize elementary-level students with these benefits.

TEACHING GUIDELINES FOR MUSCULAR STRENGTH AND ENDURANCE

As with each area of health-related fitness, the principles of training (progression, overload, specificity, regularity, and individuality) should be incorporated into the activity. Manipulate the FITT guidelines based on the age of the child. Keep in mind that chronological age may not match physiological maturation. Note that the guidelines in table 4.1 are only guiding principles for development of muscular strength and endurance. Kraemer and Fleck (1993) suggested the following guidelines for resistance exercise:

- 7 years old and younger—Introduce the child to basic exercises with little or no weight; develop the concept of a training session; teach exercise techniques; progress from body weight calisthenics, partner exercise, and lightly resisted exercises; and keep volume low.

- 8 to 10 years old—Gradually increase the number of exercises; practice exercise technique in all lifts; start gradual progressive loading of exercises; keep exercises simple;

gradually increase training volume; and carefully monitor toleration of exercise stress.

▶ 11 to 13 years old—Teach all basic exercise techniques; continue progressive loading of each exercise; emphasize exercise techniques; and use little or no resistance when introducing more advanced exercises.

TRAINING METHODS FOR MUSCULAR STRENGTH AND ENDURANCE

A child with no resistance training experience should begin at the previous level, regardless of age, and move to the next level as he or she develops exercise tolerance, skill, and understanding of the lifting techniques.

Several recommendations or position stands are available for resistance and strength training. See the *Physical Education for Lifelong Fitness: The Physical Best Teacher's Guide, Third Edition* to provide guidance in developing children's resistance training programs (ACSM, 2000; AAP, 2001; Hass et al., 2001; NSCA, 1985). Use these guidelines to assist you in developing a safe and developmentally appropriate muscular strength and endurance unit. Both the American Academy of Pediatrics (AAP) and the ACSM recommend strength training for children as young as six years old.

Beginning students, especially elementary students, should engage primarily in circuit training using their own body weight, partners, or light medicine balls. The volume should be low and the intensity very low (Bompa, 2000; Graham et

al., 2010). Children should try performing reverse curl-ups or the lowering phase of the push-up (holding the lower position) if they have difficulty performing the regular curl-up or push-up. Upper elementary students may begin to participate in partner-resisted exercises and resistance band training.

MOTOR-SKILL DEVELOPMENT THROUGH MUSCULAR STRENGTH AND ENDURANCE ACTIVITIES

Using the weight room to develop muscular strength and endurance is not always necessary or appropriate. According to Graham et al. (2010), "weight training is not appropriate for elementary students; overload of muscles and bones can be accomplished through physical activity" (p. 52). Graham et al. (2010) encourage educators to utilize activities that motivate children to move and lift their body weight. Students may engage in a variety of motor skills to increase muscular strength and endurance. For example, primary students engaged in a tag game may be using locomotor skills such as hopping or skipping that improve muscular strength and endurance of the leg muscles. Older students may enjoy team-building activities that necessitate arm strength for success. Motor-skill development through fitness activity is the perfect area for you to consider the abilities and disabilities of all students.

Table 4.1   FITT Guidelines Applied to Muscular Fitness

Ages	9–11 yr[a, b]	12–14 yr[a, b]
Frequency	Two or three times per week	Two or three times per week
Intensity	Very light weight	Light weight
Time	At least one set (may do two sets) 6–15 reps At least 20–30 minutes	At least one set (may do three sets) 6–15 reps At least 20–30 minutes
Type	Major muscle groups, one exercise per muscle or muscle group	Major muscle groups, one exercise per muscle or muscle group

[a] Modified from AAP 2001.

[b] Modified from Faigenbaum, et al. 1996.

Some are high achievers, others are low achievers, and still others have physical or intellectual disabilities. Provide opportunities for all students to develop physical skills and be successful in your classroom. If a student is severely disabled, you may need to contact someone who specializes in adapted physical education for assistance in developing an individualized education plan. Many of the Physical Best activities either incorporate a variety of motor skills or allow you to create modifications to the activity to address the motor development needs of your students.

MUSCULAR STRENGTH AND ENDURANCE NEWSLETTER

Use the Muscular Strength and Endurance Newsletter (located on the CD-ROM) to introduce, reinforce, and extend the concepts behind developing and maintaining good muscular strength and endurance. The following are ways you might consider using this tool:

▶ Send the newsletter home as a guardian-involvement tool during a mini unit focusing on muscular strength and endurance.

▶ Use the newsletter to help you feature muscular strength and endurance as the "Health-Related Fitness Component of the Month."

▶ Introduce the activity ideas as a whole-group task. Ask students to choose one activity to perform outside class in the next week. They should report their progress through a log, journal, a guardian's signature on the newsletter, or other means.

▶ Validate and promote student involvement in physical activity outside class time and the school setting.

▶ Among students who can read, promote reading to learn across your curriculum, further supporting the elementary school mission.

▶ Use the newsletter as a model or springboard to create your own newsletters, tailored specifically to your students' needs.

▶ Feel free to use the Muscular Strength and Endurance Newsletter (see figure 4.1) in a way that helps you teach more effectively to the specific needs of your students and their guardians.

See table 4.2 for a grid of activities in this chapter.

Figure 4.1 Becoming Your Physical Best: Muscular Strength and Endurance Newsletter.

Table 4.2 Chapter 4 Activities Grid

Activity number	Activity title	Activity page	Concept	Primary	Intermediate	Reproducibles (on CD-ROM)
4.1	Hit the Deck	80	Muscular strength and endurance	•		Hit the Deck Exercise Cards
4.2	Muscle Hustle	82	Muscular strength and endurance		•	Muscle Hustle Station Signs
						Muscle Hustle Scoresheet
4.3	Super Hero Muscles	85	Health benefits		•	Muscular Strength and Endurance Benefit Sheet
						Super Hero Muscles Puzzle Pieces
						Super Hero Cards
4.4	Sport Roundup	88	Health benefits		•	Sport Roundup Station Cards
						Muscular Strength and Endurance Health Benefit Cards
						Sport Roundup Task Sheet
4.5	Opposing Force	92	Frequency	•		Exercise Picture Chart for Runner
						Exercise Picture Chart for Sitter
4.6	Muscular Strength and Endurance Activity Log	95	Frequency		•	Muscular Strength and Endurance Activity Log
4.7	Animal Tag	97	Intensity	•		Animal Cards
						You Are It! Cards
4.8	Survivor Course	100	Intensity		•	Survivor Course Station Signs
						My Intensity Training
4.9	Time Your Workout	102	Repetition and time	•		Practicing Sets and Reps and Learning About Time
						Set and Reps Chart
4.10	Clean the Beach	105	Specificity	•		None
4.11	Shuffle and Hustle	107	Specificity		•	Shuffle and Hustle Suit Posters
4.12	Push-Up Curl-Up Challenge	109	Progression		•	Push-Up Challenge Poster
						Curl-Up Challenge Poster
						Push-Up Curl-Up Challenge Log
4.13	Stability Progression	112	Progression		•	Push-Up Progression With a Stability Ball
						Curl-Up Progression With a Stability Ball
						Push-Up and Curl-Up Challenge Handout
4.14	Lower-Body Challenge	115	Specificity	•	•	Lower-Body Challenge: Teacher's Guide for Station Setup and Utilization
						Lower-Body Challenge Station Level 1 Signs
						Lower-Body Challenge Station Level 2 Signs
4.15	Upper-Body Challenge	119	Specificity	•	•	Upper-Body Challenge: Teacher's Guide for Station Setup and Utilization
						Upper-Body Challenge Station Level 1 Signs
						Upper-Body Challenge Station Level 2 Signs
4.16	Muscular Strength and Endurance FITT Log	123	Progression		•	FITT Log
						FITT Log Worksheet

HIT THE DECK

PRIMARY

Muscular strength and endurance—Muscular strength is the strongest force possible that a group of muscles can produce to perform a task. Muscular endurance is the ability to move your body or an object repeatedly without getting tired. For most activities, you use both muscular strength and endurance.

Purpose

Students will identify and perform activities that emphasize two of the health-related fitness components: muscular strength and muscular endurance.

Relationship to National Standards

▶ Physical education standard 2: Demonstrates understanding of movement concepts, principles, strategies, and tactics as they apply to the learning and performance of physical activities.

▶ Physical education standard 4: Achieves and maintains a health-enhancing level of physical fitness.

Equipment

▶ Upbeat music and player

▶ Mats to use for floor work

Procedure

1. Ask students how important muscles are and have them point to a muscle and state how that muscle helps them. The answer is that a muscle helps do all kinds of movements and that strong muscles help us do things better and easier.

2. Go over the definitions of muscular strength and muscular endurance and explain that some exercises from the activity will use primarily muscular endurance and some will use primarily muscular strength.

3. Look at the exercise cards that show the exercises. Review each exercise and discuss briefly those that emphasize muscular endurance and those that emphasize muscular strength.

4. When you say, "Go," students should scatter. When the music starts they move about the room using a locomotor movement of your choice.

5. When the music stops, they are to "hit the deck," drop to the ground on their bellies, and then listen for the name of the exercise that they need to perform. They do the exercise until the music starts again. This process is fun for the students and they listen better when in a specific position on the floor. When the music starts they resume the locomotor activity.

6. Repeat the cycle until you have used all the Hit the Deck Exercise Cards.

Hit the Deck Exercise Cards.

Teaching Hints

▶ Reinforce which type of muscle ability they are using during each exercise.

▶ The activity can be used as a circuit using the folded cards.

Sample Inclusion Tips

▶ Students who are physically unable to move to the ground need to freeze when the music stops and prepare for appropriate exercises.

▶ Light free weights or sandbags can be used in place of body weight for exercises.

▶ Students with special needs can look at the exercise cards ahead of time to better prepare for performing them. If alternative exercises are used these could be shared with the class after the activity so that they can learn these as well.

Variations

▶ Change the locomotor movement each time to develop skills and to keep the interest of the students.

Students learn the difference between muscular strength and muscular endurance by performing various exercises in Hit the Deck.

▶ Name additional exercises. After the students perform the new exercises, help students decide whether they are muscular strength, muscular endurance, or something else, perhaps flexibility or aerobic exercises.

▶ Have students work in groups to identify a muscular strength exercise for the class or a muscular endurance exercise. They can share these between the locomotor activities and see whether the rest of the class agrees with the classifications.

Home Extensions

▶ Encourage the students to tell their families about the two types of abilities of muscles, strength and endurance, and why they are important. Students can perform some of these activities with their families.

▶ Have students look at various sports on TV and decide whether muscular strength or muscular endurance is more important in that sport. They can share their thoughts with others and see whether they agree.

Assessment

▶ Ask students to give you examples of a muscular strength exercise that they did. Do the same for muscular endurance.

▶ Ask the students to name activities they do that need lots of muscular strength. Have them name some that require a lot of muscular endurance.

▶ Ask students how they would use muscular strength or muscular endurance in a specific sport; for example, in football they would need endurance to run, strength to hold the line or to throw the ball far.

INTERMEDIATE

Muscular strength and endurance—Muscular strength involves the strongest force possible that a group of muscles can produce to perform a task. Muscular endurance is the ability to move your body or an object repeatedly without getting tired. For most activities, you use both muscular strength and endurance. If you do not use your muscles regularly, they can lose strength and endurance.

Purpose

Students will understand the definitions of muscular strength and muscular endurance by participating in several circuit activities that develop or demonstrate these components.

Relationship to National Standards

Physical education standard 4: Achieves and maintains a health-enhancing level of physical fitness.

Equipment

▶ Equipment needed for stations: basketballs, light volleyballs, soccer balls, cones, lightweight medicine ball, beanbags, mats, tape (to create a square box for target pitches), and containers

▶ Fast-moving, segmented music and player (optional)

▶ Pedometers (optional)

Procedure

1. Define muscular strength and endurance. Share or have students share a few examples of each. Explain that today students will participate in a circuit designed to build muscular strength or endurance or both, which in turn will enhance physical activity and motor performance. Describe the station activities to students. See page 84 for sample stations.

2. Divide students into small groups and have each group go to a station, with a scoresheet and a pencil for each student.

3. Signal students to perform the activity on the Muscle Hustle Station Sign at their station for 30 seconds and record their total time or repetitions. Working individually or as a group, they check off muscular strength or endurance or both.

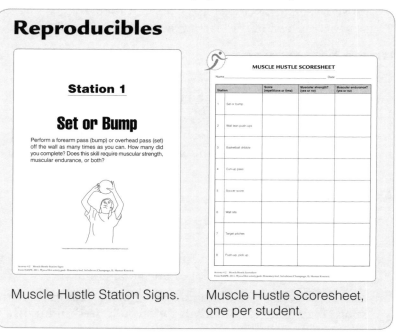

Muscle Hustle Station Signs.

Muscle Hustle Scoresheet, one per student.

4. Have students rotate from station to station.

5. Continue as long as desired.

Teaching Hints

▶ Vary the objects thrown and their size.

▶ Make the targets closer or larger if necessary.

Sample Inclusion Tips

▶ Station 1

  • Change color of ball or use an auditory signal for students with visual impairment.

  • Change the size of the ball.

▶ Station 3—Students can air dribble by tossing and catching the ball.

▶ Station 4—Students can pass a lighter ball back and forth.

▶ Station 5

  • Make the target larger or change the distance from the target.

  • Change the object thrown to a beanbag or a yarn ball.

Variations

▶ Have students bring in pictures of athletes performing muscular strength and endurance activities in their sport and use the activities of the sports for the circuit stations.

▶ Use pedometers to determine the number of steps taken during all activities.

The circuit activities in Muscle Hustle help develop both muscular strength and endurance.

Home Extension

Have students pick a muscular strength or endurance activity and perform it for a week. Ask these questions: Do you think that you made the right decision? Why or why not?

Assessment

▶ Ask students to refer to their Muscle Hustle Scoresheets and tell you for each activity whether they thought it used muscular strength, muscular endurance, or both, and why.

▶ Have students write short definitions of muscular strength and muscular endurance and give two examples of physical activities or sports that require muscular strength and endurance.

▶ Provide students with a list of physical activities and have them identify skills that require muscular strength and endurance. This example will give you a start:

  • Activity—baseball and softball

  • Muscular strength—throwing the ball from center field

  • Muscular endurance—pitching for an inning

MUSCLE HUSTLE SAMPLE STATIONS

Station 1—Set or Bump

Students perform a forearm pass (bump) or overhead pass (set) off a wall as many times as they can during their 30 seconds at the station. They count total bumps or sets.

Station 2—Wall Lean Push-Ups

Students stand with feet shoulder-width apart and lean into a wall with the elbows straight but not locked. They perform as many wall lean push-ups as they can during their 30 seconds at the station.

Station 3—Basketball Dribble

Students continually practice dribbling a basketball. They count how many successful dribbles they made during the 30 seconds at the station.

Station 4—Curl-Up Pass

Students lie in the curl-up position toe to toe with a partner with one holding a utility ball or slightly heavier ball such as a soccer ball. Partners perform curl-ups together, and on each curl-up they pass the ball from one to the other. How many successful passes did they make in 30 seconds?

Station 5—Soccer Score

Using the inside of the foot, students try to "score" by hitting a cone with the ball. They count the number of goals scored during the 30 seconds. They kick the ball from different distances from the cone.

Station 6—Wall Sits

Students sit in a chair position with their backs against the wall and hold the position as long as they can during their 30 seconds at the station.

Station 7—Target Pitches

Students pitch a ball as fast as possible yet under control at a target to score a hit. They count how many successful strikes they made into the target during their 30 seconds at the station.

Station 8—Push-Up, Pick Up

In a push-up position, students pick up beanbags and fill a container. They count how many beanbags they placed in the container during their 30 seconds at the station.

INTERMEDIATE

Health benefits—Strong muscles allow us to participate in a variety of activities, including chores, work, and play. Muscles that have good endurance allow us to play and work safely for long periods. Among the many benefits to having good muscular strength and endurance are good posture, strong bones, and strong muscles.

Purpose

Students will be able to list and discuss information about the benefits of muscular strength and endurance.

Relationship to National Standards

▶ Physical education standard 4: Achieves and maintains a health-enhancing level of physical fitness.

▶ Health education standard 3: Students will demonstrate the ability to practice health-enhancing behaviors and reduce health risks.

Equipment

▶ Domes or poly spots, eight per team

▶ Balls for dribbling

▶ Aerobic steps or benches

▶ Jump ropes

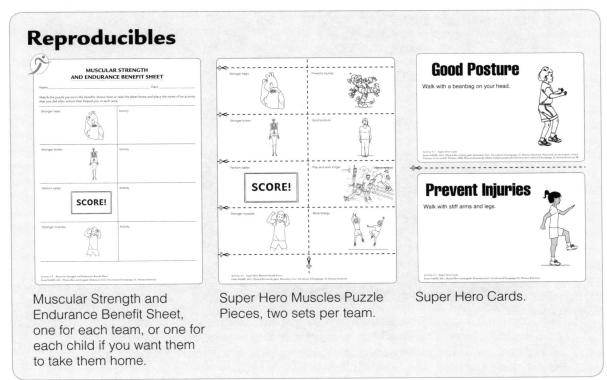

Reproducibles

Muscular Strength and Endurance Benefit Sheet, one for each team, or one for each child if you want them to take them home.

Super Hero Muscles Puzzle Pieces, two sets per team.

Super Hero Cards.

▶ Beanbags

▶ Buckets for holding the Super Hero Cards

▶ Mats for curl-up and push-up areas

Procedure

1. The room is set up as in a concentration game. Domes or poly spots are placed in eight lines down the gym with five in each line. Under the domes are the Muscular Strength and Endurance Puzzle Pieces.

2. Students are in groups of four.

3. Talk to students about the benefits of muscular strength and endurance and why they are important. Compare these benefits to the abilities of the super heroes they see in cartoons and on TV.

4. Tell them that they are going to be working on strengthening their muscles today while they are learning why it is important. They will do this with the various walks that they use to get to the other end. Review the walks and the benefits and meaning of each.

5. Give each team a Muscular Strength and Endurance Benefit Sheet and go over the benefits of muscular strength and endurance.

6. One student in each group picks a Super Hero Card, looks at the movement to use to move to the other end of the gym, puts the card back in the bucket, and performs the movement while moving down the court to touch the end wall.

7. After touching the wall, the child does either five curl-ups or five push-ups and looks under any dome cone to find a puzzle piece to bring back. The child uses the movement form to come back to the team. The team then matches the piece on the Muscular Strength and Endurance Benefit Sheet.

Using familiar symbols like the super heroes that kids see in cartoons helps them to understand the health benefits of muscular strength and endurance. The exercises on the Super Hero Cards give students the chance to learn how to become big and strong like their heroes.

8. After a student touches the wall, the next person looks at a movement card and starts the trip to the far end wall to do his or her exercise and pick up another piece of the puzzle and come back to the team.

9. When a team has all eight pieces of the puzzle, they are finished. Finished groups must be able to name all eight muscular strength and endurance benefits. Have students test each other.

Teaching Hints

▸ Encourage students to be ready to run to get a movement card as soon as the person in front of them touches the wall.

▸ Encourage teamwork; students can take turns reading the puzzle pieces and trying to help partners find the missing piece.

Sample Inclusion Tips

▸ Have students with motor problems go only halfway down the gym before picking up a puzzle piece. They do not need to touch the wall, but they should be given a specific exercise ahead of time that they can do five times before coming back (for example, arm push-ups on their chair handles). If needed, assign a partner to go with the student and help pick up the piece and bring it back.

▸ Puzzle pieces can be placed on a chair or stool at a higher level than the ground for students with balance problems.

Variations

▸ Make the Muscular Strength and Endurance Benefit Sheets and puzzle pieces different colors.

▸ Students need to get all matching colors to be finished.

▸ Students need to get a different color in each area to be finished.

Home Extension

Ask students to go home and do a muscular fitness activity for 15 minutes or more. A Muscular Strength and Endurance Benefit Sheet can go home with each student. After performing the activity, students write the name of the activity next to the benefit picture. After they list six different activities students return the sheet to school. The homework sheet has a place for a guardian to sign and to make comments about the activity to enhance two-way way communication between yourself and the guardian.

Assessment

▸ Check each team to see whether everyone can name the benefits of muscular strength and endurance used in the activity.

▸ Ask what types of activities contribute to muscular strength and endurance.

SPORT ROUNDUP

INTERMEDIATE

Health benefits—Strong muscles allow us to participate in a variety of activities, including chores, work, play, and sport. Muscles that have good endurance allow us to work or play safely for long periods. In addition to having the benefit of playing and working harder and longer, good muscular strength and endurance can have many other benefits, including stronger bones, a stronger heart, good posture, and fewer injuries.

Purpose

- ▶ Students will understand the health benefits associated with muscular strength and endurance.
- ▶ Students will identify connections between specific activities and muscular fitness.
- ▶ Students will participate in physical activities that help develop muscular fitness through specific physical activities.

Relationship to National Standards

- ▶ Physical education standard 4: Achieves and maintains a health-enhancing level of physical fitness.
- ▶ Health education standard 1: Students will comprehend concepts related to health promotion and disease prevention.
- ▶ Health education standard 3: Students will demonstrate the ability to practice health-enhancing behaviors and reduce health risks.

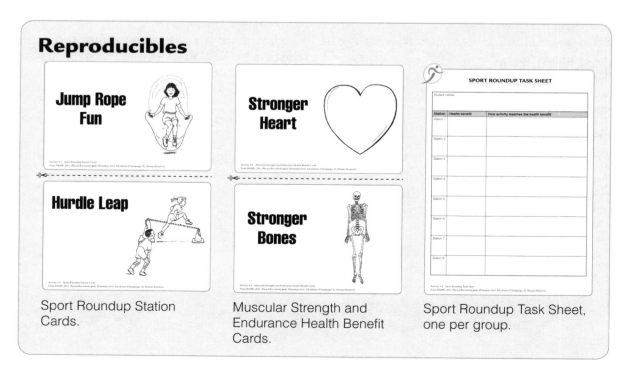

Reproducibles

Sport Roundup Station Cards.

Muscular Strength and Endurance Health Benefit Cards.

Sport Roundup Task Sheet, one per group.

Equipment

- ▶ Energetic, upbeat music and player
- ▶ Clipboards and pencils (one per group)
- ▶ Jump ropes, one for each student at a station
- ▶ Five low hurdles or small cones (lines on the floor may be substituted if needed)
- ▶ Ball, stick, puck, and so on, needed to practice goal scoring for any sport, enough for one person at a station
- ▶ Paper plates, enough for each student at a station to have two
- ▶ Stopwatch
- ▶ Mats for floor work

SAMPLE STATION IDEAS

Jump Rope Fun

Students jump rope, using multiple repetitions and sets to develop leg strength and endurance. Health benefit—stronger heart.

Hurdle Leap

Students leap over a series of low obstacles on the ground, such as low hurdles or small cones, to improve leg strength. Health benefit—stronger bones.

Score That Goal

Students take several shots on goal in a row (any sport). Health benefit—perform better.

Kick Boxing

Students perform a variety of kicks and punches to develop upper- and lower-body strength and endurance. Health benefit—stronger muscles.

Strike Out

Students practice throwing form. Health benefit—prevents injuries.

Core Moves

Seated in the V seat position, clap hands together and then touch them to the floor repeatedly. From the pelvic raise position, alternately lift the right leg and the left leg. Health benefit—good posture.

Skating

Students pretend to skate in a pattern between and around cones, keeping the legs low to work the leg muscles. Use paper plates under their feet to help them slide better. Health benefit—play and work longer.

Line Dance

Have students perform a basic line dance routine or other dance moves (such as those used in the You Should Be Dancing activity from the aerobic fitness chapter). Health benefit—more energy.

Procedure

1. Use the Sport Roundup Station Cards and the Health Benefit Cards to set up the stations around the activity space. Place the station activity and corresponding Health Benefit Cards side by side at each station. You may also create your own station signs for various sports and lifetime activities that interest your students.

2. Briefly review with the class the definitions of muscular strength and muscular endurance. Also, discuss the health benefits often associated with good muscular strength and endurance.

3. Divide students into groups of four to six. Assign each group to a station.

4. Start music to signal students to perform the activity at that station. Stop the music to signal groups to stop and fill in their Sport Roundup Task Sheets for that station. They should write in the health benefit that corresponds with the activity and a brief explanation of how the activity relates to the health benefit (for example, jumping rope works the leg muscles but also increases the heart rate, working the heart and making it stronger).

5. Start music again to signal students to proceed to the next station. They continue through the stations or until you reach a predetermined time.

6. Discuss the task sheets as a group.

Teaching Hint

Make sure that the stations are equal in time needed to do the activities. Use a stopwatch or segmented or interval music to ensure consistent timing.

Sample Inclusion Tips

▶ Modifications to each activity:

- Jump Rope Fun—have students jump over lines, a secured hula hoop, or a short rope for students to jump continuously.
- Hurdle Leap—change the height of the hurdle.
- Score That Goal—change the size of the puck, use a handled hockey stick, add color to the goal.
- Kick Boxing—have students perform a sitting curl-up in a wheelchair; add weight if needed by using a medicine ball.
- Strike Out—change the size and weight of the ball; use a yarn ball or beanbags.
- Skating—a student in a wheelchair can move in a pattern between and around cones.

▶ When changing stations, use visual cues, such as red and green flags, for students with hearing impairments.

Variation

To promote critical thinking by older students, scatter the Health Benefit Cards in the center of the activity space. After performing the station, students look through the health benefits, select one that matches their activity, and fill that in along with the explanation of their choice on their task card.

Sport Roundup introduces a variety of fun activities, like line dance, that can provide the health benefits of muscular strength and endurance.

Home Extension

Have students see whether they can do an activity for one week to improve their muscle strength.

Assessment

▶ Collect task sheets after first asking students to identify which health benefits are most important to them. They should write an answer on their task sheets.

▶ Have groups create their own stations to improve muscular strength and endurance. They should explain why they chose that activity, how it relates to muscular strength and endurance of that particular sport or activity, and what health benefits may be associated with that activity.

OPPOSING FORCE

PRIMARY

Frequency—How many days a week you perform muscular strength and endurance activities. You should participate in strength and endurance activities a minimum of two or three times a week. Daily chores and tasks require muscular strength and endurance.

Purpose

▶ Students will identify activities that use muscular strength daily.

▶ Students will identify that the recommended frequency of doing muscular strength and endurance activities is three times a week.

Relationship to National Standards

▶ Physical education standard 2: Demonstrates understanding of movement concepts, principles, strategies, and tactics as they apply to the learning and performance of physical activities.

▶ Physical education standard 3: Participates regularly in physical activity.

▶ Physical education standard 4: Achieves and maintains a health-enhancing level of physical fitness.

Equipment

Needs are based on how many groups of two you have in a class. Each group should have the following:

▶ One hockey stick and puck to represent raking leaves

▶ Student backpack with one or two books in it (bring from classroom)

▶ Basketballs

▶ Milk crate with jerseys inside to represent laundry basket

▶ Scooter with a towel to put into a student's hand to represent washing the floor

▶ Wastebaskets or cans with wadded up paper to represent trash cans

▶ Mats for floor work

Exercise Picture Chart for Runner, one per runner.

Exercise Picture Chart for Sitter, one per sitter.

Procedure

1. The students pair off. One partner sits facing the wall. The other partner stands with one hand touching the same wall.

2. On the "Go" signal, the standing partner should run to the far wall and perform the first exercise on the list until you direct them to return. During this time the sitting partner performs the first exercise on his or her list until the partner returns.

3. When the sprinting partner returns, they quickly switch positions and exercises. Partners continue to run and exchange tasks as directed.

4. Each exercise set should be continued for one to two minutes.

Teaching Hints

▶ Review the definition of muscular strength and endurance.

▶ Talk to students about how they use their muscles every day.

▶ Tell them that to make muscles stronger, sometimes they have to get tired.

▶ This activity will show how to use muscles during everyday activities as well as how students can make muscles stronger by doing exercises.

▶ Students work with partners so that they can remind each other to do strengthening activities two to three times a week minimum.

Opposing Force helps students acquire the recommended frequency of muscular fitness activity.

© BOLD STOCK / age fotostock

Sample Inclusion Tip

Depending on the mobility of the child the distance that must be traveled on the sprint can be modified, and depending on the needs of the child the exercises on the wall can be altered.

Variations

▶ Change the strength activities to work on different muscle groups.

▶ Vary the locomotor movement used while traveling to and from the opposite wall.

▶ Vary the amount of time that students perform the activity based on ability and grade level.

Home Extension

Encourage students to perform one or more of the activities introduced during this lesson at home at least three times during the week. They should ask a family member to do the activity with them and talk with the family member about the benefits of both daily activities and planned exercise.

Assessment

▶ Ask students to name some activities that use their muscles daily.

▶ Ask students how many days each week they should do strengthening exercises.

▶ Ask them to name some strengthening exercises.

▶ Talk to students during the activities and see whether they can tell you how many days a week they need to be doing muscular strength and endurance activities.

MUSCULAR STRENGTH AND ENDURANCE ACTIVITY LOG

INTERMEDIATE

Frequency—Frequency describes how often you perform the targeted health-related physical activity. For muscular strength and endurance activity sessions, frequency should be two or three times per week, although daily activities such as carrying groceries, a backpack, or raking leaves also develop muscular strength and endurance.

Purpose

Students will understand and demonstrate how many days per week they should perform muscular strength and endurance activities.

Relationship to National Standards

▶ Physical education standard 3: Participates regularly in physical activity.

▶ Health education standard 3: Students will demonstrate the ability to practice health-enhancing behaviors and reduce health risks.

Equipment

Everyday items for stations are suggested in "Variations."

Procedure

1. Review or define frequency. Have the students brainstorm some ways that they perform muscular strength and endurance activities in their everyday lives (for example, carrying groceries into the house will build both muscular strength and endurance, raking leaves will build muscular endurance in arm muscles, and riding a bike will build muscular endurance of the legs). Encourage them to use physical activity examples from outside physical education class. (See also Sport Roundup examples, on page 89.)

2. Pass out the Muscular Strength and Endurance Activity Log and ask students to work with their guardians at home to fill it out for the next one to two weeks.

Teaching Hints

▶ Use class time effectively by having students brainstorm during a cool-down or stretch.

▶ Construct a bulletin board with student drawings or magazine pictures of the various activities that students found to do.

Sample Inclusion Tips

▶ Provide guardians and students with a list of agencies (departments of parks and recreation or therapeutic

Reproducible

MUSCULAR STRENGTH AND ENDURANCE ACTIVITY LOG

Name _____ Date _____

Date	Description of activity (what kind)	Time (how long)	Your initials

Activity 4.6 Muscular Strength and Endurance Activity Log
From NASPE, 2011, *Physical Best activity guide: Elementary level, 3rd edition* (Champaign, IL: Human Kinetics).

Muscular Strength and Endurance Activity Log, one per student.

Students explore how frequently they address muscular strength and endurance outside the classroom with the Muscular Strength and Endurance Activity Log.

recreation programs) that offer programs for students with disabilities outside the school environment.

▶ For students with significant delays, modify the Muscular Strength and Endurance Activity Log using pictures so that students are able to circle the choices that they made and want to record.

Variations

▶ Create stations using everyday items to show how students can get a workout using items in their homes (for example, lifting canned foods onto a shelf, sweeping dirt and objects into a dustpan, climbing steps or climbing one step repeatedly to simulate a staircase).

▶ Have a family day in physical education when family members join students in activities that the family can do at home to keep in shape.

Home Extension

Check with students during the week to make sure that they are doing the Muscular Strength and Endurance Activity Log. Have them record on the sheet whether other family members join in their activities. Encourage students to do the log and return it to school later.

Assessment

▶ Have students tell or write a definition of frequency and compare their log to the number of days per week they should participate in muscular strength and endurance activities.

▶ Collect the homework sheet and lead a class discussion on activities that the students participate in most frequently.

ANIMAL TAG

PRIMARY

Intensity—Intensity is how hard you work your muscles during an activity. Working muscles harder than usual will make them stronger and able to perform longer. Specificity is doing certain movements to help a particular muscle get stronger.

Purpose

▶ Students will evaluate the intensity level of their movements, and discuss whether the intensity level would help them gain muscular strength and endurance.

▶ Students will also identify which muscles are working and therefore gaining in muscular strength.

Relationship to National Standards

▶ Physical education standard 2: Demonstrates understanding of movement concepts, principles, strategies, and tactics as they apply to the learning and performance of physical activities.

▶ Physical education standard 4: Achieves and maintains a health-enhancing level of physical fitness.

Equipment

▶ A bucket to hold used Animal Cards, or a designated card area

▶ If available, animal beanbags

▶ Pedometers (optional) to keep track of steps

Procedure

Choose three or four students to be taggers. The other students are runners.

1. The taggers are given three Animal Cards and one You Are It! Card.

2. After tagging a runner, the tagger gives that student an animal card. The runner must do that animal movement for a count of 20. When the runner finishes the exercise, she or he takes the card to the card area and then returns to the activity.

Reproducibles

Bear Walk

Bear walk with straight arms and legs facing the floor. Hands and feet are on the floor.

Benefit: strength in arms and legs

You are it!

You are it!

Animal Cards, three per tagger.

You Are It! Cards, one per tagger.

3. The tagger continues until he or she has given all three animal cards to other students. The tagger then gives the You Are It! Card to the next runner he or she captures, and that person becomes the new tagger. The new tagger must get three Animal Cards from the card area and then take a turn at tagging others.

Teaching Hints

▶ Talk to students about using muscles to make them stronger.

▶ Many animals have strong muscles and use them every day, just as we need to do.

▶ To make a muscle stronger, they must work the muscle and use it in a harder way than they usually do—frogs must jump farther or more frequently, bears must go farther or faster.

▶ Review the animal walks and tell the students they will be using various muscles during this activity. At the end of class you will discuss which muscles they used and how tired they became with each animal walk.

Performing animal movements is a fun way for students to experience the intensity of muscular strength and endurance.

Sample Inclusion Tips

▶ Have students with special needs who are tagged come up with alternative activities to suit their needs and abilities.

▶ If a tagger has a physical disability then it might be appropriate for the tagger to walk rather than jog when trying to tag a runner or for the tagger to call out the runner's name, signaling them to go to the tagger and get a card.

▶ Add additional types of animal walks that meet the needs of your students.

Variations

▶ If you have beanbag animals, use them instead of cards.

▶ Make this a stuffed animal day and have students bring in animals. Design walks for each animal and play the game. Taggers carry the stuffed animals and pass them to the person tagged. After a tag, the animal is returned to the pile.

▶ If they are wearing pedometers, students can check how many steps they used when playing the activity. Talk about intensity and aerobic fitness. If students have a lot of steps, ask them to explain why they have so many.

Home Extension

Students can use stuffed animals at home and continue the activity by developing different movements of other animals not used in class. Have students bring their ideas back to class.

Assessment

Explain to students that intensity is how hard they work their muscles during an activity. Ask these questions:

▶ How do you know when you work your muscles hard? What signs did you feel from your body that told you how hard you worked?

▶ What muscles did you use for each animal walk? (Name each walk and ask.)

▶ Which walks made you the most tired? What could you do to help yourself get stronger so that you don't feel as tired when you do these types of walks?

SURVIVOR COURSE

INTERMEDIATE

Intensity—Intensity is how hard you work your muscles during and activity.

Purpose

Students will perform muscular strength and endurance activities to learn about the concept of intensity and the ways in which the body senses intensity.

Relationship to National Standards

▶ Physical education standard 4: Achieves and maintains a health enhancing level of physical fitness.

▶ Physical education standard 5: Exhibits responsible personal and social behavior that respects self and others in a physical activity setting.

Equipment

Equipment is based on groups of five at six stations:

▶ Two medicine balls or similar weighted objects

▶ Five stability balls (optional)

▶ Five basketballs or playground balls

▶ Five volleyballs or lightweight volleyballs

▶ Two ladders or two taped ladder patterns on the floor

▶ Pedometers (optional)

▶ Heart rate monitor (optional) to add an aerobic fitness component

▶ Mats to use for floor work

▶ Stopwatch

Procedure

1. Discuss the definition of a survivor. Ask what they need to be a survivor.

2. Tell students that they are on a survivor course and will be doing the exercises at each station for one full minute. They will be traveling around the course twice.

3. Explain each station to the students and place them in six groups.

4. Time each event for one minute and tell students when to rotate.

Reproducibles

Station 1

Group Over and Under Line Drill

The group forms a straight line and uses a playground ball. Go over your head and under your legs to pass the ball down the line. After you have passed the ball, go to the end of the line and wait for the ball to come to you again.

Activity 4.8   Survivor Course Station Signs
From NASPE, 2011, *Physical Best activity guide: Elementary level, 3rd edition* (Champaign, IL: Human Kinetics).

Survivor Course Station Signs.

MY INTENSITY TRAINING

Name _____   Date _____

Fill in the following tables with three different exercises to help you develop greater muscular strength and endurance. Your teacher can give you ideas if you need help. You are to do these exercises two different times during the week, and is it better not to do the exercises two days in a row. Record your workouts and return to your teacher when you have completed your intensity training!

Day of the week:		
Exercise name	Number of times repeated	Time spent doing activity
1		
2		
3		

How did your muscles feel when you were done?

Do you think that you can increase the time or number on the second day that you perform the exercises? Yes or no? Why or why not?

Day of the week:		
Exercise name	Number of times repeated	Time spent doing activity
1		
2		
3		

How did your muscles feel when you were done?

Were you able to increase the time or number on the second day that you performed the exercises? Yes or no? Why or why not?

Activity 4.8   My Intensity Training
From NASPE, 2011, *Physical Best activity guide: Elementary level, 3rd edition* (Champaign, IL: Human Kinetics).

My Intensity Training, one per student.

Teaching Hints

▶ Talk to students about the definition of intensity and signs of an intense workout. What are some signs of intensity? (Answers: breathing harder, sweating, muscles getting tired, losing concentration, possibly others.) Briefly discuss how much is enough with intensity. Remind students that it is OK for the signs to appear because that means that the muscles are becoming stronger, but if they think that they are working too hard then they should check with you.

▶ Tell students that at times they may need a short rest before beginning again, but they should keep working the muscles at these stations as much and as long as they can. Remind them that survivors work really hard to survive!

▶ If stability balls are not available then use push-ups on the floor (modified push-ups, 90-degree push-ups) or a bridge activity.

▶ Coach them to a higher intensity level if needed.

Sample Inclusion Tips

▶ Vary the exercises and the equipment to meet the needs of the students.

Students experience intensity firsthand while trying to survive this challenging circuit course.

▶ Students with balance problems may find it easier to pass the ball over their heads at station 1.

▶ Students with limited mobility, balance, and strength should be supported on the stability balls at station 2.

▶ Straight paths moving forward or sideways with larger step areas may be used instead of the agility ladder at station 6. Tape can be used on the floor to mark lines for a ladder.

Variations

▶ Increase the time at the stations.

▶ Reverse the order of exercises for a change.

▶ Have students work with a partner and push each other to a higher level of performance.

Home Extension

Give students the My Intensity Training worksheet to take home. In class, help students set goals and identify three exercises that they want to do at home. Remind them that they are working on intensity and that they will have to perform these exercises until they get very tired. Students are to record the exercises for two days out of a week.

Assessment

▶ Walk around the room and ask individual students what intensity means and whether they are applying it to the exercise that they are doing. Ask how they are applying intensity.

▶ Ask students what is meant by intensity when working out. Ask how it helps them.

▶ Ask students to give you several signs that they would use to tell how intensely they are working.

TIME YOUR WORKOUT

PRIMARY

Repetition and time—Repetition refers to one complete movement of an activity. A set is a fixed number of repetitions. Time is how long an activity takes. In the case of muscular strength and endurance time may be the time needed to perform the sets and reps plus the rest between the sets.

Purpose

▶ Students will be able to define what repetitions, sets, and time mean with respect to a muscular strength and endurance workout.

▶ Students will be able to identify which parts of a muscular strength and endurance workout are the repetitions, which parts are the sets, and what components make up the time.

Relationship to National Standards

▶ Physical education standard 2: Demonstrates understanding of movement concepts, principles, strategies, and tactics as they apply to the learning and performance of physical activities.

▶ Physical education standard 4: Achieves and maintains a health-enhancing level of physical fitness.

Equipment

▶ 50 or more fleece balls or soft throwing objects

▶ Lines, cones, or tape to mark the throwing line

▶ 10 hula hoops

▶ Upbeat music and player

▶ Mats to use for floor work

Procedure

1. Divide the gym in half and place half of the students on each side. They cannot cross the center line during the activity.

2. Spread out 8 to 10 hula hoops along one side of the gym. Determine the distance from the throwing line by the ability of the students participating (see figure 4.2).

3. When the music starts, students do 10 push-ups.

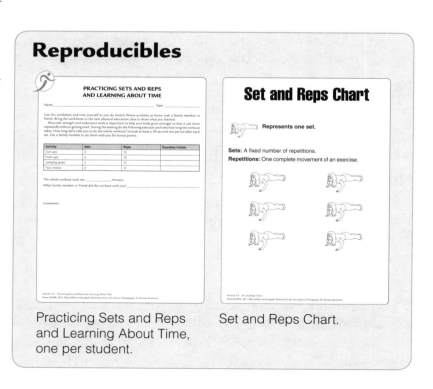

Practicing Sets and Reps and Learning About Time, one per student.

Set and Reps Chart.

4. Each student then picks up one ball and goes to the throwing line.

5. Students use an underhand throw to toss the ball into a hula hoop.

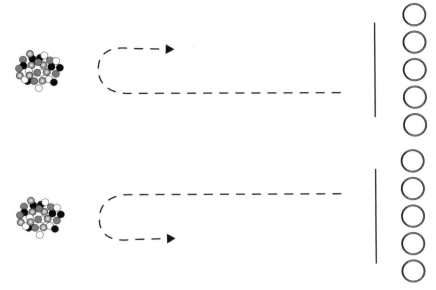

6. After throwing a ball, they go back to the start line and repeat the activity, beginning with 10 push-ups.

7. After all the balls have been thrown at the hoops, stop the music. Students then return to the start line.

8. Discuss sets, reps, and time. Use the Set and

Figure 4.2   Floor setup for Time Your Workout.

Rep Chart to help students understand the concepts. The sets were the number of different times that they did push-ups. The reps were the number, 10, that they did in each group. The rest period after each set was going up to throw a ball. Here the arms were at rest. Time was the amount of time it took to do the exercises and throw the balls. Having a rest period after each set is important.

9. Students should know that when doing muscular strength and endurance exercises, the amount of time it takes them to perform the whole activity includes doing the exercise (repetitions) and the rests after the sets.

10. Repeat the whole activity using a different exercise, such as curl-ups or jumping jacks.

Teaching Hints

▶ Ask students how hard they have to work their muscles to get them stronger. Ask them how they know when they are working hard. (Answer: A sign is that the muscle gets tired.) Discuss what repetitions, sets, and time mean with regard to enhancing muscular strength and endurance. Tell the students that today they will play an activity in which they will use many repetitions and at least two sets of repetitions to help make their arm and leg muscles stronger.

▶ Using the Set and Rep Chart again can help to reinforce the concepts.

▶ Use the terms during the activity so that students make connections between the activity and the definitions.

▶ Remind students that muscles get stronger when they repeat an exercise several times in a row.

▶ Stop the activity when all the balls have been thrown. Point out that not all students move in the same way. Some try to move faster than others do. Some students may have done more sets and reps of the exercise than others did. Remind them that everyone is different and that they are to move at their own pace, but that they should always use the proper form.

▶ Remind students that working muscles will feel tired. This feeling will also be different for each person. After their muscles become stronger, they can go longer before they get tired.

Sample Inclusion Tips

▶ Shorten the distance that a student has to go to reach the throwing line.

▶ Decrease the number of repetitions that a student has to do.

▶ Change the exercise to match the ability of a student with a handicap.

▶ Have other students pick up two balls and give one to a student in a wheelchair.

▶ Use a grab extender for a student with balance or mobility problems to aid in picking up the items.

Variations

▶ Have students give you an exercise to use.

▶ Use overhead throwing.

▶ Time the throwing event to see how long it takes to get all balls in the hoops along with doing the exercises. When all the balls are out at the back line, students can pick up the missed balls to throw into the hoops. Repeat and see whether it takes longer after muscles become tired.

▶ If students are using pedometers, compare the number of steps to demonstrate that each student is also different in this area. Remind them that workouts are different for everyone.

Home Extension

Distribute the Practicing Sets and Reps and Learning About Time handout to students. Have students do the homework sheet with a family member at home. They should do the exercises together and be sure to time how long it takes. After they have completed the work, students should return the paper to school for a discussion on what they learned from the assignment.

Assessment

▶ Ask why sets and reps are important. (Answer: More reps and sets increase our strength because we are working longer.)

▶ Ask them to define what a repetition means and give an example of how they used repetitions in this activity.

▶ Ask what a set is. Have them give an example of how they used a set in the activity.

▶ Ask students to put their thumbs up if they think that they did many repetitions in this activity and to put their thumbs down if they think that they did not do many repetitions.

▶ Ask them to put their thumbs up if they think that they did a lot of sets in this activity and to put their thumbs down if they think that they did only a few sets.

▶ Ask students to explain the Set and Rep Classroom Visual Chart.

▶ Ask them whether they know how many sets they did in this activity.

▶ Ask them to tell you how time is calculated for this activity. (Answer: It is a combination of sets, reps, and recovery time before the exercise is repeated.)

PRIMARY

Specificity—Specificity refers to the kind of activity that you do. When you do an activity, the muscles that you use to perform the movements get stronger while other muscles do not. When working on muscles, the muscles that you exercise are specific to the activity.

Purpose

Students will evaluate which muscle groups are worked in what exercises.

Relationship to National Standards

▶ Physical education standard 3: Participates regularly in physical activity.

▶ Physical education standard 4: Achieves and maintains a health-enhancing level of physical fitness.

Equipment

▶ 5 hoops

▶ 50 yarn balls, beanbags, or pieces of paper wadded up in a ball

▶ Ocean sounds or "Under the Sea" music from *The Little Mermaid*

▶ Scooters (optional)

Procedure

1. Explain to the students that if they support their body weight with their arms and legs, those muscles will get stronger.

2. Tell a story explaining that an accident has occurred and piles of trash have been thrown about the ocean. The trash is being washed onto the beach. The students' job is to clean up the beach.

3. Have the students seat themselves along a wall facing objects in the middle of the gym. Place hula hoops representing trash cans near the ends of the gym or at an appropriate distance for the age group. This setup will force students to travel a distance to pick up trash and put it away.

4. Spread various yarn balls and beanbags throughout the play area.

5. When the music begins the students walk in crab position to a ball (piece of trash). They place the trash on their bellies and transport it to their hoop (trash can).

6. They continue until they have collected all the trash.

7. Repeat the activity using various locomotor movements that focus on different muscle groups.

   • Hop on one foot and squat to pick up the trash.

   • Hurt puppy: Place two hands and one foot on the floor and one foot in the air.

   • Use big bunny jumps to move around the gym, going for distance with each standing broad jump.

   • Walk on tiptoes or heels.

Reproducible

None.

Teaching Hints

▶ Review with students the definition of specificity. Tell them that they will be working with various locomotor movements to increase the muscular strength and endurance of specific muscles.

▶ During the activity you want them to focus on what muscles are getting tired as they perform the activity. You will ask them to identify these working muscles after the beach is clean and tie it to specificity of increasing the muscular endurance and strength of used muscles.

▶ Explain that as they travel in crab position they must keep their belly flat and seat up to keep the trash from falling off them. This position will force them to use their abdominals and gluteus maximus as well as their arm strength.

▶ They can transport only one piece of trash at a time (requiring them to make more trips to the hoops).

Clean the Beach does more than teach students about the training principle of specificity; it also provides a lesson in protecting the environment.

Sample Inclusion Tips

▶ A student with mobility issues may use a grip extender or a lacrosse stick to gather trash, depending on muscular strength capabilities.

▶ A student who is unable to hold crab position could propel a scooter using the arms or legs.

▶ Use lacrosse sticks to gather paper.

Variations

▶ The activity could be performed using scooters:
  • Belly—alligator walk
  • Seated with hands and feet on the floor—crab
  • One knee on scooter—hurt puppy

▶ Time the event to encourage work at a higher level of intensity.

▶ Ask questions regarding whether they think that taking care of the earth is important and what they can do to help.

Home Extensions

▶ Ask students what they could do at home to help clean up the earth.

▶ Encourage them to pick up litter that they see because doing so not only helps the earth but also helps them use their muscles more and get stronger. They should report back at the next class.

Assessment

▶ Evaluate answers to these questions: What muscle groups were used with this locomotor activity? What does specificity mean with regard to these muscle groups and getting stronger?

▶ Give them other exercises not used in the activity and see whether they can tell you what muscles are getting stronger (for example, push-ups, curl-ups).

INTERMEDIATE

Specificity—Specificity, or type, refers to the kind of physical activity that you do. In muscular strength and endurance activities, the muscles worked are specific to the exercises performed.

Purpose

▶ Students will be able to define specificity (type) with respect to muscular strength and endurance.

▶ Students will be able to list exercises or activities that develop specific muscle groups.

Relationship to National Standards

Physical education standard 4: Achieves and maintains a health-enhancing level of physical fitness.

Equipment

▶ A deck of cards

▶ Upbeat music and player (optional)

▶ Any equipment needed for the exercises at each station; for those provided on the CD-ROM, you will need the following:

• Lightweight dumbbells

• Stretch bands

• Step benches

• Mats

Procedure

1. Place a poster with a different playing card suit symbol and list of exercises for specific muscle groups on each of the four walls of the activity area to create four stations. If conducting the activity outdoors, use slotted cones or another means to secure the posters. Use the posters provided on the CD-ROM reproducible or create your own.

2. As a group, practice the exercises that coincide with each of the four muscle groupings selected. While doing this, introduce students to the anatomical names for the muscle groups and focus on teaching proper form for executing the exercises. Also, explain that different exercises work different muscles (concept of specificity).

3. Break the class into small groups of two or three students.

4. Place a deck of cards with face cards removed in the center of the activity space. Have each group draw a card from the deck and go to the poster that has that suit.

Reproducible

A
♥

♥

A
♥

Ace of Hearts

♥ Squats
♥ Wall sits
♥ Step-ups
♥ Calf raises

Activity 4.11   Shuffle and Hustle Suit Posters
From NASPE, 2011, *Physical Best activity guide: Elementary level, 3rd edition* (Champaign, IL: Human Kinetics).

Shuffle and Hustle Suit Posters.

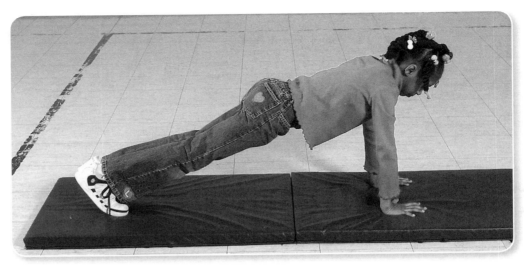

Students learn how to work specific muscles during Shuffle and Hustle.

5. They then choose a specific exercise from that suit's designated muscle groups and perform the number of repetitions that correspond with the number on their card.

6. Students come back, place their card in a bucket, and draw a new card from the remaining stack. They continue until all cards have been used, at which point the cards can be reshuffled for a second round. Continue until you've reached a designated time or number of rounds.

Teaching Hints

▶ Look for extra large playing cards—they will be easier to handle and keep together.

▶ Move around the room throughout the activity to provide assistance and feedback with the exercises. Talk to students about the exercise they are doing and what group of muscles it uses.

Sample Inclusion Tips

▶ Assign a peer assistant to a child with a visual impairment to help the child travel safely to and from the walls as well as to read the number of the shuffled card and perform the activity.

▶ Add pictures next to the writing on the wall charts for nonreaders.

Variations

▶ Use the activity as a circuit with posters at the stations and the matching suit of the cards already at the station.

▶ Put face cards in the decks as wild cards. A student who draws a wild card chooses any station and does 10 repetitions of the station exercise.

Home Extension

Have students find four exercises to improve the upper body or lower body. They should perform the exercises three times a week with a partner and report their success to you.

Assessment

▶ Point to a muscle group on your body and ask students to name an exercise that they did during the activity that worked those muscles.

▶ Ask students to name the muscles used for the activity Shuffle and Hustle.

INTERMEDIATE

Progression—Progression refers to how a person should increase overload. Proper progression involves a gradual increase in the level of exercise manipulated by increasing frequency, intensity, time, or a combination of all three components.

Purpose

Students will practice the concept and skill of applying progression as it relates to muscular strength and endurance.

Relationship to National Standards

▶ Physical education standard 3: Participates regularly in physical activity.

▶ Physical education standard 4: Achieves and maintains a health-enhancing level of physical fitness.

▶ Health education standard 3: Students will demonstrate the ability to practice health-enhancing behaviors and reduce health risks.

▶ Health education standard 6: Students will demonstrate the ability to use goal-setting and decision-making skills to enhance health.

Equipment

▶ Curl-up strips

▶ Mats

Reproducibles

Push-Up Challenge Poster

In the modified or regular push-up position, do the following:
- Do "Mississippi" count push-up
- Move hands back and forth over a line
- Perform sailor salutes
- Pass an object back and forth between hands
- Wave hello, switching hands
- Alternately raise feet
- Stack beanbags (or rocks) in a bucket

From the modified or regular push-up position, do the following:
- Inchworm push-up (walk hands out and in)
- Push-up with an object balanced on your back
- Narrow-hands push-up
- Wide-hands push-up
- Four-count push-up (two down, two up)

From the regular push-up position, do the following:
- Wide-leg push-up
- Push-up with one foot on top of the other

From a standing position, do the following:
- Wall push-up

Push-Up Challenge Poster.

Curl-Up Challenge Poster

Individual curl-ups:
- Four-count curl-up (knees, toes, knees, floor)
- Angled curl-ups (alternating toward the right knee and then the left knee)
- Reverse curl-ups
- Legs in air curl-ups
- Chant curl-up ("1, 2, 3, 4, strength is what we're looking for!") going up and then repeat going down

Partner curl-ups—facing each other:
- High fives
- Shake hands
- Pass the object

Curl-Up Challenge Poster.

PUSH-UP CURL-UP CHALLENGE LOG

Name _____ Date _____

Name of push-up challenge selected: _____

Name of curl-up challenge selected: _____

	Curl-up total count (three sets)	Push-up total count (three sets)
Week 1		
Day 1		
Day 2		
Day 3		
Week 2		
Day 1		
Day 2		
Day 3		

Initial curl-up result: _____ Final curl-up result: _____

Initial push-up result: _____ Final push-up result: _____

Push-Up Curl-Up Challenge Log, one per student.

▶ Balls

▶ Beanbags

▶ Buckets

Procedure

1. Describe progression as it relates to frequency, intensity, time, and type. Teach and allow students to practice the basic curl-up position and 90-degree push-up position to ensure correct technique. Remind students that each person must work from his or her current ability to gradually progress and achieve better performance. Remind students that they are each improving as individuals, not competing with one another.

2. Have them write down in their Push-Up Curl-Up Challenge Logs how many push-ups and curl-ups they currently can perform according to the Fitnessgram protocols. You may also help them select a reasonable goal that they would like to achieve on their follow-up assessment. If they have not recently performed the assessments, conduct them as a class and have them record the numbers on their logs.

3. Introduce students to the activities on the Push-Up Challenge Poster and Curl-Up Challenge Poster.

4. Direct each student to work in a personal space. Have each student choose one push-up challenge from the poster and, beginning slowly, perform the exercise for a predetermined time or for a range of repetitions. Students rest and then repeat the same exercise challenge for a second set and then a third set (depending on individual ability). Students should record their results on their logs—writing the challenge selected and the total number of repetitions completed.

5. Repeat step 3, this time having students choose one curl-up challenge.

6. Bring students together as a group and assign them an out-of-class challenge. They should perform their push-up and curl-up challenges for three nonconsecutive days per week over the next two weeks and record the results on their logs (they will have completed their first day of week 1 in class). They should aim to meet or exceed the total repetitions completed in class.

7. At the conclusion of the two weeks, have students bring in their completed logs to class, repeat the Fitnessgram push-up and curl-up assessments, and write the results on their logs.

The Push-Up Curl-Up Challenge introduces students to the idea of progression and increasing overload.

Teaching Hints

▶ Review the concept of a workout: Repetitions + sets = workout.

▶ If class is held at least three times per week, the challenges and logging can be done in class.

▶ Ask the school's after-school care providers to provide for space, time, and other support for students to work on their logs.

▶ To reinforce the concept of progression, repeat the activity periodically throughout the school year and compare logs.

Sample Inclusion Tips

Modifications and alternatives to push-ups:

▶ Use weights while maintaining flexed arms and muscle contractions.

▶ Pick up a weighted object tied to a rope.

▶ Do wrist curls by holding a rod with a rope attached to a weight. Wrap the rope around the rod using only wrist movements.

▶ Do wall push-ups.

▶ Start in static push up-position with a small wedge under the student to train the student to maintain the mechanics of the push-up position.

Modifications to curl-ups:

▶ Perform a seated curl-up using weight if needed; can also twist side to side.

▶ Have a partner hold the student's feet.

▶ Perform a curl-up with arms placed at the sides and touch the back of the heels.

Variation

After students are familiar with the various types of push-ups and curl-ups, make a circuit with stations that alternate push-up and curl-up exercises from the challenge posters. Post the Push-Up Challenge Posters at the push-up stations and the Curl-Up Challenge Posters at the curl-up stations so that students can refer to them to choose a push-up or curl-up exercise to do. Students go clockwise from station to station doing one set of the various push-ups and curl-ups *that they can do with good form.* They do no more than 10 repetitions at each station. Use music in the background.

Home Extension

Have students create at least three different push-ups and curl-ups. They should write them down and bring them to class for everyone to try. They should use the Push-Up Curl-Up Challenge Log to record their challenges.

Assessment

▶ Collect the Push-Up Curl-Up Challenge Logs to evaluate the number of times that students practiced the challenges.

▶ Ask students to describe what progression means in terms of health-related fitness and the FITT guidelines.

▶ Discuss with the class why they may have progressed. For example, they may have been doing activities that helped them progress in the assessments. Also, discuss why they may not have progressed. For example, on some days they may feel better and stronger than on other days and they may have had a better day at the start of the challenge; progression can take more time; or perhaps they chose a challenge that did not provide enough overload to progress.

STABILITY PROGRESSION

INTERMEDIATE

Progression—Progression refers to how a person should increase overload. Proper progression involves a gradual increase in the level of exercise manipulated by increasing frequency, intensity, time, or a combination of all three components.

Purpose

Students will practice the concept and skill of applying progression as it relates to muscle strength and endurance.

Relationship to National Standards

- ▶ Physical education standard 4: Achieves and maintains a health-enhancing level of physical fitness.
- ▶ Health education standard 3: Students will demonstrate the ability to practice health-enhancing behaviors and reduce health risks.

Equipment

- ▶ One stability ball per person (for options in equipment see "Sample Inclusion Tips" and "Variations")
- ▶ Fast-moving music and player
- ▶ Mats for floor work

Reproducibles

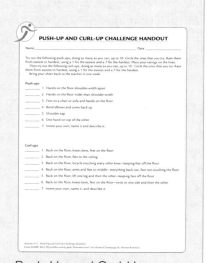

Push-Up Progression With a Stability Ball.

Curl-Up Progression With a Stability Ball.

Push-Up and Curl-Up Challenge Handout, one per student. Students can use this take-home handout even if they do not have access to a stability ball because the exercises can be done without a stability ball if necessary.

Procedure

1. Demonstrate, or have a student demonstrate, each push-up.
2. Start with an easy push-up on the stability ball where the thighs are on the ball. Students do the push-up as many times as they can up to 10 times with good form.
3. A second push-up is done with the ankles on the ball. Students do as many as they can with good form up to 10.
4. A third push-up is done with the hands on the ball and the feet on the floor. Students do as many as they can with good form up to 10.
5. Each student selects the push-up that is the most challenging one that he or she can perform with good form.
6. When the music starts, students jog around the room, each carrying a stability ball.
7. When the music stops, students do the push-up that they selected with good form 10 times.
8. When the music starts, students dribble their balls around the room.
9. When the music stops, they do the progressive push-up of choice again.
10. When the music starts, students dribble their stability balls around the room.
11. They stop and do all of the progressive push-ups again.

Teaching Hints

▶ Have a discussion before students begin working. Include the following:
  • Discuss why some of the push-ups are harder than others.
  • Talk about why they would want to do an exercise that is hard for them to do; overload is an important principle in strength training, and intensity is one factor of overload.
▶ Observe students doing the exercises. Coach them into the level that they need to be performing during this activity.

The use of stability balls can help to increase overload on specific muscle groups. Students can progress using various positions on the stability ball and increase intensity as they work.

Sample Inclusion Tips

▶ Students in wheelchairs can use round sand weights as dumbbells or medicine balls of different weight if they are able to hold them. This activity would still work arm strength and would represent something round and different like a stability ball.

▶ For students with poor muscular strength and endurance, a small wedge can be placed under the student's chest or belly area. For progression, slowly shift the wedge, giving less support each time until the student no longer needs the wedge.

Variations

▶ Repeat the previous activity pattern but use the curl-up progression from the poster. If the curl-up progression is used, mats will be needed for floor work.

▶ If stability balls are not available for every student, have them pair up and take turns. The person without the ball can do the exercise on a mat on the ground. When dribbling, partners should pass the ball back and forth.

Home Extension

Send home the Push-Up and Curl-Up Challenge Handout for students to experiment with at home. Students will rate the push-ups and curl-ups from easiest to hardest.

Assessment

▶ Ask students to give examples of how they used overload, or made the exercise harder, during the activity.

▶ Have students give examples of other exercises and how they would make them harder or easier for themselves.

▶ Have students tell the various ways to overload a muscle and list the various indicators that tell them that they are overloading the muscle.

LOWER-BODY CHALLENGE

PRIMARY AND INTERMEDIATE

Specificity—The principle of specificity says that if a person wants to increase the strength of a muscle, she or he must use that specific muscle when performing exercises and activities. The principle of overload says that for a muscle to get stronger and endure longer, it must be used at a level that is harder than normal.

Purpose

▶ Students will be able to identify specific exercises that help increase the strength of specific muscles.

▶ Students will be able to discuss how to increase muscle strength and endurance by using the overload principle (variations of weight or repetitions, or modifications to the exercise).

Relationship to National Standards

▶ Physical education standard 2: Demonstrates understanding of movement concepts, principles, strategies, and tactics as they apply to the learning and performance of physical activities.

▶ Physical education standard 4: Achieves and maintains a health-enhancing level of physical fitness.

Reproducibles

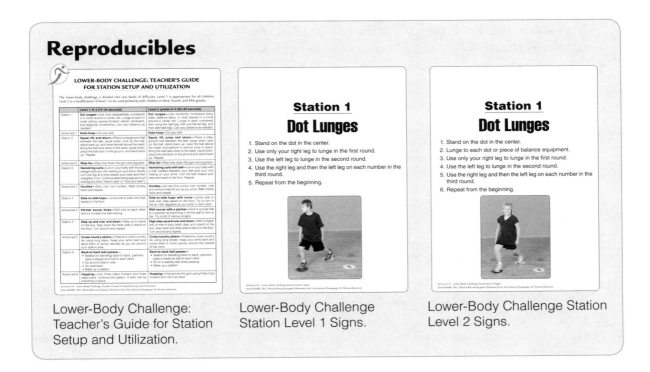

Lower-Body Challenge: Teacher's Guide for Station Setup and Utilization.

Lower-Body Challenge Station Level 1 Signs.

Lower-Body Challenge Station Level 2 Signs.

Equipment

For 26 children you would need approximately the following:

- ▶ 8 cones
- ▶ 10 playground balls
- ▶ 6 low hurdles
- ▶ 4 balance domes (bosu balls), balance discs, small stacked mats, steps, or boxes
- ▶ 4 hula hoops
- ▶ 6 stability balls or playground balls
- ▶ 6 soccer balls
- ▶ Poly spots, dot mats, or tape to mark dot patterns
- ▶ 6 jump ropes
- ▶ For advanced levels, 6 lightweight medicine balls
- ▶ Upbeat, fast-moving music and music player
- ▶ Stopwatch
- ▶ Mats for floor work
- ▶ Pedometers (optional)

Procedure

1. Place stations in a clockwise pattern around the room. Use the Lower-Body Challenge: Teacher's Guide for Station Setup and Utilization reproducible to help you with setup of stations, equipment needed for various stations, and additional information regarding how to perform many of the activities.

2. Discuss with the students why it is important to have strong muscles and ask them to name muscles that they think need to be strong.

3. Discuss the idea of muscle fitness training circuits that focus on upper-body muscles versus lower-body muscles. What parts of the body make up the lower body? Discuss the importance of a strong lower body and list some of the muscles.

4. State that this lesson will focus on learning and practicing several exercises that will help specific muscles of the lower body get stronger. When we target certain muscles and do exercises for them so that they can get stronger, we are using the principle of specificity. Give examples.

5. Ask students what they need to do to make their muscles stronger besides making sure that they use the specific muscles that they want to strengthen. Discuss the principle of overload. Also, discuss the need to rest worked muscles so that they are able to work hard again. During the circuit, active rest periods will occur after the muscle fitness activity at each station. The active rest will allow worked muscles to rest while other muscles are used to perform physical activity.

6. Show the students the circuit station signs and point out that each sign contains a muscle fitness activity and an active rest activity. Teach and practice each activity.

7. Tell students that they will try to do each activity for 30 seconds. If they cannot perform the exercise for all of the 30 seconds, they can take a very short rest and continue.

8. Explain that whenever music is playing they should be performing an activity on the station sign. They will first perform the muscle fitness activity for 30 seconds to music. Then the music will stop, and they will prepare to do the active rest activity when the music starts

again. When the music stops a second time they need to put all equipment back in its appropriate place, go quickly to their next station, and be ready to start performing the next muscle fitness activity when the music starts again.

9. Have students do a general warm-up around the perimeter of the room using activities such as brisk walking, easy jogging, or high marching steps.

10. Divide the students into groups and have them move to assigned stations where they can check the circuit card and ascertain the muscle fitness activity that they will perform when the music starts.

11. When the music plays, students perform the muscle fitness activity at their stations; when the music stops, they set down the equipment and prepare for the active rest activity. When the music starts, they perform the active rest activity for 30 seconds. When the music stops a second time, the students rotate to the next station and prepare to begin working on the next muscle fitness activity. Music bouts will be 30 seconds for grades K through 2 and 30 to 60 seconds for grades 3 through 5.

Teaching Hints

▶ Ensure that students understand the correct form for all the activities, and continually check their form throughout the activity. If some students cannot use correct form with the equipment chosen for the entire time, they need to know that they can change the equipment used to a lighter type, use a different type of movement, or take a rest and start again.

▶ Move around the room and encourage students to perform their best to ensure that they are overloading the muscles.

▶ Not all stations need to be included in one session, and other stations could be substituted depending on the experience of the children regarding the exercises and special equipment.

▶ Two stations may be combined into a single station, and students could be allowed to choose which exercise they do.

▶ If adequate time is available, two or three rounds may be used.

Sample Inclusion Tips

▶ Have various pieces of equipment of different sizes at the stations.

▶ Active resting for those with mobility problems might include substituting large palms-up arm circles and other arm movements that emphasize arm strength to help them with activities of daily life.

Knowing which exercises target particular parts of the body can help students increase their muscular endurance and strength in specific muscles.

Variations

- ▶ Start with only a few stations per lesson and gradually add more activities as students learn the correct form for each movement.

- ▶ Students who are ready and capable of enhancing their overload can use modifications listed for the upper grades (level 2). Students who are weak can remain at level 1 and progress more slowly, even if they are older. Emphasize that form is more important than how much they can lift or do.

Home Extension

Encourage the students to pick two of the exercises that they performed today for their lower body and do them at home every other day for a week. Encourage them to work on overloading the muscles by adding at least one or two repetitions per day or adding more time to their exercise each day so that they will get stronger.

Assessment

- ▶ Hold up each station card and ask what specific body parts and muscles were being worked at that station. Ask whether this is an upper-body strength activity or a lower-body activity or both. Why?

- ▶ Ask them to tell you two things that they can do to help get muscles stronger. (Answer: Target muscles with specific exercises and work them harder than usual.)

- ▶ Ask them to tell you what specificity means with regard to working out.

- ▶ Ask them to tell you what is meant by overloading a muscle. Ask them how they overload a muscle, and what overloading feels like.

- ▶ Ask them to point to a lower-body muscle that they worked today. Can they tell you the name of the exercise that they did for that muscle?

PRIMARY AND INTERMEDIATE

Specificity—The principle of specificity says that if a person wants to increase the strength of a muscle, he or she must use that specific muscle when performing exercises and activities. The principle of overload says that for the muscle to get stronger and endure longer, it must be used at a level that is harder than normal.

Purpose

▶ Students will be able to identify specific exercises that help increase the strength of specific muscles.

▶ Students will be able to discuss how to increase muscle strength and endurance by using the overload principle (variations of weight or repetitions, or modifications to the exercise).

Relationship to National Standards

▶ Physical education standard 2: Demonstrates understanding of movement concepts, principles, strategies, and tactics as they apply to the learning and performance of physical activities.

▶ Physical education standard 4: Achieves and maintains a health-enhancing level of physical fitness.

Upper-Body Challenge: Teacher's Guide for Station Setup and Utilization.

Upper-Body Challenge Station Level 1 Signs.

Upper-Body Challenge Station Level 2 Signs.

Equipment

For 26 children you would need approximately:

- ► 18 playground balls
- ► 4 balance domes (bosu balls) or small stacked mats
- ► Hula hoops
- ► 6 stability balls or playground balls
- ► Poly spots, dot mats, or tape to mark dot patterns
- ► 6 jump ropes
- ► For advanced levels, 6 medicine balls (optional) and 8 resistance bands (optional)
- ► Fast, upbeat music and music player
- ► Stopwatch
- ► Mats for floor work

Procedure

1. Place stations in a clockwise pattern around the room. Use the Upper-Body Challenge: Teacher's Guide for Station Setup and Utilization reproducible to help you with setup of stations, equipment needed for various stations, and additional information regarding how to perform many of the activities.

2. Ask the students why it is important to have strong muscles. Have them name muscles that they think need to be strong and tell why.

3. Discuss the idea of muscle fitness training circuits that focus on upper-body muscles versus lower-body muscles. What parts of the body make up the upper body? Discuss the importance of strong arms, back, chest, and neck.

4. State that in this lesson they are going to perform several exercises that will help specific muscles of the upper body get stronger. When we target certain muscles and do exercises for them so that they can get stronger, we are using the principle of specificity. Give examples.

5. Ask students what they need to do to make their muscles stronger besides making sure that they use the specific muscles that they want to strengthen. They need to work the muscles harder than they normally do, even to where they feel very tired. This is the principle of overload. Also, discuss the need to rest worked muscles so that they are able to work hard again. During the circuit, active rest periods will occur after the muscle fitness activity at each station. The active rest will allow worked muscles to rest while other muscles are used to perform physical activity.

6. Show the students the circuit station signs. Teach each of the exercises and activities that they will be doing during the activity and have the students practice them. Tell them that they will try to do the activity for 30 seconds. If they cannot perform the exercise for 30 seconds, they can take a very short rest and continue.

7. Have students begin with a general warm-up that includes not only aerobic activity for the total body but also some upper-body movements such as jumping jacks, pretend boxing, and body hugs.

8. Divide the students into equal groups and send them to the various stations. Play music while students perform the activities. When the music stops, students look on the circuit sign to see what active rest activity to do. When the music starts, they begin this activity until the music stops again. Then they rotate to their next station.

Teaching Hints

▶ Ensure that students understand the correct form for all the activities, and continually check their form throughout the activity. If some students cannot use correct form with the equipment chosen for the entire time, they need to know that they can change the equipment used to a lighter type, use a different type of movement, or take a rest and start again.

▶ Move around the room and encourage students to perform their best to ensure that they are overloading the muscles.

▶ Not all stations need to be included in one session, and other stations could be substituted depending on the experience of the children regarding the exercises and special equipment.

▶ You could combine two stations into one spot on the circuit and allow the students to choose which exercise they do.

Sample Inclusion Tips

▶ Have various pieces of equipment of different sizes at the stations where tossing and lifting of balls is undertaken.

▶ Active resting for those with mobility problems might include substituting large arm circles with the palms up and other arm movements that emphasize rhythmical large-muscle work in place of the leg exercises.

In Upper-Body Challenge, students learn exercises that increase their upper-body strength and endurance.

Variations

▶ To make the exercise harder or easier, students can use the alternative ways to perform the activities as noted on the station signs.

▶ Start with only a few stations per lesson and gradually add more activities as students learn the correct form for each movement.

▶ Students who are ready and capable of enhancing their overload can use modifications listed for the upper grades (level 2). Students who are weak can remain at the level 1 and progress more slowly, even if they are older.

Home Extension

Encourage the students to pick two of the exercises that they performed today for their upper body and do them at home every other day for a week. Encourage them to work on overloading the muscles by adding at least one or two repetitions or adding more time to their exercise each day so that they will get stronger.

Assessment

▶ Hold up each station sign and ask what specific body parts and muscles were being worked at that station. Ask whether this is an upper-body strength activity or a lower-body activity or both. Why?

▶ Ask them to tell you two things that they can do to help get muscles stronger. (Answer: Target muscles with specific exercises and work them harder than usual.)

▶ Ask them to tell you what specificity means with regard to working out.

▶ Ask them to tell you what is meant by overloading a muscle. Ask them how they overload a muscle and what overloading feels like.

▶ Ask them to point to an upper-body muscle that they worked today. Can they tell you the name of the exercise that they did for that muscle?

INTERMEDIATE

Progression—Progression refers to how a person should increase overload. Proper progression involves a gradual increase in the level of exercise that is manipulated by increasing frequency, intensity, time, type, or a combination of all four components.

Purpose

► Students will learn and apply the training principles of progression and overload.

► Students will learn and apply the training principles of progression and overload for muscular strength and endurance by completing a FITT Log and FITT Log Worksheet.

Relationship to National Standards

► Physical education standard 3: Participates regularly in physical activity.

► Physical education standard 4: Achieves and maintains a health-enhancing level of physical fitness.

► Health education standard 3: Students will demonstrate the ability to practice health-enhancing behaviors and reduce health risks.

Equipment

Pencil for each student

Procedure

1. Briefly review the two-word definitions of the aspects of FITT—frequency (how often), intensity (how hard), time (how long), and type (what kind).

2. Ask students to offer brief examples of how they applied the FITT guidelines to muscular strength and endurance in previous health-related fitness activities.

3. Share descriptions of the concepts of progression and overload.

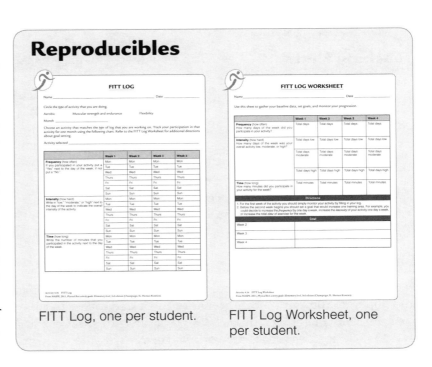

FITT Log, one per student.

FITT Log Worksheet, one per student.

4. Distribute one blank FITT Log to each student. Review each category and how it relates to each aspect of FITT.

5. Ask the class to share muscular activities that they enjoy and tell them to choose one and write it in the log.

6. Ask each child to circle "muscular strength and endurance" on the FITT Log to indicate the type of activity that they are tracking. Have them also write their name on the log.

7. Assign students to log the muscular strength and endurance physical activity that they performed outside class during one week.

8. Have students complete week 1 of the FITT Log and FITT Log Worksheet.

9. Guide students in setting goals for progression and overload and writing them on the worksheet.

10. At the end of each week, meet with the class to discuss their progress and set new goals.

Teaching Hints

▶ Ask students at each class meeting how their logs are coming along.

▶ If necessary, require guardian initials to encourage participation.

▶ Have students demonstrate the home-based activity ideas at an open house.

An important lifelong lesson for students is that even fun activities outside of the classroom help them improve their muscular strength and endurance.

▶ Ask the school's after-school care providers to provide space, time, and other support for students to add to their logs.

▶ Tie in the Fitnessgram muscular strength and endurance assessments with this activity.

Sample Inclusion Tip

Help students with special circumstances come up with alternative activities to suit their needs and abilities. You can modify activities suggested earlier in this chapter, provide suggestions for students who must stay indoors because of safety or space constraints, or otherwise help students develop activity ideas that will work for them.

Variations

- ▶ Have students keep their logs at school and fill them out at the beginning of the class period.
- ▶ Have students perform some muscular strength and endurance activities in class. Have them discuss what activities they do after school to use the same muscles that they used in class.

Home Extension

This activity is a home extension.

Assessment

After the month, have students review their logs with you and write about their experience by answering questions such as the following:

- ▶ Were you able to build up safely to a higher level of intensity over the course of the month, do the activities more frequently each week, or spend more time doing each activity? Which changes did you make, if any?
- ▶ If you were able to make changes, how might the changes have affected your muscular fitness?
- ▶ If you did not make changes, what might you be able to do differently in the future?

Realize that many factors, such as the child's initial level of fitness and participation (if already high, the child may not progress for that reason), and other personal factors may affect the answers to these question. Keeping this in mind, focus on the assessment as a means to teach and reinforce the concepts of progression and overload.

Flexibility

Chapter Contents

Flexibility is the ability to move a joint through its complete range of motion. Children can get an idea of how flexible they are by answering the question, "How well do you bend, stretch, and twist?" The goal of flexibility is to develop and maintain normal joint range of motion. Keep in mind that having too much mobility predisposes people to injury and can be just as bad as having too little.

Being flexible can bring about many benefits:

▶ Decreased muscle tension and increased relaxation (I can sleep better.)

▶ Greater ease of movement (I can move easier.)

▶ Improved coordination (I can perform better in sport or dance.)

▶ Increased range of motion (I can bend, stretch, and twist into many positions.)

▶ Reduced risk of injury (I can move safely.)

▶ Better body awareness and postural alignment (I can stand tall.)

▶ Improved circulation and air exchange (I can breathe easier.)

▶ Smoother and easier contractions (My muscles work better.)

▶ Decreased muscle soreness (I am less sore after playing hard.)

▶ Possible prevention of low back pain and other spinal problems (I can sit at my desk all morning without my back feeling sore.)

▶ Improved personal appearance and self-image (I feel good about myself.)

▶ Enhanced ability to develop and maintain motor skills (I can do a variety of activities.)

DEFINING FLEXIBILITY

Flexibility is the ability of a joint to move freely in every direction and through a full range of motion. Two types of flexibility (static and dynamic) and four types of stretches (static, active, PNF, and passive) can be used to foster the development of flexibility and improved range of motion.

▶ Static flexibility, the amount of motion at a joint, is limited by the person's tolerance to the stretch.

▶ Dynamic (ballistic) flexibility is the rate of increase in tension in a relaxed muscle as the person stretches it (Knudson, Magnusson, & McHugh, 2000).

▶ A static stretch is a slow, sustained stretch of the muscle held for 10 to 30 seconds at the point of mild discomfort and backed off slightly (or held just before reaching the point of discomfort). In static stretching, the muscles gradually lengthen through the joint's range of motion (Hoegers & Hoegers, 2010).

▶ In an active static stretch, the participant provides the force of the stretch (for example, in the sit-and-reach, the person leans forward and reaches as far as possible).

▶ In a passive static stretch, the person, a partner, gravity, or an implement provides the force of the stretch (see figure 7.3 in *Physical Education for Lifelong Fitness: The Physical Best Teacher's Guide, Third Edition*).

▶ Proprioceptive neuromuscular facilitation (PNF) is a static stretch using combinations of the active and passive stretching techniques. PNF is a "mode of stretching that uses reflexes and neuromuscular principles to relax the muscles being stretched" (Hoeger & Hoeger, 2010, p. 267). The PNF technique is often described as "contract, relax, stretch." The muscle to be stretched is first contracted against resistance from a partner or object, then the muscle is relaxed, and finally the passive stretch technique described earlier is used to stretch the muscle that was first contracted and relaxed (see figure 7.4 in *Physical Education for Lifelong Fitness: The Physical Best Teacher's Guide, Third Edition*). This type of stretch should not be performed by children 6 to 10 years old. At the elementary level, the focus is on active static stretching, not dynamic (ballistic) stretching. Also, at this level, children are not ready to work with partners to improve flexibility or to perform PNF exercises.

TEACHING GUIDELINES FOR FLEXIBILITY

As in all areas of health-related fitness, the principles of training (progression, overload, specificity, regularity, and individuality) must be applied when teaching flexibility concepts to students. The FITT guidelines (see table 5.1) also play a key role in improving flexibility. In applying the principles of training and the FITT guidelines, be aware of the factors that affect flexibility (see *Physical Education for Lifelong Fitness: The Physical Best Teacher's Guide, Third Edition*) and recognize that you may or may not observe improvement.

According to Hoeger and Hoeger (2010), muscular flexibility is primarily related to genetic factors and to physical activity. Factors that affect flexibility include the following:

- ▶ Failure to adhere to a regular program of stretching.
- ▶ Muscle temperature—raising the temperature causes the muscle tissue to become more pliable and therefore enhances stretching.
- ▶ Gender and age (Knudson, Magnusson, & McHugh, 2000)—females tend to possess more flexibility than males, and as people age they lose flexibility and range of motion unless they devote appropriate attention to stretching.
- ▶ Tissue interference (Hoeger & Hoeger, 2010)—excess adipose tissue and tissue injury in and around muscle joints may hinder range of motion.
- ▶ Muscle tension—a relaxed muscle can stretch farther because the stretch reflex is not engaged.
- ▶ Poor coordination and strength during active movement may cause imbalances and injury.
- ▶ Pain can increase tightness in soft tissues because the stretch reflex becomes engaged.

Therefore, pain should be avoided when stretching; stretch only to mild discomfort.

- ▶ Lack of proper warm-up or cool temperatures (Hoeger & Hoeger, 2010)—ideally, a full-body warm-up should be performed before stretching. A low-level aerobic activity that raises the heart rate, causes perspiration and heavier breathing to start, and continues for a minimum of 5 to 10 minutes should be undertaken before stretching.
- ▶ Certain diseases (Blanchard, 1999) or physical conditions such as arthritis, injuries, scar tissue from past injuries, cerebral palsy, and joint structure or shape of the bones (Hoeger & Hoeger, 2010).

TRAINING METHODS FOR FLEXIBILITY

Choose a variety of flexibility exercises and a variety of avenues to teach flexibility concepts to prevent boredom and the drudgery of performing the same old stretches day after day. Explain to students the relationship between flexibility exercises performed in class and the back-saver sit-and-reach test and shoulder-stretch test (Fitnessgram) performed during the fitness assessment portion of your program. When teaching flexibility concepts, stress safety and proper technique. Adequate warm-up of the parts to be stretched must be undertaken before stretching them. A warm muscle can be stretched farther and more safely than a cold muscle. Students should use slow, controlled movements when stretching, holding each stretch to the point of mild discomfort (and perhaps backing off slightly) for 10 to 30 seconds. Holding the stretch at the point

Table 5.1 FITT Guidelines Applied to Flexibility

Frequency	Three times per week minimum but preferably daily and after a full-body warm-up to raise muscle temperature.
Intensity	Slow elongation of the muscle to the point of mild discomfort and backing off slightly.
Time	Up to four or five stretches per muscle or muscle group. Hold each stretch for 10 to 30 seconds. Always warm-up properly before stretching.
Type	The preferred stretch for the classroom is slow static stretching for all muscles or muscle groups.

Note: Although 10 to 30 seconds is recommended as the length of time to hold a stretch, an advanced student may hold a stretch up to 60 seconds.

Adapted from American College of Sports Medicine 2001.

of discomfort and backing off slightly ensures application of the overload principle.

Other safety precautions include the following:

- ▶ Avoid locking any joint (maintain soft knees, soft joints).
- ▶ Do not overstretch a joint (pay attention to the tightness felt during the stretch).
- ▶ Never stretch the neck or spine too far.
- ▶ Do not perform ballistic stretches (reserved for controlled, sport-specific training of secondary students and adults).
- ▶ Be sure to raise the temperature of the muscles before stretching. Stretches performed to enhance range of motion and length should be undertaken only after warming up the part. Warm-up ideally is 5 to 10 minutes of light aerobic activity for the total body. Stretching to enhance range of motion is especially effective after the most vigorous part of the lesson or activity is completed.
- ▶ A trained health care professional should check a student who has excessive mobility.

Along with these safety precautions, be aware of questionable exercises or contraindicated exercises as presented in *Physical Education for Lifelong Fitness: The Physical Best Teacher's Guide, Third Edition.*

Flexibility is an important component of health-related fitness, so resist the temptation to relegate it to warm-ups and cool-downs. The activities that follow provide many opportunities to use flexibility as the focus of your lesson or add variety to your warm-ups and cool-downs.

MOTOR-SKILL DEVELOPMENT THROUGH FLEXIBILITY ACTIVITIES

Normal full range of motion (ROM) is essential to learning and perfecting motor skills, and a student with limited ROM will have difficulty mastering a motor skill that a classmate with normal mobility will learn easily. The specificity principle applies here. For example, if a student wants to be able to punt a football or perform a high kick in a soccer game, he or she must have good leg flexibility. Good flexibility, then, enhances motor-skill development. Motor-skill development through fitness

activity is the perfect area for you to consider the abilities and disabilities of all students. Some are high achievers, others are low achievers, and still others have physical or intellectual disabilities. Provide opportunities for all students to develop physical skills and be successful in your classroom. If a student is severely disabled, you may need to contact a person who specializes in adapted physical education for assistance in developing an individualized education plan. When students see the connections between flexibility and the physical activities that they are engaging in, they are more likely to continue working on enhancing flexibility as a lifestyle choice. In short, you create a deeper awareness of the need for flexibility.

FLEXIBILITY NEWSLETTER

Use the Flexibility Newsletter (see figure 5.1) to introduce, reinforce, and extend the concepts behind developing and maintaining good flexibility. The following are ways in which you might use this tool:

- ▶ Send the newsletter home as a guardian-involvement tool during a mini unit focusing on flexibility.
- ▶ Use the newsletter to help you feature flexibility as the "Health-Related Fitness Component of the Month."
- ▶ Introduce the activity ideas as a whole-group task. Ask students to choose one to perform outside class in the next week. They should report their progress through a log, a journal,

Figure 5.1 Becoming Your Physical Best Flexibility Newsletter.

a guardian's signature on the newsletter, or other means.

▶ Validate and promote student involvement in physical activity outside class time and the school setting.

▶ Among students who can read, promote reading to learn across your curriculum, further supporting the elementary school mission.

▶ Use the newsletter as a model or springboard to create your own newsletters, tailored specifically to your students' needs.

Feel free to use the Flexibility Newsletter in a way that helps you teach more effectively to the specific needs of your students and their guardians. See table 5.2 for a grid of activities in this chapter.

Table 5.2   Chapter 5 Activities Grid

Activity number	Activity title	Activity page	Concept	Primary	Intermediate	Reproducibles (on CD-ROM)
5.1	You Can Bend	132	Flexibility	•		You Can Bend Pictures
						You Can Bend Homework Worksheet
5.2	Flexible Fun	135	Flexibility		•	Definition Cards
5.3	Beginning Yoga Poses	138	Health benefits	•		Beginning Yoga Pose Signs
						Flexibility Health Benefits Poster
5.4	Intermediate Yoga Poses	140	Health benefits		•	Intermediate Yoga Pose Signs
						Flexibility Health Benefits Poster
5.5	Stability Ball With Flexibility	142	Warm-up	•		Stability Ball Exercise Pictures
5.6	Stretching Out Tag	145	Warm-up and cool-down		•	Warm-Up Wall Chart
						Warm-Up Station Signs
						Static Stretching Exercise Signs
						Cool-Down Wall Chart
5.7	Flexibility Activity Picture Chart	149	Frequency	•		Flexibility Activity Picture Chart
5.8	Towel Stretching for Flexibility	151	Frequency		•	Towel Stretching for Flexibility Sign
						Towel Stretches for the Day Homework
						Towel Stretching for Flexibility Log
5.9	Caterpillar Stretch	154	Intensity	•		Human Caterpillar Picture
5.10	At Least 10 Leopard Cats	157	Time	•		Stretching Reminders
						At Least 10 Leopard Cats Sign
						At Least 10 Leopard Cats Stretch Signs
5.11	Roll the Stretch	159	Specificity, or type	•	•	Stretching Picture Sign (Primary)
						Stretching Picture Sign (Intermediate)
						Roll the Stretch Assessment Rubric
5.12	Stretch Marks the Spot	161	Specificity, or type		•	Stretch Activity Station Signs
						Stretch Activity Worksheet
						Stretch Evaluation Sheet
5.13	Flexibility FITT Log	163	Progression		•	FITT Log
						FITT Log Worksheet

PRIMARY

Flexibility—Flexibility is the ability to bend, stretch, and twist the body.

Purpose

▶ Students will perform stretching exercises and will be able to define flexibility.

▶ Students will be able to identify the importance of stretching to physical activity and daily life.

Relationship to National Standards

▶ Physical education standard 3: Participates regularly in physical activity.

▶ Physical education standard 4: Achieves and maintains a health-enhancing level of physical fitness.

Equipment

If you do not have this equipment, use the You Can Bend Pictures in the reproducible.

▶ PowerPoint, picture screen saver, or video editing program

▶ Computer

▶ LCD projector

▶ Pictures of your students performing flexibility exercises or doing daily chores

▶ Slow, relaxing music and player

▶ Mats for floor work

Procedure

1. Talk about the body and point out the joints. Joints are where bones meet other bones and movement occurs: hip, wrist, knee, elbow, shoulder, and ankle.

2. Go over the definition of flexibility and add movements to the words. Flexibility is the ability to bend (hands on hips and bend at the waist forward), stretch (lift arms to the ceiling), and move easily around a joint (big arm circles).

Reproducibles

You Can Bend Pictures. Use these if you don't have access to technical equipment.

You Can Bend Homework Worksheet, one per student.

3. Perform a full range of movement around the joints for students to understand this concept. Discuss that stretching muscles will give you more flexibility or make it easier to bend without hurting yourself.

4. Take digital pictures of flexibility exercises and save them so that you can transport them. In your pictures, show where the range of motion depends on the joints and the ability of the muscles to stretch, such as reaching behind the back to touch hands or sitting and reaching for the toes.

5. Use a PowerPoint program to place each photo in sequential order. Adjust timing to suit the needs of the class for each picture. Add music if the computer program permits.

6. Use the program projection to provide directions and pictures for students to see so that they can perform the stretches. Move around the class to provide feedback or give individual aid to students.

Teaching Hints

▶ Point out to students the wide range of movement that they must perform. They bend, stretch, and twist at many joints. Having adequate range of motion depends on the joints and the ability of the muscles to stretch.

▶ Time is needed in advance to take photos and set up the flexibility exercise pictures.

Using pictures helps young students understand the definition of flexibility and the proper way to perform stretches.

▶ Make sure that guardian release permission is granted before using individual pictures outside of school.

▶ Give safety directions for stretching. Students should reach to a point of mild discomfort but not pain.

Sample Inclusion Tips

▶ Use some additional pictures for students with alternative needs.

▶ Modify stretches for students with physical or orthopedic problems as well as those who may be using wheelchairs, walkers, or canes.

▶ Always consult the physical therapist who is working with specific students. Some stretching may be contraindicated for particular students.

Variations

▶ Use a video camera and a screen to project the active learning taking place. Here students can view their stretches and see what they are doing. Select a student and focus the camera on her or his movement. Have the class perform the exercise.

▶ After a stretch ask students when this ability would be important in their lives. For example, ask, "What sport would this help?" and "How would this help in daily life?"

Home Extension

Have the students complete the You Can Bend Homework Worksheet at home and then bring it back to school to be put on a wall in the gym.

Assessment

▶ Have students give you the definition of flexibility with body movements.

▶ Ask them why it is important to stretch—to bend, stretch, and twist the body.

▶ Have students tell you something that they are able to do when they are flexible.

FLEXIBLE FUN

INTERMEDIATE

Flexibility—Flexibility is the ability to bend, stretch, and twist the body with ease, through a full range of motion.

Purpose

Students will learn or review the definition of flexibility as a component of health-related fitness.

Relationship to National Standards

▶ Physical education standard 4: Achieves and maintains a health-enhancing level of physical fitness.

▶ Physical education standard 5: Exhibits responsible personal and social behavior that respects self and others in physical activity settings.

Equipment

▶ Mats

▶ Heart rate monitors (optional)

▶ Pedometers (optional)

Procedure

1. Print the Definition Cards available on the CD-ROM. These cards contain the definition for each component of health-related fitness. Cut each segment into strips and laminate them. For the activity, you will need one set of Definition Cards for each group of students. Choose how many sets of the other health-related fitness cards you wish to use. Scatter the Definition Cards facedown in the center of the activity space.

2. Ask students to define flexibility as a component of health-related fitness. Alternatively, offer the definition for flexibility provided by Physical Best—flexibility is the ability to bend, stretch, and twist the body with ease, through a full range of motion. Briefly brainstorm examples of how flexibility helps us in sports, other physical activities, and daily life. Also review the definitions for the other components of health-related fitness (as provided on the Definition Cards).

3. Divide students into small groups of three or four students per group and have them form relay lines.

4. On your signal, one student from each group runs out, picks up a Definition Card, and then runs back to the group. The other students in the group jog in place until the runner returns. The group then determines

Reproducible

Flexibility

The ability to bend, stretch,

and twist the body with ease

through a full range of motion.

Definition Cards for each component of health-related fitness. One set for each group of three students. Five additional flexibility definition cards can be made to make the activity go faster.

Flexible Fun lets students puzzle out the definition of flexibility and enjoy group stretching.

whether the words are part of the flexibility definition and whether the part of the definition is still needed. If not, the next runner returns the card, places it facedown, and picks up another card.

5. The relay continues until the group has all the word cards needed to complete the definition for flexibility. Then they put the cards in the correct order and sit and stretch to signal that their group is finished.

6. This activity can be used as part of a warm-up. Complete the activity by finishing with a group stretch.

Teaching Hints

▶ When first introducing the activity, provide each group with the definition of flexibility or place the cards faceup.

▶ Strongly emphasize safety whenever stretching. Never encourage competition among students or groups.

▶ For all class flexibility activities, always strive to relate stretching to other activities that students are interested in or must do (for example, favorite sports or other physical activities and everyday life activities).

Sample Inclusion Tips

▶ Substitute locomotor movements and adjust placement of cards for students with limited mobility.

▶ Place some strips at a higher level (on a chair or stool) for those students that cannot bend over to retrieve the strips at a low level.

Variations

▶ If using the activity as a warm-up, consider substituting a locomotor movement that is more suitable for a warm-up, such as a fast walk.

▶ Have the student who just returned with the paper jog around the playing area after he or she has returned with part of the right or wrong definition. This movement will help students warm up before stretching.

▶ Use this activity when teaching the other components of fitness as well.

▶ Heart rate monitors can be used to keep track of how hard the students' hearts worked during the activity or during different parts of the activity like the waiting section or the running relay section.

▶ Pedometers can be used to determine how many steps it took to complete the activity.

Home Extension

Have the students do one to three stretches at home every day. Provide them with examples of general stretches as well as the proper guidelines to perform them.

Assessment

▶ Ask students for an oral or written definition of flexibility.

▶ Offer an oral or written list of the definitions (but not terms) of muscular strength and endurance, aerobic fitness, and flexibility. Ask students to identify which definition describes flexibility.

▶ Have students apply the definition of flexibility to themselves by having them record in their journals how flexibility may help them in their favorite physical activity or required daily activities. Repeat this assessment periodically throughout the school year to monitor how students are assimilating the information into their lives.

BEGINNING YOGA POSES

PRIMARY

Health benefits—Good flexibility can have many health benefits, such as helping with good posture and helping to feel relaxed.

Purpose

Students will identify several benefits of using yoga as a way to increase flexibility for a healthy, active life.

Relationship to National Standards

▶ Physical education standard 6: Values physical activity for health, enjoyment, challenge, self-expression, and/or social interaction.

▶ Health education standard 3: Students will demonstrate the ability to practice health-enhancing behaviors and reduce health risks.

Equipment

▶ Soft, soothing music and player

▶ Mats

Procedure

1. Explain to students that many of the balances and stretches in which we participate during physical education are similar to yoga. Yoga offers many benefits associated with good flexibility (read Flexibility Health Benefits Poster or the following list):

   - Increased flexibility
   - Increased oxygen because of breathing deeply
   - Increased blood flow
   - Increased ability to focus
   - Increased ability to think clearer and make better decisions

2. Select, or have a student select, a yoga picture.

3. Explain to students how to take position, how to balance, and where to focus.

Beginning Yoga Pose Signs.

Flexibility Health Benefits Poster.

Students experience the flexibility and mental benefits of yoga. Classroom teachers can continue to use yoga outside of the gym to help students experience the mind–body benefits of yoga.

4. Encourage students to feel their chests rise and fall with their breathing.
5. Repeat with the selection of a new picture.

Teaching Hint

Teach classroom teachers yoga poses so that students can do yoga movements before or after intense learning in the classroom.

Sample Inclusion Tip

Try to offer poses and modifications that will be appropriate for students with disabilities. For example, allow students to use a wall or chair for balance and support as needed.

Variations

▶ Make yoga fun for primary students by using the imagery of the pose.
▶ Have the students give names to the poses.

Home Extensions

▶ Ask the students to pick their favorite pose and practice it at home.
▶ The students can also teach the pose to family members and teach them about its benefits.

Assessment

▶ Have the students demonstrate a pose that they like and tell you what parts of the body it stretches.
▶ Ask students to state one benefit of good flexibility.

INTERMEDIATE

Health benefits—Good flexibility has many health benefits, such as reduced tension and improved posture.

Purpose

Students will become aware of the benefits of flexibility in a variety of poses.

Relationship to National Standards

- ▶ Physical education standard 6: Values physical activity for health, enjoyment, challenge, self-expression, and/or social interaction.
- ▶ Health education standard 3: Students will demonstrate the ability to practice health-enhancing behaviors and reduce health risks.

Equipment

- ▶ Soft, soothing music and player
- ▶ Mats

Procedure

1. Explain to students that many of the balances and stretches in which we participate during physical education are similar to yoga and that practicing yoga can assist in gaining the benefits of flexibility (display Flexibility Health Benefits Poster).

2. Tell students that everyone has a different flexibility potential. Emphasize that they should not feel pain when stretching or holding a pose, but that the muscles should feel like they are being stretched.

3. Select, or have a student select, a yoga picture.

4. Explain to students how to take position, how to balance, and where to focus.

5. Encourage students to feel their chests rise and fall as they breathe in and out.

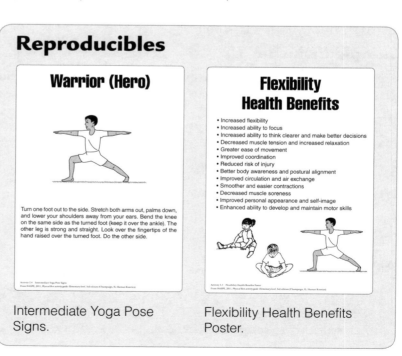

Intermediate Yoga Pose Signs.

Flexibility Health Benefits Poster.

6. To work on the ability to focus, students should be very quiet as they do the poses.

7. Repeat with the selection of a new picture.

Teaching Hints

▶ For stress management, students need to be quiet and ignore distractions around them.

▶ Caution: Students of this age tend to try to impress each other by outdoing one another. A reminder about the importance of being aware of your own sensations and not pushing yourself to the point of pain or great discomfort might help.

▶ Teach students to exhale when moving into a stretch and to use the exhalation to push the stretch a little farther. This method will help them overload their muscles slowly to increase range of motion and will enhance the health benefit of relaxation. Inhaling deeply in the rest phase of multiple stretch repetitions takes the relaxation aspect even further.

Yoga has many benefits for students, including reduced tension and improved posture and balance.

Sample Inclusion Tips

▶ Try to offer poses and modifications that will be appropriate for students with disabilities.

▶ Allow students to use a wall or chair for balance or support as needed.

▶ Provide the opportunity for students with disabilities to practice poses and adaptations before class.

Variations

▶ After you have introduced students to the poses, this could be a station activity.

▶ Talk to the classroom teachers about using yoga on stressful test days before testing to help students relax and focus. Yoga can also be beneficial after testing.

Home Extension

Have students teach their guardians, babysitters, or grandparents a yoga pose that could enhance their health-related fitness.

Assessment

▶ Ask students how they could use yoga to help maintain health-related fitness.

▶ Ask students to explain how yoga can help increase flexibility.

STABILITY BALL WITH FLEXIBILITY

PRIMARY

Warm-up—The purpose of a warm-up is to get the muscles ready for activity and avoid injury. A good warm-up before flexibility exercises consists of light aerobic activity for about five minutes that includes movements that will help to stretch muscles.

Purpose

▶ Students will identify exercises to warm up the body gradually before doing activity.

▶ Students will explain the importance of a warm-up.

Relationship to National Standards

▶ Physical education standard 4: Achieves and maintains a health-enhancing level of physical fitness.

▶ Health education standard 3: Students will demonstrate the ability to practice health-enhancing behaviors and reduce health risks.

Equipment

▶ A stability ball for each student

▶ Slow, relaxing music and player

Procedure

1. Show students stiff spaghetti and explain how it is like their muscles before they have warmed up.

2. When the music starts, students travel in any pathway, each carrying a stability ball around the room. Arms and legs need to be straight and knees or elbows should not bend.

3. When the music stops, students put the ball down and sit on it.

4. Lead the students in an exercise. Begin with jumping jack arms.

5. Begin the music. Tell the students that jumping jack arms have now loosened up their arms and they can bend them. Have students hand dribble the ball with stiff legs around the room or turning in a circle.

6. Stop. Students sit on the ball and reach for their toes. They count to 10, three times.

7. Students are now able to bend their arms and legs while moving.

8. Continue the warm-up, changing movement activities with the ball and flexibility exercises on the ball.

Reproducible

Stability Ball Jumping Jacks

Stability Ball Exercise Pictures.

9. Students walk or jog around the room holding the ball. They then sit on the ball and do jumping jacks with their arms only.

10. Students walk and dribble the ball with two hands around the room. They stop, sit on the ball, and do a triceps stretch.

11. Students jog and dribble the ball with one hand. They then stop, sit on the ball, and do a straddle stretch.

12. Students toss the ball up and let it bounce once before catching it. They stop, sit on the ball, and do a side bend.

Stability balls can help students gain balance and flexibility while they warm up or cool down.

13. At the end of the workout, show the students cooked spaghetti to demonstrate how their muscles become more flexible after they are warmed up.

Teaching Hints

▶ Discuss that a warm-up is light activity that helps warm up the muscles by gradually increasing physical activity. The warm-up prepares the heart and other muscles of the body for vigorous activity and avoids adding stress.

▶ The purpose of the warm-up is to (1) prevent muscle strain, (2) prevent soreness, (3) increase the elasticity of the muscles, and (4) warm up the body for activity.

▶ Instruct students that when they are sitting on a stability ball they should always remain in contact with the ball.

▶ Caution students that high bouncing while sitting on the ball could cause the ball to roll away, resulting in a fall on the floor.

▶ While the students are stretching, talk about the importance of a warm-up and show students uncooked and cooked spaghetti to represent cold and warm muscles.

▶ Discuss the purpose of a cool-down. It is a time to slow down the body and to prevent muscle soreness and muscle stiffness. The cool-down consists of less-vigorous activity and stretching.

▶ Talk about specificity with exercises. Certain exercises can help specific muscle groups. For example, reaching for the toes will stretch the leg muscles. A triceps stretch will help loosen up the arms.

Sample Inclusion Tips

▶ Students in wheelchairs can be given a smaller ball for the stretches and active moving. Assign two students to take turns retrieving the ball when needed.

▶ Students can use a smaller ball to dribble while sitting or they can toss a ball against a wall.

▶ Students can do actions such as lifting the ball high and then low, touching the belly and then stretching the ball forward as far as possible, or using the ball to touch the toes or twisting to the sides and touching the arms of the wheelchair with the ball.

Variation

Ask students to give you stretching exercises to do while sitting on the ball. This variation can also be used to teach specificity with flexibility exercises.

Home Extension

Ask students to sit in a chair at home and pretend that the chair is a stability ball. Ask them to do the exercises that they did in class on the ball. Ask them to come up with new exercises and bring them to class next time.

Assessment

Ask students these questions:

▶ Why is it important to warm up before exercise?

▶ Why is it important to cool down after exercise?

▶ What exercises would you do for soccer to warm up the body? Why? Select another sport and repeat the question.

INTERMEDIATE

Warm-up and cool-down—A warm-up gets the body ready for activity and prevents injuries by increasing the elasticity of the muscles and tendons. A warm-up also gradually speeds up the heart and breathing so blood and oxygen can move through the body faster and bring nutrients to the muscles. A cool-down helps slow the body down gradually after activity and can help prevent injuries. Stretching once the muscles are warmed up, and especially during a cool-down when muscles are very warm, helps relax muscles, increase their length, and increase the range of motion in muscles and joints, thereby reducing the chances of suffering tight and sore muscles.

Purpose

▶ Students will understand why warming up, cooling down, and stretching are important parts of a workout and that warming up is important prior to stretching.

▶ Students will be able to list exercises to use for warm-up, for cool-down, and for stretching.

▶ Students will be able to discuss how to stretch correctly.

Relationship to National Standards

▶ Physical education standard 3: Participates regularly in physical activity.

▶ Physical education standard 4: Achieves and maintains a health-enhancing level of physical fitness.

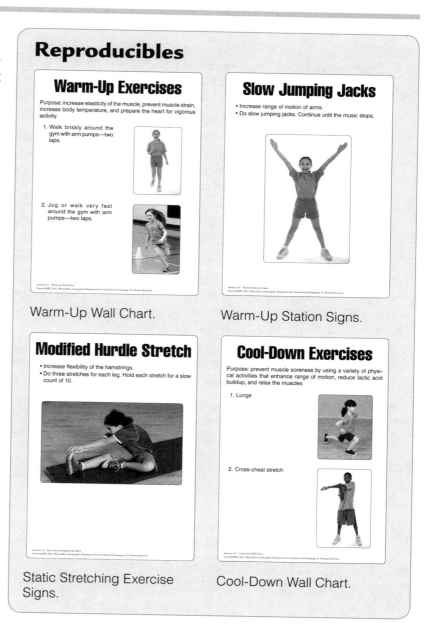

Reproducibles

Warm-Up Wall Chart.

Warm-Up Station Signs.

Static Stretching Exercise Signs.

Cool-Down Wall Chart.

Equipment

▶ Pedometers (optional) to keep track of steps

▶ Mats

▶ Music player and soothing music

Procedure

1. Before starting class, place a Warm-Up Station Sign and a Static Stretching Exercise Sign at each station around the perimeter of the room.

2. Discuss the definition of flexibility, the benefits of flexibility, and the principles for enhancing flexibility. Also review what static stretching involves and why it should be used.

3. Go over the six warm-up activities using the Warm-Up Wall Chart so students are familiar with the group warm-up activities that will be performed first. Then play music while students go around the perimeter of the room doing each warm-up activity for 30 seconds as you call them out. Stop the music to signal the students to end their activity and listen for instructions.

4. At the end of the group warm-up, bring the students together and ask them if they feel signs of warming up. Ask students to name these signs (e.g., differences in heart rate, breathing, sweating).

5. Before starting the second part of the warm-up, show students the Warm-Up Station Signs and explain that these warm-up activities emphasize specific areas of the body. Assign students to stations and play music while they perform the exercise on their station cards. When the music stops they should move clockwise to the next station. Continue this rotation until students have had a chance to try all the stations.

6. Bring the students together again and discuss the signs of warming up.

7. Now that the warm-up exercises have been completed, it is time to play Stretching Out Tag. In Stretching Out Tag, everyone chases each other. When a student is tagged, he or she goes to one of the six stations and performs the exercise given on the Static Stretching Exercise Sign. Remind students to hold the stretch for 10 slow counts and not to bounce. Students should go to a different station each time they are tagged and should not repeat a station until they have been to all six. If necessary, review the Static Stretching Exercise Signs. Plan to play Stretching Out Tag for several minutes.

8. Once you have called an end to Stretching Out Tag, have students perform a cool-down by walking two or three laps clockwise around the gym. Then take students through the activities listed on the Cool-Down Wall Chart to finish the cool-down.

9. Ask students whether they think that they have cooled down enough. Why or why not? Use the signs of exertion: how hard are students breathing, how fast are their hearts beating, are they still sweating? If needed, use additional stations to allow for more cool-down time.

Teaching Hints

▶ Remind students to pay attention to signs that the body is warming up so that they are successful in helping the body prepare for the workout and the stretching to come.

▶ Emphasize the importance of warming up and cooling down and what each should feel like. The warm-up should be a gradual warming of the body with signs like increased heart rate and sweating. The cool-down should be a gradual slowing of the body. Again, use the signs of exertion to see if students are actually cooling down slowly and effectively.

Stretching Out Tag helps students learn just how an effective warm-up and cool-down should feel.

▶ It is important for students to understand that immediately after a hard workout they need to do large muscle activity to help slow the bodily functions gradually. Point out that the cool-down stretching should be static stretching held long enough to be effective.

▶ Have students be mindful of how their stretching feels and how far they can stretch when they first start playing tag. Have them compare this to how the stretching feels during the game and after they finish the game. Point out that flexibility usually increases after the muscles have warmed up through hard work due to the warming of the body.

Sample Inclusion Tips

▶ During Stretching Out Tag, students who use wheelchairs, canes, or walkers can use a noodle to extend their arm length.

▶ To avoid being tagged, hands go above the head. Have these students think about whether their arms and other upper body parts can stretch further after warming up and after the tag activity.

▶ Develop and place appropriate exercises on the wall to select and perform when tagged.

Variation

Students can create new flexibility cards to place at the stations. Review the stretches so that all students will know them.

Home Extension

Pass out index cards so that students can create new flexibility or warm-up exercises to bring in for the next class. They should include three things: name of the exercise, how long to hold it or perform it, and why it is important.

Assessment

▶ Ask students why it is important to warm up before exercising and stretching.

▶ Ask students why it is important to cool down after an activity.

▶ Ask students to list the differences between active stretching and dynamic or ballistic stretching and to give examples.

▶ Ask students when the best time to stretch is and why.

▶ Ask students if they were able to stretch further after the workout. Should they be able to stretch further after the tag activity than after the warm-up? Why or why not?

▶ Have students list exercises appropriate for a warm-up and a cool-down.

PRIMARY

Frequency—Frequency is the number of times per week that you need to stretch for good flexibility. Experts recommend that to make and keep your body flexible, you should stretch at least three times a week.

Purpose

Students will understand and participate in stretching activities at least three times a week.

Relationship to National Standards

▶ Physical education standard 3: Participates regularly in physical activity.

▶ Health education standard 3: Students will demonstrate the ability to practice health-enhancing behaviors and reduce health risks.

Equipment

Pencils

Procedure

1. Have the students brainstorm ways that they stretch in their everyday lives. Encourage them to use examples from outside physical education class.

2. Pass out the Flexibility Activity Picture Chart, explain how to fill it out, and ask students to work with their guardians at home to fill it out for the next one to two weeks.

Teaching Hints

▶ Construct a bulletin board with hand-drawn or magazine pictures of the various activities that students found to do.

▶ You may want to complete a chart to show students as an example.

Sample Inclusion Tip

Use this activity as an opportunity for diversity training. Have students with disabilities share or demonstrate the activities that they participate in outside of school.

Variation

Encourage students to find different ways to stay flexible. Give them examples that fit within their community.

Home Extension

Have a family day in physical education when family members join the students in activities that the family can do at home to keep in shape.

Flexibility Activity Picture Chart, one per student.

Flexibility is crucial to a variety of sports and activities. In this activity, students learn the importance of stretching at least three times per week.

Assessment

▶ Have students tell you how many days per week they perform flexibility activities.

▶ Have students name a flexibility activity that they could do every day.

▶ Collect the Flexibility Activity Picture Chart and lead a class discussion on the activities circled and added.

▶ Have students discuss their favorite flexibility activity with the class.

INTERMEDIATE

Frequency—Frequency is the number of times per week that you need to stretch for good flexibility. Experts recommend that to make and keep your body flexible, you should stretch at least three times a week. Even better is stretching daily.

Purpose

▶ Students will participate in flexibility stretching activities at least three times a week.

▶ Students will identify the benefits of flexibility exercises when doing them at least three times a week.

Relationship to National Standards

▶ Physical education standard 4: Achieves and maintains a health-enhancing level of physical fitness.

▶ Health education standard 3: Students will demonstrate the ability to practice health-enhancing behaviors and reduce health risks.

Equipment

▶ A towel for each student

▶ Slow music and player

▶ Mats

Reproducibles

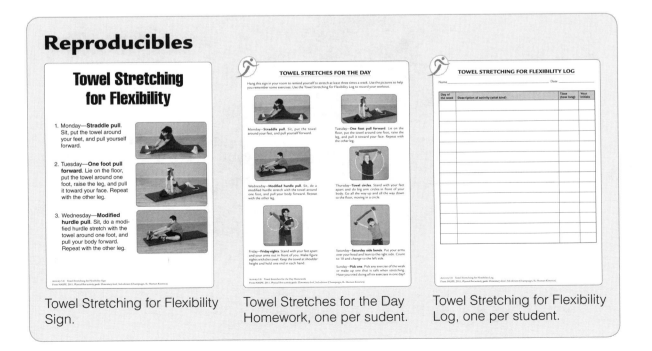

Towel Stretching for Flexibility Sign.

Towel Stretches for the Day Homework, one per sudent.

Towel Stretching for Flexibility Log, one per student.

Procedure

1. Place Towel Stretching for Flexibility Sign on the walls for students to see.

2. Give each student a towel to use during this activity. When moving around the gym students need to carry one end of the towel in each hand to avoid creating a tripping hazard.

3. Talk about the timing of the stretches. Students should hold them for 10 to 30 seconds and not bounce. Sustained stretching is the best type of stretch to perform.

4. When the music begins, students slowly jog two laps around the gym with the end of a towel in each hand to warm up the body before stretching.

5. When the music stops, call out a day of the week so that students can perform the flexibility exercise for that day written on the Towel Stretching for Flexibility Sign. Have students tell you what muscle group they are stretching.

6. When the music begins again, select, or have a student select, a different locomotor movement for the students to perform. Encourage students to use the towel to move with, swaying it side to side, up and down, high and low. They use the arms to make the locomotor movements interesting. Remind them that one end of the towel needs to remain in each hand.

7. When the music stops, call out another day of the week so that students can perform the flexibility exercise for that day written on the Towel Stretching for Flexibility Sign. Have students tell you what muscle group they are stretching.

8. Continue until the exercises for all days of the week have been performed.

Stretching with towels is a fun way to introduce the idea of using objects to aid flexibility frequency.

Teaching Hints

▶ Before you begin, discuss with students the safety of keeping the towel to themselves. The towel is only to be used as something to stretch with in this warm-up activity.

▶ Discuss with students why it is important to warm up the body first before stretching.

▶ Discuss that stretching a variety of muscle groups should be done three times a week or every day to help keep the body loose and flexible.

▶ Check for correct stretching form because students are expected to repeat the exercise at home.

▶ The recommendation is to stretch at least three times a week, but preferably to stretch every day and focus on different muscle groups each day. Stretching seven days a week can help students remember to stretch some part of the body daily.

Sample Inclusion Tips

▶ Most stretches can be modified and performed while seated in a wheelchair.

▶ Locomotor skills can be modified to each student's level of ability. They use arms only on movements if necessary.

Variations

▶ Stretch bands can be used later to demonstrate another way to stretch.

▶ Reinforce the flexibility exercise of the day by doing that activity when students have class. By repeating the exercises for a month, students have a better chance of remembering them all year.

▶ Discuss the safety of keeping the towel to themselves and then have students hold on to only one end of the towel and create dance moves before stretching.

▶ Have students form a circle of three and perform various stretching exercises together. They might reach high, reach low, and develop a wave going up and down one person at a time.

Home Extension

Have students take home the Towel Stretches for the Day Homework. They can use the pictures to remind them of a stretch that they can do each day of the week. They use the Towel Stretching for Flexibility Log to keep track of what they have done. After one week they bring the log back to school to talk about their flexibility workouts.

Assessment

▶ Review the exercise for each day and see whether they can remember the stretching exercise for each day.

▶ Ask how many times they should stretch in a week and discuss the answers.

▶ Ask students why stretching often is important and what stretching can do for the body. Stretching helps keep the body flexible so that they can bend, stretch, and move easily during the day with daily activities and when playing sports.

CATERPILLAR STRETCH

PRIMARY

Intensity—Intensity in flexibility exercises refers to how hard you need to stretch to improve or maintain flexibility. Adequate range of motion in all joints allows us to enjoy a variety of physical activities that can, in turn, contribute to a healthful life.

Purpose

▶ Students will define intensity as stretching as far as they can without feeling pain or trembling of the muscle. They should feel only mild discomfort.

▶ Students will participate in stretching activities and identify the stretch of the muscle.

Relationship to National Standards

▶ Physical education standard 4: Achieves and maintains a health-enhancing level of physical fitness.

▶ Health education standard 3: Students will demonstrate the ability to practice health-enhancing behaviors and reduce health risks.

Equipment

▶ One rubber band

▶ Music player and music

▶ Mats for floor work

▶ *The Very Hungry Caterpillar*, board book and CD (April 19, 2007) by Eric Carle

Procedure

1. Show students a rubber band and bend it in all directions.

2. Ask them what would happen if the rubber band were pulled too tightly. Why?

3. Tell them that it is important to be safe when stretching so that they won't hurt themselves. Make sure that they understand that some students will be more flexible than others, but that everyone needs to stretch safely to loosen and lengthen muscles. Stretching can help them move better and not pull their muscles when moving in activities.

4. Have students do a modified hurdle stretch position (see photo on page 155) and touch the knee. Do they feel a pull in the back of the leg? Have them reach below the knee. Now do they feel a pull in the back of the leg?

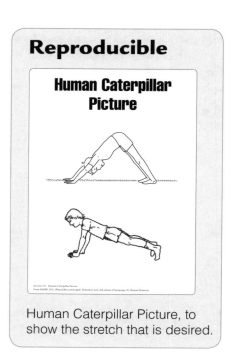

Reproducible

Human Caterpillar Picture

Human Caterpillar Picture, to show the stretch that is desired.

5. Have students pretend that their fingers walking down the leg are an inchworm.

6. Have students go down until they feel a pull in the back of the leg. This is where the caterpillar wants to stop and count its feet. A caterpillar has three pairs of feet on the front end and three pairs on the back end. They will count to 12 to represent every foot on the caterpillar.

7. Now they move like a caterpillar with the whole body moving down the gym. They move the hands out as far as they can. Then they bring the straight legs up as close to their hands as they can until they feel a pull in the back of the legs. They hold this position and count aloud the number of feet on a caterpillar. They repeat the sequence, stretching the body out, coming together, and holding for a 12 count as they go down the gym. Use the Human Caterpillar Picture to show students what they will be doing.

8. Ask them to show you what muscles they are stretching. (Answer: back of the leg, calf, gastrocnemius.) Ask how long they should hold a stretch. (Answer: Stretch should be held to the count of 12 for the inchworm.) Most stretches should be held between 10 and 30 seconds.

Teaching Hints

▶ Remind students that to make muscles more flexible, they should stretch until the muscle feels tight but doesn't hurt. If they don't stretch it to that point, their flexibility won't improve. If they stretch too far and the muscle hurts, they could injure it. They should listen to the message that the body gives them.

▶ Remind students that each person is different. Some people can stretch farther than others. Flexibility depends on how often they stretch the body, their body makeup, their age, and other factors.

It is important to use proper form when stretching to avoid injury and to make sure joints are stretched at the proper intensity. The proper form for a modified hurdle stretch is to keep the knee bent with the leg turned inward.

Sample Inclusion Tips

▶ Students with little mobility can stretch the arms, neck, sides, shoulders, back, and other areas of the body.

▶ Students with poor flexibility can use a bolster to hold them in a static caterpillar position.

▶ Students unable to do the inchworm to move down the gym can manipulate a pool noodle, bending and flexing it like an inchworm.

Variations

▶ Stretch bands or rubber bands can be used so that students can see how the muscle looks when it is stretched out.

▶ Inform the classroom teacher what you are doing and have them read the book *The Very Hungry Caterpillar* by Eric Carle.

Home Extension

Ask students to go home and find out how many caterpillar walks it takes to go across their front yard.

Assessment

▶ Ask, "How do you know that you are stretching a muscle?" (Answers: Reach until you feel a little discomfort and back off slightly. Feel tightness in the muscle.)

▶ Ask, "Should you feel a lot of pain?" Ask them to put their thumbs up if yes and thumbs down if no. (Answer: No, thumbs down.)

▶ Ask them to put their hands on the muscle that they were stretching.

AT LEAST 10 LEOPARD CATS

PRIMARY

Time—Time is how long you need to hold a stretch to improve or maintain flexibility. Experts recommend that you hold each stretch, without bouncing or jerking, for 10 seconds (progressing to 30 seconds).

Purpose

Students will demonstrate an understanding that to stretch safely they must not bounce and that to improve or maintain flexibility they must hold stretches for 10 seconds or longer.

Relationship to National Standards

▶ Physical education standard 4: Achieves and maintains a health-enhancing level of physical fitness.

▶ Health education standard 1: Students will comprehend concepts related to health promotion and disease prevention.

Equipment

Mats for floor work

Procedure

1. Instruct students about the importance of not bouncing or jerking as they perform each stretch. Remind them that everyone has a different level of flexibility and that they should not compare their bodies to the bodies of other. They should not stretch to a point of undue discomfort. Tell them that today they will practice holding stretches for at least 10 seconds. Display the Stretching Reminders so that students are reminded of these safety tips.

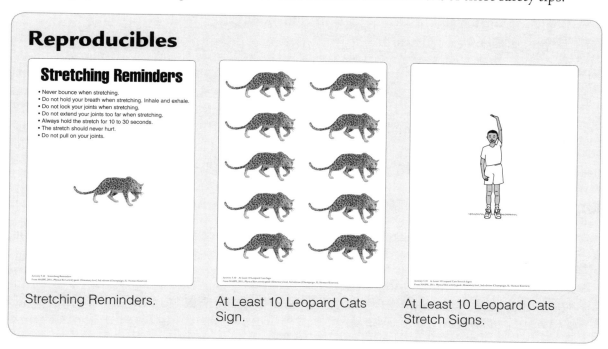

Reproducibles

Stretching Reminders
- Never bounce when stretching.
- Do not hold your breath when stretching. Inhale and exhale.
- Do not lock your joints when stretching.
- Do not extend your joints too far when stretching.
- Always hold the stretch for 10 to 30 seconds.
- The stretch should never hurt.
- Do not pull on your joints.

Stretching Reminders.

At Least 10 Leopard Cats Sign.

At Least 10 Leopard Cats Stretch Signs.

2. On your signal, students move in an activity area using a locomotor skill.

3. On your signal "Stop!" students freeze and you ask, "What do you see?" As you show the sign they respond, "At least 10 leopard cats."

4. Immediately after they say, "At least 10 leopard cats," you assume a stretch position of your choice or hold up one of the At Least 10 Leopard Cats Stretch Cards for a specific group of muscles. Then the students take the position. You cue the students to count the leopard cats by saying, "One leopard cat, two leopard cats, three leopard cats . . ." until they reach 10.

5. Repeat the activity by choosing another locomotor pattern, calling, "Stop," and asking, "What do you see?" They respond the same way by saying, "At least 10 leopard cats. . ."

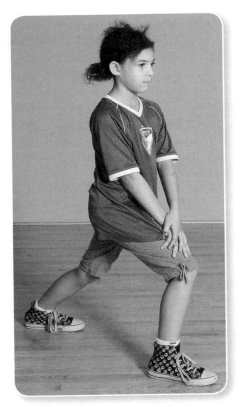

The At Least 10 Leopard Cats activity helps teach primary-level students how to count time while holding a stretch.

Teaching Hints

▶ Monitor students closely to ensure that they do not bounce or jerk when stretching. Invite students who are stretching correctly to demonstrate for others.

▶ Create a bulletin board depicting pictures of various stretch poses. The title of the board could be "At Least 10 Leopard Cats," and numbers 1 through 10 could connect the pictures.

▶ Explain to students that the first *T* in FITT stands for time. Remind them to hold stretching activities for at least 10 seconds, gradually working up to 30 seconds. Turn the first *T* on the FITT bulletin board into "Time = How Long!" Place a clock on the bulletin board next to the *T* for time.

Sample Inclusion Tips

▶ Allow students to vary the locomotor skills and modify the stretch as needed.

▶ Use peer assistance when possible.

Variations

▶ Use other methods that are popular or create ones that will take 10 seconds. For example, you could use 1 Mississippi, 2 Mississippi, 3 Mississippi, . . . 10 Mississippi or 1 one thousand, 2 one thousand, 3 one thousand, . . . 10 one thousand.

▶ Have students work in pairs; one watches the second hand of a clock and counts while the other stretches. This would also be a great time to review time keeping and digital or second hand timing devices.

Home Extensions

Ask the students to do at least one of the stretches at home and increase the hold time to 15 seconds.

Assessment

▶ Ask students how long they should hold a stretch position.

▶ Have students demonstrate other stretches. Each stretch should last for at least 10 seconds and be free of bouncing and jerking.

ROLL THE STRETCH

PRIMARY AND INTERMEDIATE

Specificity, or type—Specificity, or type, in relation to flexibility means that only the joint and muscle group that you are stretching will become more flexible. That is, if you do stretching activities for your arms, your legs will not become more flexible.

Purpose

- ▶ Students will understand that there are many muscle groups that need to be stretched.
- ▶ Students will understand that stretches are specific to particular muscle groups.

Relationship to National Standards

- ▶ Physical education standard 4: Achieves and maintains a health-enhancing level of physical fitness.
- ▶ Health education standard 3: Students will demonstrate the ability to practice health-enhancing behaviors and reduce health risks.

Equipment

- ▶ A pair of dice per group
- ▶ Relaxing music and player
- ▶ Mats

Reproducibles

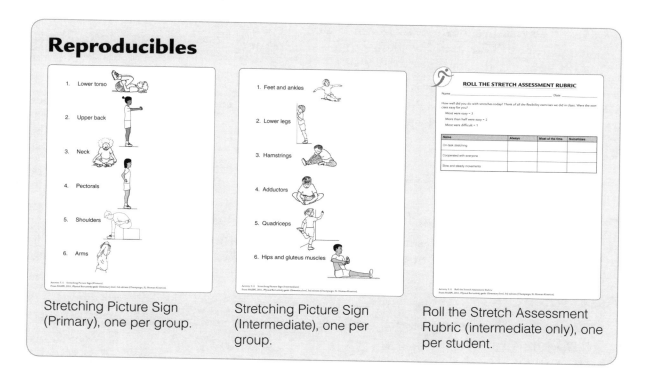

Stretching Picture Sign (Primary), one per group.

Stretching Picture Sign (Intermediate), one per group.

Roll the Stretch Assessment Rubric (intermediate only), one per student.

Procedure

1. Have students participate in an activity that will warm up their bodies and prepare them for stretching.

2. Divide students into small groups. Give each group a Stretching Picture Sign and a pair of dice.

3. Explain that they will use a slow, steady movement when performing all stretches to help prevent injury.

4. One student rolls the dice and reads the number. That student then locates the picture on the sign. With a slow, steady count (30 seconds), the student leads the group in performing the stretch.

5. The sign and dice are then passed to the next student, who becomes the roller and leader.

6. Make sure that all students have a chance to lead.

7. After completing the activity, intermediate students should complete the Roll the Stretch Assessment Rubric.

Teaching Hints

▶ Perform the activity as a class for the first lesson and in small groups for the second lesson.

▶ Ask the leaders to count softly aloud so that you can hear whether they are speeding up.

▶ To help prevent overuse of one muscle group, have students reroll the dice if the same exercise number comes up twice in a row.

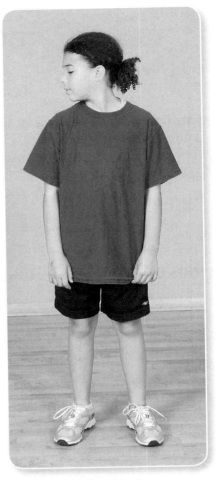

Students roll the dice to determine which stretches to perform for specific muscles.

Sample Inclusion Tips

▶ Place the music in a location where a child with an attention deficit can hear soothing sounds that will help him or her be able to do slow, steady stretches.

▶ Secure a resistance band for a student who is not able to perform the designated stretch.

▶ Provide two stretches for each body part and allow the student to choose one of the stretches (be conscious of meeting the needs of all students).

Variation

Encourage students to find different ways to stay flexible. Give them examples that will work within their community.

Home Extension

Have the students select one to three flexibility exercise that they can do at home and ask them to stretch every day for a week. Suggest that they do the stretches during commercials or at any time during the day.

Assessment

▶ Select a body part or muscle group and ask students to demonstrate or write a stretch for that body part.

▶ Use the Roll the Stretch Assessment Rubric to assess intermediate students. Discuss the results.

STRETCH MARKS THE SPOT

INTERMEDIATE

Specificity, or type—Specificity, or type, in relation to flexibility means that only the joint and muscle group that you are stretching will become more flexible. That is, if you do stretching activities for your arms, your legs will not become more flexible.

Purpose

▶ Students will be able to identify specific flexibility exercises for various body parts.

▶ Students will apply the stretch used to prepare for various sports.

Relationship to National Standards

▶ Physical education standard 2: Demonstrates understanding of movement concepts, principles, strategies, and tactics as they apply to the learning and performance of physical activities.

▶ Physical education standard 3: Participates regularly in physical activity.

▶ Health education standard 3: Students will demonstrate the ability to practice health-enhancing behaviors and reduce health risks.

Equipment

▶ Pencil

▶ Mats

▶ Upbeat music and player

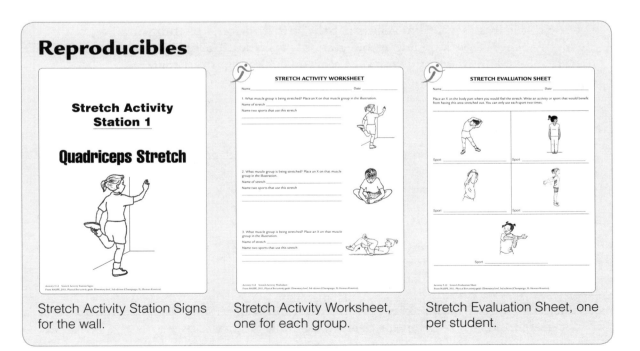

Reproducibles

Stretch Activity Station Signs for the wall.

Stretch Activity Worksheet, one for each group.

Stretch Evaluation Sheet, one per student.

Procedure

1. Explain to students the importance of flexibility exercises and their role in maintaining normal joint range of motion. To stretch a muscle properly, each exercise should be performed slowly and carefully. To improve flexibility, they should use a slow elongation of the muscle to the point of a mild discomfort and then back off slightly.

2. Place six flexibility stations around the gym.

3. Place students in even-sized groups at the stations.

4. When the music starts, students perform the flexibility exercise as pictured on the Stretch Activity Station Signs. Be sure that they hold the stretch for a count of 10 to 30 seconds. They do one side of the body and then the other, alternating until the music stops.

5. When the music stops, the group does four things with their Stretch Activity Worksheets: (1) decides what muscle group they were stretching, (2) places an X on that muscle, (3) writes in the name of the exercise below the picture, and (4) lists two sports that use that exercise.

6. The groups rotate around to the next station and begin a new activity. After completing each activity they rotate to the next station until they have completed all stations.

Stretch Marks the Spot challenges students to identify what specific muscle groups are worked during various stretches.

Teaching Hints

▶ Remind students that they must warm up the muscles before stretching. Say, "Jog around the gym two times before stopping at your stations. Then do 10 large arm circles backward with the palms up and 10 forward with the palms up before beginning the stretch."

▶ Review with students a variety of sports so that they won't continue to use the same sport for each exercise.

Sample Inclusion Tips

▶ If mobility is a problem, shorten the distance that the student travels during the warm-up.

▶ Have students use a partner to help with the stretches. The partner models and talks the student through the stretch if additional visual and verbal cues are necessary.

Variation

Change the flexibility exercises and repeat. Make exercises only for the upper body or for the lower body to focus on specific muscle groups.

Home Extension

Ask students to practice the stretches performed in class at home. Ask them to come back with a different stretch and be able to tell the class what muscle group was used.

Assessment

Have each student fill out the Stretch Evaluation Sheet to check for understanding.

INTERMEDIATE

Progression—Progression refers to how a person should increase overload. Proper progression involves a gradual increase in the level of exercise that is manipulated by increasing frequency, intensity, or time, or a combination of all three components. The overload principle states that a body system (cardiorespiratory, muscular, or skeletal) must perform at a level beyond normal in order to adapt and improve physiological function and fitness.

Purpose

Students will learn and apply the training principles of progression and overload to flexibility by completing a FITT Log and FITT Log Worksheet.

Relationship to National Standards

▶ Physical education standard 3: Participates regularly in physical activity.

▶ Physical education standard 4: Achieves and maintains a health-enhancing level of physical fitness.

▶ Health education standard 3: Students will demonstrate the ability to practice health-enhancing behaviors and reduce health risks.

Equipment

▶ Pencils

▶ Any equipment required by the assessment selected

Procedure

1. Briefly review the two-word definitions of the aspects of FITT—frequency (how often), intensity (how hard), time (how long), and type (what kind).

2. Ask students to offer brief examples of how they have applied the FITT guidelines to flexibility in previous health-related fitness activities.

3. Share descriptions of the concepts of progression and overload.

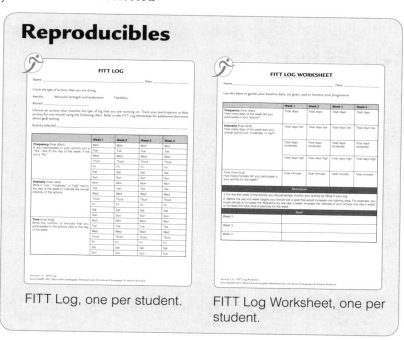

Reproducibles

FITT Log, one per student.

FITT Log Worksheet, one per student.

4. Distribute one blank FITT Log to each student. Review each category and how it relates to FITT. Outline how students can apply progression as they use the form.

5. Ask the class to share flexibility activities, choose two to three stretches for various body parts, and write them on the "Activity selected" line of their logs.

6. Have each student write her or his name on the log.

7. Assign students to log their flexibility physical activity performed outside class for one week.

8. Have students fill in one week of the FITT Log.

9. Guide students in setting goals for progression and overload and have them write their goals on the FITT Log Worksheet.

10. At the end of each week, meet and discuss their progress and set new goals.

The FITT Log helps students to realize that activities they take part in outside of the classroom help them to progress in their flexibility health.

Teaching Hints

▶ Ask students at each class meeting how their logs are coming along.

▶ Require guardian initials if necessary to encourage participation.

Sample Inclusion Tips

▶ Help students with special needs develop alternative activities based on their level of ability.

▶ Students with special needs can modify activities and keep a basic log as required by other students.

▶ Students with special needs also need to set a personal goal under the guidance of an adult.

Variations

▶ Ask the school's after-school care providers to provide space, time, and other support for students to add to their logs.

▶ Tie in the Fitnessgram flexibility assessments.

Home Extension

The lesson and the variations give the extension of the activity outside of class.

Assessment

After the month, have students review their logs with you and write about their experiences by answering questions such as the following:

▶ Were you able to build up safely to a higher level of intensity over the course of the month, did you do the activities more frequently each week, or spend more time doing each activity? Which changes did you make, if any?

▶ If you were able to make changes, how do you think the changes have affected your flexibility fitness?

▶ If you did not make changes, what might you be able to do differently in the future?

Realize that many factors, such as the child's initial level of fitness and participation (if already high, she or he may not progress for that reason), and other personal factors may affect the answers to these questions. Keeping this in mind, focus on the assessment as a means to teach and reinforce the concepts of progression and overload.

Body Composition

Chapter Contents

© Monkey Business/fotolia.com

The activities in this chapter explore body composition, an important component of fitness. At the elementary level, students should understand the major concepts regarding body composition, including energy intake and expenditure, guidelines for healthy eating such as the Food Guide Pyramid, and factors that affect body composition such as genetics, diet, and physical activity. When completing these activities, students should understand how their behaviors will affect their body composition. The following information introduces the subject of body composition at the elementary level. For more information on this topic, refer to the chapters about body composition and nutrition in *Physical Education for Lifelong Fitness: The Physical Best Teacher's Guide, Third Edition*.

DEFINING BODY COMPOSITION

Body composition is the amount of lean body mass (all tissues other than fat, such as bone, muscle, organs, and body fluids) compared with the amount of body fat, usually expressed in terms of percent body fat. Among the common ways of assessing whether body composition is appropriate are BMI-for-age tables, skinfold caliper testing, and waist-to-hip ratio. When assessing body composition in elementary-level students, remember that body composition may change rapidly with growth spurts, so an assessment method must accommodate these changes.

RELATING BODY COMPOSITION TO THE OTHER HEALTH-RELATED COMPONENTS

As with any other component of health-related fitness, a person's body composition does not develop in isolation from the other components. Indeed, you should show students the connections among all health-related fitness components so that they can clearly see how their personal choices affect this area of health-related fitness. Although genetics, environment, and culture play significant roles, body composition

results largely from physical activity levels in the other components:

▶ Aerobic fitness—aerobic activities burn calories.

▶ Muscular strength and endurance—muscle cells burn (metabolize) more calories at rest than fat cells do. To increase the likelihood that students will maintain appropriate body composition, emphasize physical activity that follows the principles of training.

▶ Flexibility—a flexible body can better tolerate aerobic fitness and muscular strength and endurance activities.

NUTRITION

Nutrition also plays an important role in body composition. Besides reviewing the Food Guide Pyramid, discuss appropriate portion size. In the United States, portion sizes have been increasing for the last three decades. The Western diet includes many highly processed, high-fat, high-sugar, and high-salt foods. The human body was designed to work best with whole grains, vegetables, and fruits.

Nutrients fall into six classes: carbohydrate, protein, fat, vitamins, minerals, and water. Because all are essential for good health, the diet must provide all six.

▶ Carbohydrate provides most of the energy for people across the world and represents the preferred source of energy for the body. People should obtain carbohydrate from whole grains, cereals, vegetables, and fruits. Refined grains and sugars can also provide carbohydrate.

▶ Protein serves as the structural component for vital body parts. Every cell in the body contains protein. In the United States, meat is the primary source of protein.

▶ Fat serves as a concentrated form of energy, and the human body stores excess calories as fat.

▶ Vitamins and minerals contain no calories, but small amounts are essential for good health.

▶ Many students do not realize that water is an essential nutrient. Students need to drink at least six to eight cups of water daily. Water is also found in many foods, especially fruits and vegetables.

TEACHING GUIDELINES FOR BODY COMPOSITION

Approach discussions about body composition objectively and as a topic about which students should be sensitive. Strive to point out connections among physical activity, diet, and body composition related to daily life, recreational activities, and physical education activities. Showing the students the latest Physical Activity Pyramid for Children and discussing the various types of activities that they can use to enhance body composition can help students recognize how important all types of physical activity can be in obtaining and maintaining a desired body composition and appearance.

Never use a student as a positive or negative example regarding body composition. Heavier students may become uncomfortable, so be prepared to help them approach this as a learning process, not as a negative or punitive message. Emphasize that a student who is overfat because of genetics can still greatly reduce health risks by being physically active. Remember, students will follow your lead with their peers. If you are comfortable with the topic, they will be too.

Although approaching body composition in the physical education setting can be a delicate matter, you must address this important component of fitness. Handle body composition instruction professionally and by concentrating on how a good diet and active lifestyle can positively affect it. Emphasize that normal bodies come in all sizes and encourage a positive self-image. Also, emphasize to the students that they should encourage each other to be more active, regardless of body size and shape or ability, and discuss how positive encouragement can help others become more active and stay active.

BODY COMPOSITION RESOURCES ON CD-ROM

Use the Body Composition Newsletter (see figure 6.1), the Physical Activity Pyramid (see figure 6.2

on page 170), and the MyPyramid (see figure 6.3 on page 170), all located on the CD-ROM, to introduce, reinforce, and extend the concepts behind developing and maintaining healthy body composition. The following are ways in which you might use these tools:

- ▶ Send the various resources home as a guardian-involvement tool during a mini unit focusing on body composition.
- ▶ Use the resources to help you feature body composition as the "Health-Related Fitness Component of the Month."
- ▶ Validate and promote student involvement in physical activity outside class time and the school setting.
- ▶ Among students who can read, promote reading to learn across your curriculum, further supporting the elementary school mission.
- ▶ Use the newsletter as a model or springboard to create your own newsletter, tailored specifically to your students' needs.

Use the Body Composition Newsletter and the pyramids in any way that helps you teach more effectively to the specific needs of your students and their families. See table 6.1 on page 170 for a grid of activities in this chapter.

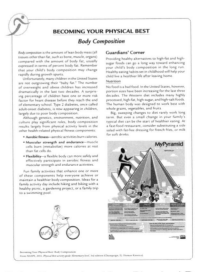

Figure 6.1 Becoming Your Physical Best: Body Composition Newsletter.

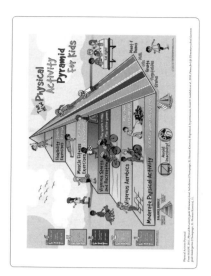

Figure 6.2 Physical Activity Pyramid.

Figure 6.3 MyPyramid.

Table 6.1 Chapter 6 Activities Grid

Activity number	Activity title	Activity page	Concept	Primary	Intermediate	Reproducibles (on CD-ROM)
6.1	Maintaining Balance	171	Body composition	•		Body Composition Benefit Signs
6.2	Disc Golf and Body Composition	173	Body composition		•	Body Composition Fact Cards
6.3	Activity Time	175	Health benefits	•		Clock Illustration
6.4	Activity Pyramid Circuit	177	Health benefits		•	Physical Activity Pyramid for Children
						Activity Pyramid Cards
						Activity Pyramid Match Cards
						Check Your Activity Pyramid Worksheet
6.5	Brown Bag Dinner	180	MyPyramid	•		MyPyramid Poster
						Food Pictures
6.6	Getting Nutrients	183	Nutrients		•	Nutrient Wall Signs
						Fuel Up the Body Homework Sheet
6.7	Hoop It Up With Food	186	Nutrition	•		Hoop It Up With Food Pictures
						MyPyramid Poster
						Hoop Cards
						Fill Your Plate Homework Sheet
6.8	A Variety of Protein	189	Nutrition		•	Protein Food Pictures
						Select Your Protein Homework Sheet
6.9	Calorie Burn-Up	191	Metabolism	•		None
6.10	Metabolism Medley	194	Metabolism		•	Physical Activity Pyramid for Children
6.11	Bowl a Snack	196	Body composition and nutrition	•		Paper Food

MAINTAINING BALANCE

PRIMARY

Body composition—Body composition is the amount of lean body mass (all tissues other than fat, such as bone, muscle, organs, and body fluids) compared with the amount of body fat. A healthy body composition involves having a healthy amount of both lean body mass and fat mass to allow you to enjoy life, be active, have energy to spare, and grow and develop.

Purpose

▶ Students will learn about healthy body composition.

▶ Students will engage in critical thinking, use teamwork, and practice following instructions.

Relationship to National Standards

▶ Physical education standard 4: Achieves and maintains a health-enhancing level of physical fitness.

▶ Health education standard 1: Students will comprehend concepts related to health promotion and disease prevention.

Equipment

▶ 30 to 35 bowling pins, two-liter bottles, or small cones

▶ Pinnies for one team, if desired (see "Teaching Hints")

Procedure

1. Using the Body Composition Benefits Signs, discuss the benefits of fat and lean body mass, and the importance of a healthy balance between the two.

2. Scatter the pins over the playing area, spacing them as far apart as possible and placing half upright and half lying down.

3. Divide the class into two teams—the "Ups-fats" and the "Downs-leans."

4. Line up the teams at opposite ends of the playing area.

5. On the signal, all members of each team try either to set the pins up or to set the pins down, depending on their assignment. After a couple of minutes call a halt and count the number of pins in each position. Record the number of pins down and the number of pins up and keep a total score through several rounds.

6. Switch teams, names, and begin another round.

7. Every time the Ups-fats set up a pin, they must circle around the pin two times.

Reproducible

Body Composition Benefits

Benefits of Fat

- Acts as an insulator, helping the body adapt to heat and cold
- Acts as a shock absorber, helping to protect internal organs and bones from injury
- Helps the body use vitamins effectively
- Acts as stored energy when the body needs energy
- Maintains healthy skin and hair
- Regulates levels of cholesterol in the blood

Activity 6.1 Body Composition Benefit Signs
From NASPE, 2011, *Physical Best activity guide: Elementary level, 3rd edition* (Champaign, IL: Human Kinetics).

Body Composition Benefit Signs.

8. Do not tell the students that up and down represent anything until they have completed all the rounds. The next time you play, review and note that the Ups must work harder to "maintain a balance."

9. Continue for several rounds and then follow up with a discussion about maintaining balance. As you switch roles for the teams, the balance of scores at the end of the round will probably shift. You can discuss how our balance also shifts during life with active and inactive periods.

10. In most cases the Leans will win, and you then discuss why they have more energy and how they can get more energy.

Teaching Hints

▶ To ensure that the Leans win most of the time, you may want to place two or three more players on their team.

▶ You can put pinnies or armbands on the teams to represent the Ups-fats and the Downs-leans and keep track of who is playing.

▶ Safety is important when knocking down pins. Remind students to put the pins down gently.

Maintaining Balance teaches students to find the balance between useful body fat and lean body mass.

▶ Students will remember benefit statements better if they are visual. Use the Body Composition Benefit Signs during the activity as a tool to present the body composition concept of fitness.

Sample Inclusion Tips

▶ Add rest (safe) areas into the game so that those who need a rest can do so.

▶ Use an extension for students seated in wheelchairs to enable them to knock down the pins.

Variation

If your teams are large, have only half the members go for a minute at a time while the other half circles the perimeter of the activity space as motivators for their teammates.

Home Extension

Ask students to discuss with their families what body composition means and the benefits of both body fat and lean body mass. Students can tell them about the activity that they played called Maintaining Balance and what this means with regard to body fat and lean body mass.

Assessment

▶ Ask, "Why is it important to have both lean mass and body fat?" (Answers include the many health benefits listed on the Body Composition Benefit Signs.)

▶ Ask, "What is meant by maintaining balance between body fat and lean mass?"

DISC GOLF AND BODY COMPOSITION — 6.2

INTERMEDIATE

Body composition—Body composition is what your body is made of. Your body is made of several components: muscles, bones, tissues, water, and fat cells. The health of your body composition depends primarily on two things: nutrition and physical activity.

Purpose

Students will be able to identify basic facts about body composition.

Relationship to National Standards

▶ Physical education standard 4: Achieves and maintains a health-enhancing level of physical fitness.

▶ Health education standard 3: Students will demonstrate the ability to practice health-enhancing behaviors and reduce health risks.

Equipment

▶ Disc golf disc (or Frisbee) for every student

▶ Nine disc golf stations—disc golf goals or a hula hoop with a cone in the middle to give visual assistance to finding the goal

Procedure

1. Students work in pairs. They proceed with a disc golf game, taking turns and trying to score in the goal.

2. At each goal is a box with a different Body Composition Fact Card.

3. Students complete the nine rounds and collect a card from each hole.

4. At the end of the disc golf game, students review the Body Composition Fact Cards with a partner.

Teaching Hints

▶ Discuss with students the definition of body composition.

▶ Help them understand what they can do to maintain a balanced body composition.

Sample Inclusion Tip

Pair students who have reading difficulties with peers who can assist.

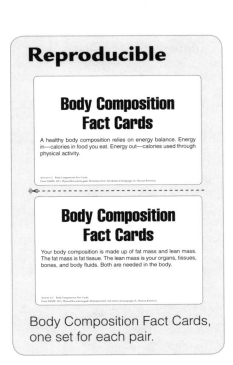

Reproducible

Body Composition Fact Cards

A healthy body composition relies on energy balance. Energy in—calories in food you eat. Energy out—calories used through physical activity.

Activity 6.2 Body Composition Fact Cards
From NASPE, 2011, *Physical Best activity guide: Elementary level, 3rd edition* (Champaign, IL: Human Kinetics).

Body Composition Fact Cards

Your body composition is made up of fat mass and lean mass. The fat mass is fat tissue. The lean mass is your organs, tissues, bones, and body fluids. Both are needed in the body.

Activity 6.2 Body Composition Fact Cards
From NASPE, 2011, *Physical Best activity guide: Elementary level, 3rd edition* (Champaign, IL: Human Kinetics).

Body Composition Fact Cards, one set for each pair.

173

Variations

▶ Create fact cards for other areas of fitness to educate students.

▶ Use a different sport with stations and use the same Body Composition Fact Cards.

Home Extension

Ask students to get a piece of paper at home and write down as many facts as they can remember from the disc golf Body Composition Fact Cards. They then bring the paper with them to the next physical education class.

Assessment

▶ Have a group of two tell another group all nine facts. See how many they can remember.

▶ Ask students to name some activities that burn calories to promote a healthy body composition.

▶ Ask students how to reduce the amount of calories consumed on a daily basis if they need to improve their body composition. (Possible answers: read the label, reduce serving size, eat when hungry.)

Photo courtesy of Gopher Sport

Introduce students to different sports like disc golf to give them a variety of choices for activities outside of school. In this activity, disc golf is combined with facts about body composition.

PRIMARY

Health benefits—Regular physical activity is a key to maintaining healthy body composition. Children and adolescents should do 60 minutes or more of daily physical activity. While most of the 60 or more minutes of daily physical activity should emphasize either moderate or vigorous aerobic physical activity, children and adolescents should be encouraged to participate in vigorous activity a minimum of 3 days per week. In addition, part of the 60 or more minutes of daily physical activity should focus on muscle and bone strengthening on at least 3 days per week (USDA, 2008).

Purpose

- ▶ Students will participate in a moderate to vigorous physical activity.
- ▶ Students will understand that to help maintain healthy body composition, physical activities should be both aerobic and muscular in nature.

Relationship to National Standards

- ▶ Physical education standard 4: Achieves and maintains a health-enhancing level of physical fitness.
- ▶ Health education standard 1: Students will comprehend concepts related to health promotion and disease prevention.

Equipment

- ▶ Beanbags (at least six per student)
- ▶ Poly spot for each student
- ▶ Upbeat music and music player
- ▶ Equipment as needed for aerobic and muscular activities

Procedure

1. Place beanbags around the edge of the room for students to pick up when the music stops.
2. Give each student a Clock Illustration and a poly spot to call home base. Have students sit by the poly spot and place the Clock Illustration (a clock divided into six sections) under it. Explain to the students that they will accumulate physical activity time by moving in and around the activity space. Discuss the importance of regular physical activity and tell them that both aerobic activity and muscular activity contribute to a healthy body composition.
3. Begin the music and direct students to start moving around the activity space, selecting a locomotor movement.
4. Stop the music and ask students to pick up one beanbag and place it by their clock and poly spot.

Reproducible

Activity 6.3   Clock Illustration
From NASPE, 2011, *Physical Best activity guide: Elementary level, 3rd edition* (Champaign, IL: Human Kinetics).

Clock Illustration, one per student.

5. Start the music and direct students to begin moving again through the activity space.

6. Continue until students have collected six beanbags, choosing a variety of locomotor movements, some of which are more aerobic in nature (walking, skipping, and so on) and some of which are more muscular in nature (biceps curls using tennis balls or animal walks). Explain that each beanbag represents 10 minutes of physical activity.

7. Have the students place the Clock Illustrations on the floor and put one beanbag in each 10-minute section to indicate a total of 60 minutes of daily physical activity.

8. When the students repeat the activity, have them play until they have picked up four beanbags. Have them take out the Clock Illustrations again and place a beanbag on four of the 10-minute sections. Have them figure out how many more minutes of activity they would need to perform to meet the recommendation for 60 minutes of daily physical activity.

Students learn how to fill a clock with 10-minute bouts of activity in order to achieve the health benefits of accumulating 60 minutes of activity each day.

Teaching Hint

Enforce safety during movement by ensuring that students watch out for others when moving.

Sample Inclusion Tip

Use a beanbag with a beeper for students who are visually impaired.

Variations

▶ Count by 10s with 6 beanbags to equal 60 minutes.

▶ Revisit this activity on another day and again stop short of collecting six beanbags. Have students calculate how many minutes of activity time a beanbag represents and how much time they will need to be active through the remainder of the day to reach the 60-minute recommendation. Brainstorm ideas for achieving the recommendation (recess and so on).

Home Extension

Ask students to decide on one way to increase the time that they stay active after school. They should try to do this activity every day for a week. Students can ask their guardians to help them meet their goals. Students then report to you whether they met their goal or not.

Assessment

▶ Review with students activities that they do in their lives that don't make their hearts beat faster or help their muscles become stronger. Some examples would be watching TV and playing video games.

▶ Ask students to tell you ways in which they can stay active through aerobic fitness and muscular fitness activities outside of the class setting.

▶ Ask what types of physical activities contribute to healthy body composition (primarily aerobic fitness and muscular activities, with flexibility contributing).

ACTIVITY PYRAMID CIRCUIT

INTERMEDIATE

Health benefits—Regular physical activity is a key to maintaining healthy body composition. Children and adolescents should do 60 minutes or more of daily physical activity. While most of the 60 or more minutes of daily physical activity should emphasize either moderate or vigorous aerobic physical activity, children and adolescents should participate in vigorous activity a minimum of 3 days per week. Part of the 60 or more minutes of daily physical activity should focus on muscle and bone strengthening on at least 3 days per week (USDA, 2008).

Purpose

Students will be able to distinguish between the different levels of physical activity and understand how they connect to a healthy body composition.

Relationship to National Standards

► Physical education standard 4: Achieves and maintains a health-enhancing level of physical fitness.

► Health education standard 3: Students will demonstrate the ability to practice health-enhancing behaviors and reduce health risks.

Equipment

► Five cones

► One stretch band for each person in a group

► One jump rope for each person in a group

► Three scarves for each person in a group

► One step bench for each person in a group

► Soccer balls, volleyballs, basketballs, ping pong balls, and tennis balls for each person in a group

Reproducibles

Physical Activity Pyramid for Children, one copy for each station.

Activity Pyramid Cards.

Activity Pyramid Match Cards.

Check Your Activity Pyramid Worksheet, one per student.

▶ Mats for floor work

▶ Poly spots

▶ Fast music and music player

▶ Interval of music: 30 seconds with a 20-second pause

Procedure

1. Post five copies of the Physical Activity Pyramid for Children on the wall by each station for reference. Place five cones around the gym with five Activity Pyramid Cards facedown on the floor. Each station represents one area of the Physical Activity Pyramid for Children.

2. Divide students into five groups. (Each station will need enough equipment for all students to be active at the same time.)

3. When the music starts, one student from each group selects an Activity Pyramid Card and the whole group performs that exercise.

4. When the music stops, one student runs to the center area. There the student should look at the Activity Pyramid Match Cards and select a card that shows the same type of activity that his or her group performed. The student takes that card back to the group.

5. Students check a Physical Activity Pyramid for Children posted on the wall to see if the Activity Pyramid Match Card they selected matches the type of activity they performed. If they have the wrong Activity Pyramid Match Card, the student should return the card to the middle and select the correct card.

6. Students take the Activity Pyramid Match Card with them when they move to the next station. By the end of the circuit, each group should have a card from each area of the Physical Activity Pyramid for Children.

Students match exercises to the correct area of the Physical Activity Pyramid.

Inclusion Tip

Use alternative exercises that fit within the activity pyramid levels that meet students' needs.

Teaching Hints

▶ Use the visual of the Physical Activity Pyramid for Children on the wall at the stations to help students see the different types of activities.

▶ Explain to students how a variety of exercises is needed to maintain aerobic fitness, muscular strength and endurance, flexibility, and body composition.

▶ If you have a blackboard or a whiteboard, have the students help draw the activity pyramid with its categories.

Variation

Give students paper and have them make up exercise sheets for a specific area on the pyramid.

Home Extension

Give students the Check Your Activity Pyramid Worksheet to take home and complete for one week. When they finish, they bring the worksheet back to you.

Assessment

▶ Have students read an Activity Pyramid Match Card and then name an exercise to go with it.

▶ Check the Activity Pyramid Match Cards to make sure each group has one from each area. If they have two from one area of the Physical Activity Pyramid for Children, review the exercises they did for each card.

▶ Check each station card before students rotate to the next station.

PRIMARY

MyPyramid—Food is the fuel that your body needs to perform well. The nutrients gained from each food group help fuel the body. The MyPyramid or MyPlate helps us decide what kinds of foods to eat each day for a healthy body composition.

Purpose

Participants will be able to identify the different types of food groups and how to use the MyPyramid or MyPlate to help make wise eating choices.

Relationship to National Standards

▶ Physical education standard 6: Values physical activity for health, enjoyment, challenge, self-expression, and/or social interaction.

▶ Health education standard 1: Students will comprehend concepts related to health promotion and disease prevention.

Equipment

▶ Brown paper bag, one per student

▶ Fast music and player

▶ Stability balls and stretch bands for choice activities, if desired

▶ Pedometers (optional) to compare the number of steps to energy input and energy output

Procedure

1. Create food bags for each student using the Food Pictures. Put five different food items in each bag, but make sure to mix up the types of food given so that the bags do not have a food item from each food group. For example, some bags may have only fruit, vegetables, or protein food items. Bags may have foods from many food groups but should not have a complete meal.

2. Show the students the MyPyramid or MyPlate and talk about the foods

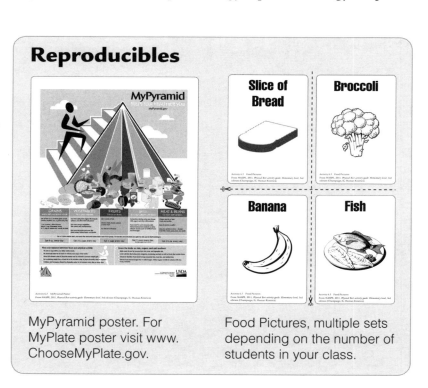

MyPyramid poster. For MyPlate poster visit www. ChooseMyPlate.gov.

Food Pictures, multiple sets depending on the number of students in your class.

found in each group. Tell them that a nutritious meal should have at least one food from each food group.

3. Show the students several of the paper Food Pictures and talk about what food group each food represents by comparing it with the MyPyramid or MyPlate.

4. Pass out the food bags and have students look to see what food group they are missing in the bag by comparing their foods to the various food groups on the MyPyramid or MyPlate.

5. When you start the music, students should move around the room using the locomotor movement of your choice. When the music stops, students should stop moving and pair up with another student. Both students must choose an exercise that they will do 10 times.

6. After students perform their exercise, they should look in their food bags and exchange one food item with their partner. The goal is to finish the activity with one food from each of the five food groups shown on the pyramid or plate so they can have a complete meal.

7. After exchanging food items, students should move on to find another classmate for another exercise of choice and an exchange of one food item. They continue this pattern until the music starts again. Students then start moving using a different locomotor movement of your choice.

8. After three rounds, have students group their foods according to the pyramid or plate and see whether they are missing any food groups because they have more than one food per group.

Students learn how to trade foods from the five food groups in MyPyramid or MyPlate in order to get a well-rounded meal.

Teaching Hints

▶ Students need to see a complete meal and know what five food groups they need to collect.

▶ Although having one to two cups of fruit and one to two-and-a-half cups of vegetables is recommended for children 2 to 13 years of age, we don't want it all at the same meal.

▶ Talk about the "sometimes foods" and how they are not to be part of this lunch: doughnut, french fries, candy bar, cookies, ice cream, and oils or fats, such as butter. Note: Some foods included in the Food Pictures are used to play a variation of this activity (see variations that follow).

▶ Before starting you may wish to discuss what types of exercises students might use for their choice exercise before trying to make a trade.

▶ Remind students that they are to get at least one food from each of the five food groups.

▶ During play, if students are able to obtain foods representing all five food groups, they should continue to exchange foods, but try to exchange for another food from the same food group so that they can continue to have five foods representing all of the MyPyramid or MyPlate categories.

▶ Expand beyond the food items included in the Food Pictures by having students bring in their own food pictures cut out from magazines.

Sample Inclusion Tip

Be sensitive to students who have food allergies or who are vegetarians by including enough Food Pictures that they can use to build a safe yet nutritious meal.

Variations

▶ Have stability balls or stretch bands around the room and use them for exercises. Tell students that they may choose exercises that can be done with a stability ball or a stretch band.

▶ Instead of having the foods for trading already in the bags, scatter all the foods facedown in the center of the room. On your signal all students go to the center and pick up five foods for their empty bags. They then have a few minutes to see what foods they chose and what foods they will need to trade in order to get other foods to complete the goal of one food in each of the five MyPyramid or MyPlate food groups. The trading and exercise activity would then continue as described earlier.

▶ Put pictures of "sometimes foods" in some of the student bags. Tell the students that if they have a "sometimes food" in their bags or receive one in a trade, they can trade the "sometimes food" from the box for a more healthy food that will help them complete a healthier five-food meal. Holders of "sometimes foods" will still have to identify and perform an exercise before the trade can be made.

Home Extension

Have students check their dinners at home to see whether foods from all five food groups are present. Have them talk with their families about the different food groups and some of the foods found in each. Students can write down their favorite meal and assess whether it includes all the food groups.

Assessment

▶ Ask students to raise their hands if they have a balanced meal. Ask why it is balanced.

▶ Ask students to list the five food groups.

▶ Ask students to give examples of various foods in each food group.

Note: Recently the USDA created a new graphic, MyPlate, to provide a better illustration of food portions. Both the MyPyramid and MyPlate graphics have educational value and can be used with Physical Best activities.

INTERMEDIATE

Nutrients—The food that you eat carries various nutrients for your body. It is important that you get six specific nutrients during a day: water, vitamins, carbohydrate, protein, minerals, and fat.

Purpose

Students will identify the six nutrients, define why they are important, and categorize foods that carry those nutrients.

Relationship to National Standards

▶ Physical education standard 3: Participates regularly in physical activity.

▶ Physical education standard 4: Achieves and maintains a health-enhancing level of physical fitness.

▶ Physical education standard 5: Exhibits responsible personal and social behavior that respects self and others in a physically active setting.

Equipment

Select an object for which you have a set of six for each group (for example, beanbags, domes, poly spots, paper, juggling scarves, dice)

▶ Home cone to mark team location

▶ Mats

▶ Pedometers (optional), used to count steps

▶ Heart rate monitors (optional), used to determine heart rate

Procedure

To set up for this activity, write the name of the object that represents the nutrient in the corner of the wall sign. For example:

▶ Beanbag—water

▶ Poly spot—carbohydrate

▶ Dome—mineral

▶ Juggling scarf—vitamin

▶ Dice—protein

▶ Yellow pool noodle—fat

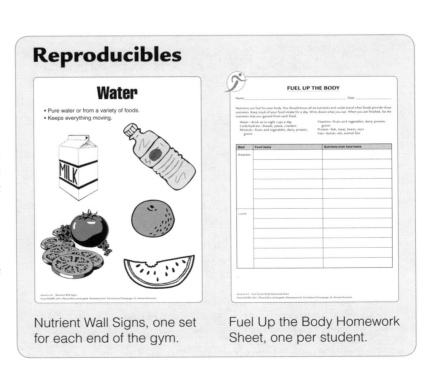

Reproducibles

Nutrient Wall Signs, one set for each end of the gym.

Fuel Up the Body Homework Sheet, one per student.

1. Place students into groups of three or four at one end of the gym. Each group has a set of six nutrient objects at the other end of the gym.

2. One team is the tag team in the middle of the gym. The object of the activity is to have a team get all six different objects that represent each nutrient. They need to be able to name all six nutrients to finish.

3. On the signal, everyone runs to the other end of the gym.

4. Each student picks up one object and returns it to their team's starting point.

5. A person who is tagged without a nutrient object in her or his hands goes to the outside wall, does five wall push-ups, and then returns to the activity.

6. A person who is tagged with a nutrient object in her or his hands goes to the outside wall and does five jumping jacks while saying the name of the nutrient that she or he is holding. After finishing the exercise, the student returns to the activity, keeping the object.

Getting Nutrients is a tag game that lets students stay active while they learn about the six nutrients: water, vitamins, carbohydrate, protein, minerals, and fat.

7. After a team has all six objects (nutrients) and no extras, they are finished. If they have two of the same object, they must return one, and in doing so they are at risk of being tagged. At this point they are to name all six nutrients to each other. After that, the team names the foods that provide each nutrient. The answers are written on the posters at both ends of the gym if the team needs to check answers.

8. Repeat the activity with a different tag team in the middle.

Teaching Hints

▶ Make sure that your students understand side vision. Because many students will be moving at the same time, they need to look out for each other.

▶ Point out all the health-related fitness areas that were used during the activity. Review what areas they developed: aerobic—running, muscle strength—wall push-ups, flexibility—jumping jacks.

▶ Talk to students about the six nutrients and go over the wall charts posted on the gym wall before beginning the activity. Remind them that after they collect all six nutrients they will have to name them and list a food group that corresponds with each nutrient.

▶ Have students problem solve in their groups about the easiest way to collect only one colored dome. To be finished, they need to have only one colored dome from each area.

Sample Inclusion Tips

▶ A student who is unable to run does arm jumping jacks while a partner goes to pick up the object and returns.

▶ A student in a wheelchair can be tagged only once when going down and back to get a nutrient. They then stop and do an exercise. A student using a wheelchair but not moving cannot be tagged.

Variations

▶ Change exercises at the end of a round so that students can work on all fitness areas.

▶ If using pedometers, discuss these questions:

• Compare number of steps per team member. Ask why they were different.

• Ask students how many steps they should take in a day.

• Ask whether this is a good activity to accumulate steps. Ask how they can change the activity to get more steps.

Home Extension

Use the Fuel Up the Body Homework Sheet.

Assessment

Make sure that each student on the team can answer the following questions:

▶ Name the six nutrients.

▶ Name a nutrient and then name a food group that has that nutrient in it.

▶ Give a reason why each nutrient is important.

PRIMARY

Nutrition—Through this activity and the use of a Food Guide Pyramid, students will learn about food groups and a balanced diet.

Purpose

Students will participate in collecting fruits, vegetables, and other foods to identify the food groups on the Food Guide Pyramid that contribute to a balanced diet.

Relationship to National Standards

▶ Physical education standard 3: Participates regularly in physical activity.

▶ Physical education standard 4: Achieves and maintains a health-enhancing level of physical fitness.

▶ Physical education standard 5: Exhibits responsible personal and social behavior that respects self and others in physical active settings.

▶ Health education standard 3: Students will demonstrate the ability to practice health-enhancing behaviors and reduce health risks.

Equipment

▶ Fast music and music player, with remote control, if available, to make playing music easier

Reproducibles

Hoop It Up With Food Pictures. Another resource is the National Dairy Council (www.nationaldairycouncil.org), which sells colored pictures the size of an actual serving with nutritional information on the back of each card. Laminate them so they will last longer.

MyPyramid Poster.

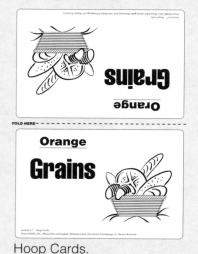

Hoop Cards.

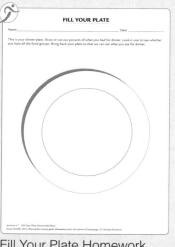

Fill Your Plate Homework Sheet, one per student.

▶ Five hula hoops, one to match each of the following colors of the Food Guide Pyramid: orange, green, red, blue, and purple

Procedure

1. This activity should be done following the preliminary introduction of the Food Guide Pyramid. Students must have basic knowledge of the food groups on the pyramid. Have students study the pyramid picture so that they can see that the size of the food group relates to the recommended daily amount for each food group.

2. Spread out Hoop It Up With Food Pictures around the gym or along the wall opposite the hula hoops.

3. Place five hula hoops in a horizontal line along one wall, allowing some space between the hoops. Lay the hoops from left to right in the order of the Food Guide Pyramid colors as follows: orange, red, green, blue, and purple. Use the Hoop Cards to label the hoops.

4. Explain to the students that as the music plays they are to move about the area using a designated locomotor movement (walk, jog, skip, hop, and so on). They are to move about without touching or stepping on any of the Hoop It Up With Food Pictures.

5. Explain to the students that when the music stops they are to reach down, pick up the food item nearest them, and decide in which hula hoop the food belongs. Students are to walk to the hoop that matches the appropriate group for the Food Guide Pyramid, place the picture inside the hoop, and stand behind the hoop in a line.

6. Start the music and repeat the activity two or three times. Give students sufficient time to move about before stopping the music. This will allow you time to make a visual assessment of locomotor skills.

7. After the students have placed several Hoop It Up With Food Pictures in the hoops, have the students at a hoop check the cards to determine whether all the cards have been placed in the appropriate hoop. Encourage discussion among groups. The MyPyramid poster on the wall can help with this activity. You should continually walk past the hoops to watch how students are doing but should remain silent if a card is placed in the wrong hoop. Initially, you should allow the students to evaluate their own hoops. When all the hoops have been completed, you can take the opportunity to discuss the results and point out some of the foods that are in each hoop. The benefits and drawbacks of the foods in each hoop can also be discussed. Ask students to show a thumbs-up, give each other high fives, or yell out a group cheer if their hoop had all correct food items.

8. Continue doing the activity until all cards have been placed in the hoops. Remember to change the locomotor skill each time the music is played.

Teaching Hint

This activity can be used as a lesson or as a warm-up before another activity.

Inclusion Tips

▶ Students with disabilities can move around at their own pace. They are allowed to have someone else pick up a card off the floor if needed.

▶ The cards can be placed at a higher level (tabletop, stool) so that they are easily accessible by students using wheelchairs or by students who have difficulties maintaining balance while bending to a low level.

▶ Peer assistance can be given if needed.

Variations

▶ To generate more discussion, you can manipulate how many cards will end up in each color hoop. Perhaps one time the game is played, the largest number of Hoop It Up With Food Pictures can end up in the orange hoop that stands for grains. The class can then discuss what might happen to a person whose diet consisted mainly of this food group. Another time, the cards can be manipulated to favor one of the other food groups. In this way, students learn about the consequences of not having a well-balanced diet.

▶ List simple exercises on the wall above each hoop. Have the largest sections of the pyramid require less exercise than the smaller sections. For example, the meats and beans may have students do 20 jumping jacks and the grains may have them do 5. Have students do the exercise when they are done evaluating their cards in the hoop. Explain why the smaller sections of the Food Guide Pyramid might require more activity to burn off the calories.

▶ Add a skill to the locomotor movement such as dribbling a basketball, kicking a spider ball, or catching a beanbag. Place the equipment and task card at each hula hoop. When you are finished discussing the Food Guide Pyramid, repeat the activity using the equipment.

▶ Provide three crates, bags, or boxes. Place a sign with a smiley face and the word "always" on one crate, a sign with a straight face and the word "sometimes" on the second crate, and a sign with a sad face and the word "sparingly" on the third crate. Let each group move their foods to the crate that they think best describes the recommended consumption of their food. Discuss the results.

Locomotor movements keep students moving while they sort pictures of food into the five food groups.

Home Extension

Distribute and instruct students to fill out the Fill Your Plate Homework Sheet. They should return it after they have completed their plates for discussion during class.

Assessment

▶ Observe the placement of Hoop It Up With Food Pictures.

▶ Facilitate group decisions when students are working with the food groups. Observe how well students are working together, correcting each other if necessary, and supporting each other when correct.

INTERMEDIATE

Nutrition—A variety of foods provides people with the needed protein for appropriate nutrition and a healthy body composition.

Purpose

Students will name ways to get protein in their diet with the focus on sources other than meat.

Relationship to National Standards

▶ Physical education standard 4: Achieves and maintains a health-enhancing level of physical fitness.

▶ Health education standard 3: Students will demonstrate the ability to practice health-enhancing behaviors and reduce health risks.

Equipment

▶ Hula hoops, one per group

▶ Upbeat music and player

Procedure

1. Divide students into groups of four.

2. Spread the hula hoops around the edge of the gym and assign each team a hula hoop as its home base.

3. In the middle of the room are various kinds of protein foods, represented by the Protein Food Pictures, including some meatless protein sources.

4. When you say, "Go," all students jog to the middle of the circle and take one piece of food back to their team's hoop.

5. When all the food is gone from the middle of the circle, students then go to other hoops to take food back to their hoop. They can take from other group's hoops, and teams cannot protect their hoops in any way.

6. When you call, "Stop," all students return to home base and look at the protein foods that they have in their hoops.

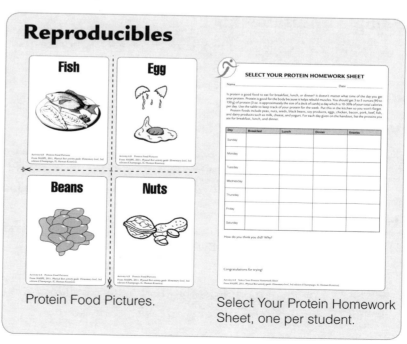

Protein Food Pictures.

Select Your Protein Homework Sheet, one per student.

7. Have student check to see whether they have at least one of each kind: fish, eggs, beans, nuts, vegetables, peanuts, and seeds.

Teaching Hints

▶ Review with student the benefits of protein to the body. Protein is good for the body because it helps rebuild muscles.

▶ Protein is in animals and plants. Protein is made up of amino acids. The body can produce 11 amino acids, whereas the other 9 are considered "essential" amino acids and must come from food.

▶ For that reason, it is important to eat a variety of whole grains, vegetable oils, beans, soy, legumes, seeds, and nuts.

▶ A 3-ounce (90 g) serving is about the size of a deck of cards. Children should have about 3 to 5 ounces (90 to 150 g) every day, or about one to two servings a day.

Students stay active while they learn meatless ways to get protein in their diets.

Sample Inclusion Tips

▶ Students with mobility problems can travel a shorter distance or take food from a special area close by.

▶ Students who move slower can take two pieces of food from a hoop because it takes them more time. Everyone else can only take one.

Variations

▶ Start with all the food spread out equally among the hula hoops. Have students look at their hoops to see what they need to have at the end of the round.

▶ Use the foods from activity 6.7 and single out a different food group.

Home Extension

Have them complete the Variety of Protein Homework Sheet.

Assessment

▶ Have students name at least four foods that provide protein.

▶ Have them show you a serving size with their hands.

CALORIE BURN-UP

PRIMARY

Metabolism—The way the body processes food into fuel is called metabolism. People with faster metabolisms burn calories faster than do those with slower metabolisms. The rate of metabolism affects body composition.

Purpose

Students will understand that although everyone needs the same nutrients, no two people have the same metabolism.

Relationship to National Standards

▶ Physical education standard 4: Achieves and maintains a health-enhancing level of physical fitness.

▶ Health education standard 1: Students will comprehend concepts related to health promotion and disease prevention.

Equipment

▶ Six different weighted objects to throw—beanbags, yarn balls, Nerf balls, Frisbees, scarves, Wiffle golf balls, or any other soft balls—enough so that each student should be able to throw five items in one round

▶ Crates or other targets

▶ Poly spots

▶ Tape and cones (if needed to create space)

Procedure

1. Place students on the long side of a gym or create a similar activity space using tape or cones. Put the beanbags or balls behind the students in a location that is easy to reach. Place crates or targets of your choice on the opposite volleyball court line or a line at a similar distance. Assign each student a specific piece of equipment: scarves, foam balls, beanbags, Frisbees, small Nerf balls, or other types of soft objects.

2. On the go signal, students throw their assigned object toward a crate or target.

3. Make or miss, the students go to get another object, but they must walk to pick up the new object and walk back to their throwing spot.

4. Give the students 30 to 60 seconds (choose your time depending on class size and the time that you have them in class). Students then stop, empty the crates, pick up loose balls or beanbags, and get ready for round 2.

5. Move the poly spot for throwing one-quarter of the way closer to the target. Have students continue to change the objects that they are throwing.

6. Make or miss, the students go to get another object.

Reproducible

None.

Students need to use a different locomotor movement than previously to pick up the new object and get back to their throwing spot.

7. Give the students 30 to 60 seconds. Students then stop, empty the crates, pick up loose balls or beanbags, and get ready for round 3.

8. Again, move the poly spot for throwing one-quarter of the way closer to the target and change the throwing object for each student.

9. Make or miss, the students go to get another object, but they must skip to pick up the new object and skip back to their throwing spot.

10. Give the students 30 to 60 seconds. Students then stop, empty the crates, pick up loose balls or beanbags, and get ready for round 4.

11. Again, move the spot for throwing one-quarter of the way closer to the target. Change the throwing object for each student.

12. Make or miss, the students go to get another beanbag or ball, but they must run to pick up the new object and run back to their throwing spot.

13. Connect the activity to the lesson on metabolism by saying the following:

    • Some objects were easier to get to the target than others. This fact can be related to a person's metabolism. For example, the balls, Frisbees, and beanbags can represent people who use food quickly and take less time to use it up. These items got to the target quickly.

By throwing objects of various weights from different distances, students learn how fast and slow metabolism rates compare. For example, it will take a ball less time to get to a target than a scarf, symbolizing that a fast metabolism will use up food faster than a slow metabolism.

- Some people use food slowly, and they use more time to use up the food that they eat. The scarves and small Nerf balls took more time to get to the target.
- The closer you were to the target, the faster you made the shot, which would show that you burned up your food quicker.
- The faster the locomotor movement was, the quicker you burned up your food, representing a fast metabolism.
- The slower the locomotor movement was, the slower you burned up your food, representing a slow metabolism. The objects could represent different people and their metabolic rates and how they burn up food.
- The scarves represent a slow-burning metabolism.
- The Frisbees represent a fast-burning metabolism.
- People burn up energy at different rates. People do not all burn energy in the same way.

Teaching Hints

▶ Use the same time throughout the activity for each throwing distance.

▶ Use a shorter time when you have more students, short class time, and limited equipment.

Sample Inclusion Tip

Alter the target (hoops, bowling pins), target location (on a table or chair), and allow other modifications (pushing instead of throwing objects) as needed to accommodate students with disabilities.

Variations

▶ You can do the same activity with kicking or striking with floor hockey sticks.

▶ You can add a final round with everyone working hard at moving. Discuss the fact that whether they have a fast metabolism or a slow metabolism, they can burn calories through activity, so it is important that they do some physical activity every day.

Home Extension

Ask students to discuss with their families what metabolism means. They can ask their family members whether they think they have fast or slow metabolism and why. Students can tell their family members what type of metabolism they think they have and why. Students should invite their families to go on a walk to help their metabolism.

Assessment

▶ Say, "The way that the body processes food into fuel is called metabolism. Thumbs-up if you agree; thumbs-down if you disagree." (Answer: thumbs-up.)

▶ Ask, "Does everyone have the same metabolism? Thumbs-up if you agree; thumbs-down if you disagree." (Answer: thumbs-down.)

METABOLISM MEDLEY

INTERMEDIATE

Metabolism—The way that the body processes food into fuel is called metabolism. People with faster metabolism burn calories faster than do those with slower metabolism. The rate of metabolism affects body composition.

Purpose

▶ Students will use the Physical Activity Pyramid for Children (Lambdin et al., 2010) to learn how participating in a variety of physical activities helps people raise their metabolism and achieve and maintain healthy body composition.

▶ Students will participate in a variety of physical activities to help them raise their metabolism, and achieve and maintain a healthy body composition.

Relationship to National Standards

▶ Physical education standard 4: Achieves and maintains a health-enhancing level of physical fitness.

▶ Health education standard 1: Students will comprehend concepts related to health promotion and disease prevention.

Equipment

▶ Equipment for enough muscular strength and endurance, flexibility, and aerobic fitness stations to keep groups small (four to six students) (see activities in chapters 3, 4, and 5 for ideas)

▶ Upbeat music and music player

▶ Pedometers (optional) to keep track of steps

Procedure

1. Tell or ask students what the word *metabolism* means as it relates to body composition. Explain that although metabolism is partly related to their individual makeup (and this part cannot be changed), part of their metabolism can be changed. Physical activity can help increase metabolism in all people.

   • *Aerobic fitness* activities burn calories, increasing metabolism.

   • Muscle cells burn (metabolize) more calories at rest than fat cells do. Having good *muscular strength and endurance* may help increase metabolism.

   • Good *flexibility* helps keep you more active overall. A flexible body helps you perform aerobic fitness and muscular strength and endurance activities better and more safely.

2. Introduce or review the Physical Activity Pyramid for Children. Point out how a variety of everyday, recreation, and sport activities helps meet everyone's needs

Reproducible

Physical Activity Pyramid for Children, one per student.

and interests while working on good body composition.

3. Send students in small groups through the stations that you develop by selecting various station ideas from chapters 3, 4, and 5.

Teaching Hint

Make the connection between the word *metamorphosis*, which students may be more familiar with, and metabolism. For example, a caterpillar or tadpole metamorphoses, or *changes*, into a butterfly or frog. We can *change* our metabolism through participating regularly in a variety of physical activities.

Sample Inclusion Tip

Modify the stations selected for the activity to provide for students with disabilities.

Variations

▶ When revisiting this activity, vary the station activities to meet your current skill unit while addressing each component of health-related fitness.

▶ Extend the lesson to tie nutrition into metabolism:

• Explain that the body is a calorie machine; if more calories go in than out (long term), the result can be a less healthy body composition.

• Remind students that physical activity can help increase metabolism, or the body's burning of calories. See "Home Extension" for a fun activity to tie in with this idea.

Select favorite stations from chapters 3, 4, and 5 to let students experience various activities that fit on the Physical Activity Pyramid for Children.

▶ You could modify several stations to include stability ball and stretch band exercises.

Home Extensions

▶ For homework over the next week, require students to mark each activity that they participate in on their photocopy of the Physical Activity Pyramid for Children. Encourage them to write in additional activity types not listed in the correct areas of the pyramid.

▶ If using the previous idea, you can give students one week to design a calorie machine diagram, drawing a gadget that shows a list of foods eaten during a day going into a machine. Have students draw a variety of physical activity choices that send calories out. Have a few students share their calorie machines during each class meeting until all have had a chance.

Assessment

Ask, "Which components of health-related fitness can you participate in to improve or keep a healthy body composition?"

BOWL A SNACK

PRIMARY

Body composition—Body composition is what your body is made of. Your body is made of several components: muscles, bones, tissues, water, and fat cells. The health of your body composition depends on two things: nutrition and physical activity.

Nutrition—Food is the fuel that your body needs to perform well. The nutrients gained from each food group help fuel the body. Choosing the right foods will help you to get the nutrition you need.

Purpose

People eat many foods as snacks, but some snacks are not as healthy for the body as others. Learning which foods are good choices for snacks can help a person make good food choices and keep the body working as well as possible.

Relationship to National Standards

▶ Physical education standard 4: Achieves and maintains a health-enhancing level of physical fitness.

▶ Health education standard 3: Students will demonstrate the ability to practice health-enhancing behaviors and reduce health risks.

Equipment

▶ A rubber bowling ball or playground ball for each group of three students

▶ 10 plastic bowling pins (or plastic water bottles with or without sand inside) for each group of three students

▶ Tape to create bowling alleys on the floor where the pins are to be placed

Procedure

1. Each group of three students works with a bowling lane, one rubber bowling ball, 10 pins, and 25 pieces of food. A bowling lane is the distance between where the bowler rolls the ball to where the pins are placed on the floor. Be sure to mark a start line.

2. Student 1 bowls the ball. Student 2 retrieves the ball and rolls it back. Student 3 moves the knocked pins out of the way.

3. After the bowler bowls two balls, the group members rotate.

4. Student 3 selects two different snacks to place under different bowling pins. One snack must be a good choice. Place the pieces of food so that they are easily accessible to student 3.

Reproducible

Paper Food, 25 pieces for each group of three students.

5. If a bowler knocks a pin down and food is under the pin, a decision needs to be made. The bowler may keep the food or leave it behind.

6. When a group runs out of food, check with the students of that group to make sure they have an understanding about good snacks. Look at each student's foods to see whether good selections were made. Help students understand good choices in food selections.

Teaching Hints

▶ Go over the snacks that students will get to select. Help them learn the better snacks to select when hungry.

▶ Tell students that they must give the body good fuel to keep it healthy and going strong.

▶ Tell them that the foods they eat can help develop a healthy body composition.

▶ Remind students that although the body needs some fat, limiting those foods is important to maintaining a healthy body composition.

Students practice selecting healthy snacks when they roll balls to knock down bowling pins and discover the food choices that are hidden under the pins. They get to decide if they want to keep the snack or keep rolling to another choice.

Sample Inclusion Tips

▶ Students who have difficulty releasing the ball can stand closer to the pins.

▶ Students using wheelchairs can use a bowling ramp designed for them.

▶ Students with difficulties maintaining balance in an upright position can be seated on the floor.

Variation

Start with the snacks divided among the students. Have them get rid of poor snacks under the pins so that they end up with all healthy foods.

Home Extension

Ask students to go home from school and eat a healthy snack. The next time that the class meets, they can report back to you.

Assessment

▶ Observe student choices when they pick up the snacks.

▶ Ask individual questions to students about what snacks are healthy.

Combined-Component Training

Chapter Contents

© Thomas Panholzer/forolia.com

The activities in this chapter reinforce the concepts presented in previous chapters. By combining fitness concepts, students can gain knowledge in a total-body workout and then begin to make choices to improve fitness. The basic principles of FITT for each fitness component can be experienced more fully when all fitness areas are integrated in an activity.

Fitness activities for primary students should have the potential to develop components of physical fitness and exercise various body parts. A variety of fitness routines and activities can help ensure all fitness components are addressed and make exercising more interesting. The principles of specificity, overload, and progression can be emphasized by varying the amount of time at a station or activity. Integrated activities can develop aerobic capacity and provide time to increase muscle fitness, improve flexibility, and address body composition. Activities that present continuous movement for all partici-

pants maximize activity time and student performance.

TEACHING GUIDELINES FOR COMBINING HEALTH-RELATED FITNESS ACTIVITIES

The activities in this chapter are designed to teach and reinforce the following:

▶ Review the basic knowledge in the components of health-related fitness
▶ Help students understand specificity of training in the various health-related fitness areas
▶ Develop and use various body parts in all areas of health-related fitness

See table 7.1 for a grid of activities in this chapter.

Table 7.1   Chapter 7 Activities Grid

Activity number	Activity title	Activity page	Concept	Primary	Intermediate	Reproducibles (on CD-ROM)
7.1	Fitness Tag	201	Fitness components	•		Fitness Tag Exercise Posters
						Health-Related Fitness Definition Posters
7.2	Fitness Four-Square	204	Specificity		•	Fitness Four-Square Exercise Cards
7.3	Mixing Fitness and Nutrition	207	Nutrition		•	Mixing Fitness and Nutrition Stretching Exercises Signs
						Nutrient Wall Signs
						Mixing Fitness and Nutrition Home Activity Sheet
7.4	Making Muscles	210	Specificity		•	Making Muscles Signs
						Muscle Muscles Signs (Labeled)
						Making Muscles Station Signs
						Making Muscles Home Extension Worksheet
7.5	Total-Body Workout	213	FITT principle		•	Total-Body Challenge Extension
7.6	Roll the Dice Fitness Routine	217	Balanced workout		•	Roll the Dice Signs
						At Work and at Play Handout
7.7	Mini Triathlon	220	Pacing		•	Pacing Your Mini Triathlon Record Sheet
						Am I Giving My Heart a Workout? Chart
7.8	Blackout Fitness Bingo	223	Total fitness workout		•	Blackout Fitness Bingo Card

FITNESS TAG

7.1

PRIMARY

Fitness components—Fitness components of muscular strength and endurance, flexibility, and aerobic fitness are all used many times in activities. Knowing the difference between each of the fitness components is important.

Purpose

▶ Students will demonstrate health-related fitness exercises.

▶ Students will identify exercises that strengthen each area of health-related fitness.

Relationship to National Standards

▶ Physical education standard 3: Participates regularly in physical activity.

▶ Physical education standard 4: Achieves and maintains a health-enhancing level of physical fitness.

Equipment

▶ Four different colored noodles cut in half and four cones to match the noodles (If noodles are not available, beanbags, poly spots, or colored paper can be used.)

▶ Two beanbags per student at the body composition station

▶ Six jump ropes

▶ Mats

▶ Heart rate monitors to keep track of heart rates

▶ Pedometers to keep track of steps

Procedure

1. Post the Fitness Tag Exercise Posters at stations around the room. Place Health-Related Fitness Definition Posters at the appropriate stations so that students will know which area of fitness each station addresses. Review these definitions with students before starting the station activities and review them again during assessment at the end of the class.

Fitness Tag Exercise Posters.

Health-Related Fitness Definition Posters.

Fitness Tag is a fun game that helps students review the health-related fitness components.

2. Select three students to be taggers.

3. Each tagger has a colored noodle that corresponds with the colored cone placed under an exercise chart. When tagged, the student will go to the cone of the same color. Here they select one exercise to do from a Fitness Tag Exercise Poster. The number of times will be listed on the poster. The next time they return to that fitness area they must pick a different exercise to perform.

4. Rotate taggers after a minute or when you think that students are getting tired so that each student has a chance to be a tagger.

Teaching Hints

▶ Talk to students about health-related fitness. Review the Health-Related Fitness Definition Posters so students understand the areas of fitness they will be working on at each of the stations.

▶ Have all students do exercises in each area to make sure that they understand the exercises and know what fitness area they represent.

▶ Define each area so that students have a good understanding of the fitness area that each exercise develops.

 • Aerobic fitness occurs when the heart, lungs, and muscles work together for an extended period.

 • Muscular strength and endurance occur when muscles come together to produce force or move an object repeatedly without getting tired.

 • Flexibility exercises are those that help the body bend, twist, and move easily in a full range of motion.

 • Body composition is the amount of lean body mass (bones, muscle, organs, and fluids) compared to the amount of body fat. Physical activity and balanced nutrition contribute to good growth and development of a healthy body composition.

Sample Inclusion Tips

▶ Use pictures along with colored paper so that all children can understand the posters.

▶ For children who have limited mobility, provide appropriate exercises and equipment to improve muscular strength and endurance such as hand-held weights, stretch bands, and stability balls.

Variations

▶ Use more taggers so more students get caught.

▶ Select various locomotor movements (such as skipping, galloping, and hopping). Change locomotor movements each time taggers are rotated.

▶ Use stability balls or bosu balls at the stations.

Home Extension

Allow students to borrow noodles at recess to play this activity in a specific area. When students are tagged, the tagger tells them what exercise they have to perform. Students can play this activity at home and report to you how many times they played and what exercises they used.

Assessment

▶ Ask questions about the definitions of muscular strength and endurance, flexibility, and aerobic fitness.

▶ Ask students what health-related fitness component they worked on today.

▶ Have students name exercises in each area of fitness.

FITNESS FOUR-SQUARE

INTERMEDIATE

Specificity—By experiencing a variety of fitness activities and then discussing them, students gain an understanding of specificity training.

Purpose

▶ Students will demonstrate exercises that develop specific areas of health-related fitness.

▶ Students will classify exercises in health-related fitness areas.

Relationship to National Standards

▶ Physical education standard 1: Demonstrates competency in motor skills and movement patterns needed to perform a variety of physical activities.

▶ Physical education standard 3: Participates regularly in physical activity.

▶ Physical education standard 4: Achieves and maintains a health-enhancing level of physical fitness.

Equipment

Each group of four needs the following:

▶ Punch ball, volleyball trainer, or beach ball

▶ Four-square area marked with tape or chalk

▶ One cone for each four-square court

▶ One die for each four-square group

▶ Pedometers (optional) to count steps during the activity

▶ Mats

Procedure

1. Demonstrate each exercise from the lists if students are not familiar with them. Explain to students that each four-square court will have a die and a cone with a Fitness Four-Square Exercise Card.

2. Divide the students into groups of four. Each student will take a turn at being the roller when they are in square 4.

3. The student in square 1 is the server and serves the ball that the group selected to anyone in the other courts. The server begins the activity by asking, "Ready?" and the team responds, "Serve."

4. The object of the activity is to keep the ball continuously passed using the forearm pass or set without letting it touch the ground. Explain that a person

Reproducible

Fitness Four-Square Exercise Card

1. Do 10 squats.
2. Power walk around your square once.
3. Do 10 jumping jacks.
4. Touch your knee to your opposite elbow 30 times.
5. Do a cross-chest stretch for a count of 20. Switch arms.
6. Do 20 high knees.

Activity 7.2   Fitness Four-Square Exercise Cards
From NASPE, 2011, *Physical Best activity guide: Elementary level, 3rd edition* (Champaign, IL: Human Kinetics)

Fitness Four-Square Exercise Card

1. Do 10 lunges.
2. Do 10 calf raises with both feet (go up on your toes and then lower yourself back down again).
3. Touch your knee to your opposite elbow 10 times on each elbow.
4. Do 10 push-ups.
5. Do 10 mountain climbers.

Activity 7.2   Fitness Four-Square Exercise Cards
From NASPE, 2011, *Physical Best activity guide: Elementary level, 3rd edition* (Champaign, IL: Human Kinetics)

Fitness Four-Square Exercise Cards, to be placed on cones.

Fitness Four-Square introduces a new way to learn about specificity and health-related fitness.

cannot hit the ball twice in succession and that students have to remain in their squares to pass the ball.

5. After the ball touches the ground, the student in square 4 rolls the die. The number that the die lands on corresponds with an exercise listed on the cone at each court. Students need to decide what area of fitness the exercise will help develop and then perform the exercise.

6. After exercising, students rotate squares. The student in square 3 rotates to square 4 and becomes the new die roller. The student in square 4 moves to square 1 and becomes the new server. All other team members move around the square.

Teaching Hints

▶ Teach the skills first and allow appropriate time for the children to practice.

▶ Talk about health-related fitness and discuss that specific exercises will strengthen or stretch certain muscle groups and enhance aerobic fitness and heart health.

▶ Help students categorize these exercises into the specific health-related fitness area: muscle strength and endurance, flexibility, and aerobic fitness.

Sample Inclusion Tips

▶ Students in wheelchairs or with low skill levels can catch and throw the ball if necessary.

▶ Students lightly toss or bounce the ball to students with special needs.

Variations

▶ Design your own exercises so that each square represents a specific fitness area.

▶ Have students rotate squares after three rounds.

▶ Have students design exercises.

▶ Use playground balls and allow them to bounce the ball.

Home Extension

Ask students to design a four-square area at home. They can use the rules followed in class and make up their own exercises. They can play the activity with just one friend, but four makes it more fun.

Assessment

▶ Students should be able to determine what area of fitness each exercise goes with. Evaluate their answers.

▶ Give students pencil and paper. Have them list three exercises and identify the part of the body that each exercise develops and the health-related fitness it primarily develops.

MIXING FITNESS AND NUTRITION

INTERMEDIATE

Nutrition—Body composition is altered by your food intake and physical activity. When you know your nutrients, you can more easily provide your body with quality fuel. Combining this knowledge with a quality workout can lead to a healthy active lifestyle.

Purpose

▶ Students will evaluate their intensity level related to aerobic fitness when playing a group activity.

▶ Student will be able to name all six nutrients and name a food that provides each nutrient.

Relationship to National Standards

▶ Physical education standard 3: Participates regularly in physical activity.

▶ Physical education standard 4: Achieves and maintains a health-enhancing level of physical fitness.

▶ Physical education standard 5: Exhibits responsible personal and social behavior that respects self and others in physical activity settings.

Equipment

▶ 12 Frisbees, 6 of one color and 6 of another, labeled with a nutrient—water, carbohydrate, minerals, vitamins, protein, or fat

▶ Four large cones to mark the center line if playing outside

▶ Four cones on each side to mark the nutrient bank area (see figure 7.1 on page 208)

Reproducibles

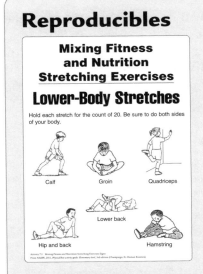

Mixing Fitness and Nutrition Stretching Exercises Signs, one set each to be placed on a cone for each team.

Nutrient Wall Signs.

Mixing Fitness and Nutrition Home Activity Sheet, one per student.

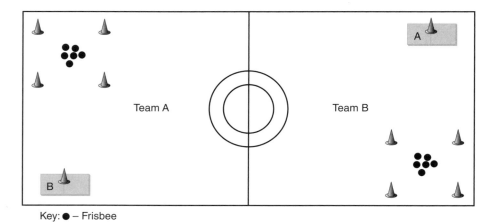

Key: ● – Frisbee

Figure 7.1   Setup for Mixing Fitness and Nutrition.

▶ Two cones for the holding area where students perform stretches

▶ Two mats for the holding areas

▶ Colored vests for one team

▶ Heart rate monitors (optional) to take heart rate averages during an activity

▶ Pedometers (optional) to check intensity level

Procedure

1. Six Frisbees per team represent the six nutrients: water, carbohydrate, minerals, vitamins, protein, and fat.

2. Each team protects the nutrients for their side.

3. The object of this activity is for a team to get all six "nutrient" Frisbees from the opposing team to their four-corner coned area on their side of the court—the "nutrient bank." This activity is played in an area the size of a basketball court.

4. Team A is on one side, and Team B is on the other side.

5. After students cross over into the other team's side, they can be tagged by anyone on the opposing team. If they are tagged they go to the opponent's holding cone area. This area, labeled A or B in the diagram, shows where students need to go. While they are waiting for the next person to be captured, they do at least one flexibility exercise. Students pick which stretching exercise to do from the Mixing Fitness and Nutrition Stretching Exercises Signs.

6. If the tagged person has a Frisbee, it is returned to where it came from.

7. Three people must be in the holding area before one can be released. If another student is tagged, this person takes the place of the person already at the cone. The student who was at the cone cannot be tagged when returning to her or his team.

8. Each round is timed. At the end of a round (five minutes), teams check to see what nutrients are missing. Teams must name a food to get that nutrient back to begin again. For example, for the Frisbee labeled *fat*, students must name a fat, such as butter.

Teaching Hints

▶ Discuss intensity in the following ways:

• Discuss what students could do to raise their heart rates in this activity.

• Discuss the benefits of getting the heart to beat faster.

- Have students check their heart rates at the end of the activity. Discuss what intensity level they played at during the activity. Ask whether they moved a lot or stood around.
- What signs will they notice in their bodies if they were working hard? (Answer: face red, breathing hard, tired, sweating)

▶ Go over the nutrients and list several foods that will provide the body with each nutrient. Nutrient Wall Signs can be placed in the gym for reference.

Sample Inclusion Tips

▶ Students can take turns pushing those who use a wheelchair. If the chair is not moving, a student in a wheelchair cannot be tagged.

▶ Students using canes or walkers or students with mobility and coordination problems may go at their own pace. When the student thinks that he or she will be tagged, the student raises a hand in the air or freezes in place to be safe. He or she may be tagged only when both arms are down or the student is moving.

Variations

▶ Students on the holding mat can do muscular strength and endurance exercises.

▶ Add a bosu ball to the holding area for exercises.

Home Extension

Children should participate in aerobic activities three or more times a week. To gain benefits for the heart, students need to remember to work at a good intensity level. They can use the Mixing Fitness and Nutrition Home Activity Sheet to list the activity that they participated in outside of school and the signs that showed their intensity level.

Assessment

▶ Check the students' heart rates after a certain period (perhaps five minutes) to initiate a discussion of intensity level. Have them name signs that show they are working hard. For example, their hearts beat faster, they breathe hard, their faces turn red, they sweat, and they feel tired.

▶ Have students tell you a flexibility exercise.

▶ Name various foods and have students tell you the nutrients that they provide for the body.

7.4 MAKING MUSCLES

INTERMEDIATE

Specificity—Students should understand specificity so that they can improve muscle strength and flexibility. By learning muscle names and location as well as specific strengthening and stretching exercises, students can begin to develop an exercise plan to meet individual needs.

Purpose

▶ Students will identify a stretch and strengthening exercise to go with a specific muscle group.

▶ Students will be able to identify the location of various muscles on the body.

Relationship to National Standards

▶ Physical education standard 4: Achieves and maintains a health-enhancing level of physical fitness.

▶ Physical education standard 5: Exhibits responsible personal and social behavior that respects self and others in physical activity settings.

Equipment

▶ One cone for each group

▶ Mats for floor exercises

▶ Upbeat music and music player

▶ Pedometers to keep track of steps

▶ Aerobic steps or benches

▶ Heart rate monitors (optional) to demonstrate to students their heart rates during the workout

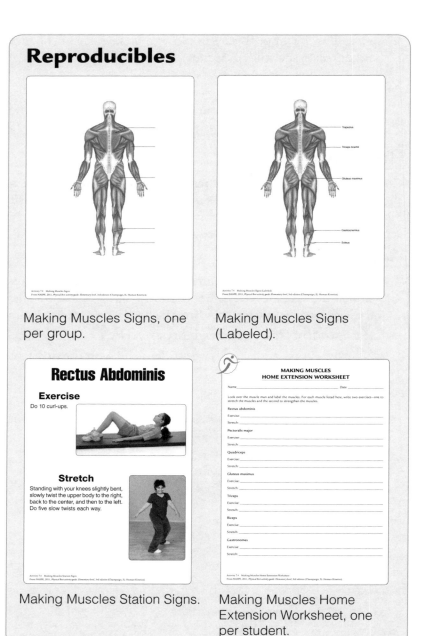

Reproducibles

Making Muscles Signs, one per group.

Making Muscles Signs (Labeled).

Making Muscles Station Signs.

Making Muscles Home Extension Worksheet, one per student.

Procedure

1. Put students into groups of equal numbers and give each group the Making Muscles Signs.

2. Students should travel to stations and perform a strengthening and stretching exercise for each muscle.

3. When students finish at a station, they should write the name of the muscle they were strengthening and stretching in the correct location on the Making Muscles Signs.

4. Students should move to the next station on your cue.

5. Once students have rotated through all of the stations, go over the answers by using the Making Muscles Signs (Labeled) so they can check to see if they have filled out the diagram correctly.

Teaching Hints

▶ Talk to students about the two areas of health-related fitness this activity emphasized and that this activity will help develop flexibility and muscular strength and endurance.

▶ Have students look at the Making Muscles Cards and go over the location of the muscles.

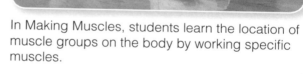

In Making Muscles, students learn the location of muscle groups on the body by working specific muscles.

▶ This activity has students perform an exercise to help locate a muscle. By doing the exercise, students use the muscle and can then locate it on the Making Muscles Signs.

▶ Some of the exercises will stretch the muscle, and others will make it stronger.

▶ At the end of class students will be asked which exercises were strengthening and which were stretching.

Sample Inclusion Tips

▶ Vary the exercises to meet the needs of students with limitations.

▶ Adjust space as needed for students to move independently.

Variation

Have students come up with a different exercise or stretch for the muscle at their station.

Home Extension

Provide students with the Making Muscles Home Extension Worksheet and have them develop exercises for each muscle group.

Assessment

▶ Students can be assessed using the worksheet done in class.

▶ At the end of the activity, name a muscle and ask students to place their hands on that muscle.

▶ At the end of the activity, name an exercise and have students name the primary muscle worked.

▶ At the end of the activity, name an exercise and have students use a thumbs-up if the exercise was for muscle strength and a thumbs-down if the exercise was for flexibility.

INTERMEDIATE

FITT principle—The FITT principle needs to be followed when working on improvement in aerobic fitness, muscular strength and endurance, and flexibility. F = frequency, I = intensity, T = time, and T = type.

Purpose

▶ Students will participate in a total-body workout that develops aerobic fitness, muscular strength and endurance, and flexibility.

▶ Student will label exercises that help develop a specific health-related fitness area.

▶ Students will understand and review the FITT principle.

Relationship to National Standards

▶ Physical education standard 2: Demonstrates understanding of movement concepts, principles, strategies, and tactics as they apply to the learning and performance of physical activities.

▶ Physical education standard 4: Achieves and maintains a health-enhancing level of physical fitness.

Equipment

▶ 20 cones

▶ 10 hoops

▶ Jump rope for each group of three students

▶ Mats for floor work

▶ Upbeat music and music player

Procedure

1. Divide the class into groups of three. Set up the groups as shown with student 1 and student 3 on one end line, student 2 on the other end line, and one hoop on the ground in the middle (see figure 7.2 on page 214).

2. The basic pattern to this activity is that when the music begins, student 1 runs to the middle, performs an exercise at the hoop, and runs to tag student 2. Student 1 then replaces student 2 and stays there. Student 2 runs to the middle, performs the skill, and then runs to tag student 3. Student 2 stays there, student 3 runs to the middle, performs the skill, and so on, continuing the pattern. After one minute, pause the music and change the challenge.

3. Pick from the list in the Total-Body Workout Class Activities sidebar on page 215 and inform students what activity they will be doing in the hoop before each round begins.

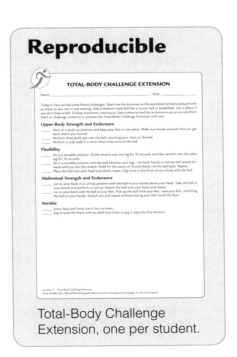

Reproducible

Total-Body Challenge Extension, one per student.

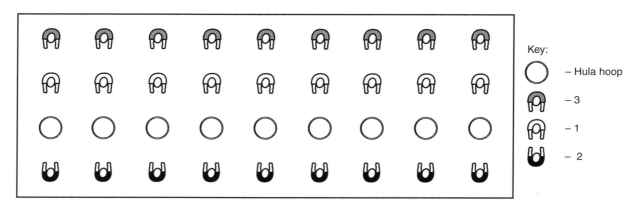

Figure 7.2 Floor diagram for Total-Body Workout.

Teaching Hints

▶ Talk about why a total-body workout is important.

▶ Keep the directions for each one-minute challenge short to maximize activity.

▶ Review health-related fitness areas before each exercise minute by referring to the FITT guidelines. For example, before students do curl-ups go over what areas of fitness they develop.

▶ FITT guideline charts can be found in the introduction to each chapter (table 3.1, page 27; table 4.1, page 77; and table 5.1, page 129).

▶ At the end of each round of exercises, go over the FITT principles for that area of fitness.

Sample Inclusion Tips

▶ Have a student with mobility difficulty be in a group of four so that two go at the same time. This student can then move at his or her own pace as the activity continues.

▶ Students in wheelchairs can do wheelchair push-ups to replace some of the specific push-up activities. Students can also hold a static push-up position with or without support from a small wedge.

▶ Students can also use a small wedge placed behind them to give support at the back when doing curl-ups.

Variations

▶ The players waiting their turn can perform an exercise—stretching, crunches, jogging in place.

▶ For abdominal strength and endurance, everyone can use a playground ball:

• Lie on your back with the ball in your hands above your head and perform a curl-up. Return the ball over your head and repeat.

• Lie on your back with the ball at your feet. Pick up the ball with your feet, raise your feet, and bring the ball to your hands. Stretch out and repeat without having your feet touch the floor.

▶ For flexibility, everyone can use a playground ball:

• Sit in a straddle position with the ball between your legs. Use both hands to roll the ball slowly forward until you feel the stretch. Hold for a count of 10 and slowly roll the ball back. Repeat.

• Sit in a butterfly stretch position (sit with bottom of feet together). Slowly roll the ball once around your body and then slowly roll the ball once around in the other direction.

TOTAL-BODY WORKOUT CLASS ACTIVITIES

Upper-Body Strength and Endurance

- Place both hands in the hoop and perform three push-ups.
- Perform three modified push-ups with your knees inside the hoop.
- Crab walk around the outside of the hoop two times.
- Start in a push-up position with your feet in the hoop. Walk your hands four steps to the right and four steps to the left.
- Start in a push-up position with your hands in the hoop. Perform a flat tire three times by slowly lowering from the up position to the down position.
- Start in a push-up position with your feet in the hoop. Lift one hand and tap your head. Repeat with the other hand. Do this three times.
- Start in a push-up position with your hands in the hoop. Perform one infinity push-up by holding a right-angle push-up position for 10 seconds.
- Start in a push-up position with your hands in the hoop. Move your hands to trace the first letter of your first name on the floor.
- Start in a crab walk position with your hands in the hoop. Perform three crab push-ups.

Abdominal Strength and Endurance

- Sit in the hoop. Lie down and perform three curl-ups.
- Sit in the hoop. Perform a V-seat and hold for five seconds. Sit with your weight balanced on your seat with your legs together. Lift your legs up straight and hold your arms straight out to the sides or in front of you (as if you were going to touch your toes with your fingers as you balance).
- Lie on your back in the hoop. Bring your knees and arms to your chest three times.
- Lie on your back in the hoop. Raise your head up far enough to look at your toes three times.

Flexibility

- Sit in the hoop in a straddle position. Slowly stretch over one leg for 10 seconds and then stretch over the other leg for 10 seconds.
- Lie on your belly in the hoop. Slowly perform a trunk raise while keeping your legs on the floor three times.
- Sit in the hoop in a modified hurdle stretch position (while sitting, one leg is straight but not locked, and the other leg is bent so that the foot of bent leg is against the straight leg). Slowly stretch over your extended leg for 10 seconds. Switch legs and slowly stretch over the other leg for 10 seconds.
- Lie on your back in the hoop. Slowly bring one knee to your chest and hug it for five seconds. Bring the other knee to your chest and hug it for five seconds.

Aerobic

- Jump in and out of the hoop three times.
- Jump rope five times with your hoop.
- Run in a circle around the hoop three times.
- Jump diagonally in and out of the hoop as you travel around the hoop.
- Do continuous vertical jumps in the hoop.

▶ For additional activities, everyone can use a playground ball. When standing, they do ball-handling skills or just dribble:

- Perform three push-ups over the ball, touching your chest to the ball.
- Perform a crab walk in a circle three times around the ball.
- Dribble the ball five times with each hand.
- Toss the ball in the air, clap your hands twice, and catch the ball. Repeat.
- Stand with your feet spread apart. Roll the ball in a figure eight around your feet three times.
- Toss the ball, let it bounce, turn around, and catch it. Repeat.
- Raise one leg over the ball while you dribble the ball.
- Dribble the ball 10 times with your nondominant hand.

Home Extension

Have students take the Total-Body Challenge home and perform the exercises. They should try to find someone to do the challenge with them.

Assessment

▶ Ask students to classify exercises into a specific health-related fitness component.

▶ Ask students to give other examples of exercises that address various fitness components.

▶ Give students a health-related fitness area and have them go through the FITT principle. For example, students could answer the following questions about aerobic fitness:

- How many times a week should you do these activities?
- How hard should you do them?
- How much time should you spend doing this area of fitness?
- Give an example of an aerobic activity.

INTERMEDIATE

Balanced workout—A fitness routine can provide students with a balanced workout that covers all components of fitness: aerobic, muscular strength and endurance, and flexibility.

Purpose

▶ Students will identify what three components can be performed for a total-body workout relating to health-related fitness.

▶ Students will identify exercises or daily living activities that go with each component of health-related fitness.

Relationship to National Standards

▶ Physical education standard 3: Participates regularly in physical activity.

▶ Physical education standard 4: Achieves and maintains a health-enhancing level of physical fitness.

Equipment

For each station, you will need the following:

▶ Three scarves for each person

▶ One basketball for each person or group

▶ Basketball hoop or target to shoot for

▶ One jump rope for each person

▶ One hula hoop for each person

▶ One Frisbee for each group

▶ One aerobic step or bench for each person

▶ Cones set up at each station to hold the instructional sign.

▶ One die for each group

▶ Mats for floor work

Procedure

1. Set up Roll the Dice Signs in a circuit around your teaching area. Each station has six activities listed on the sign.

Reproducibles

Roll the Dice Signs. You can mount signs on poster board, laminate, and adhere a strip of paper 3 inches (8 cm) wide (horizontally) to the back of the sign to help hold it on the cone.

At Work and at Play Handout, one per student.

2. Put students into four groups.

3. One student is designated to roll the die at each station.

4. The group performs the numbered activity that shows on the die in the Frisbee. (If the student rolls a 1, the group performs activity number 1 on the sign. If the student rolls a 6, the group can choose any of the activities listed on the sign.)

5. Students continue performing the activity while the music is playing (30 seconds).

6. When the music stops, students stop the activity. You say, "Move on!" and students respond by saying, "Let's go!" Each group moves to the next station, and a new person in the group rolls the die.

7. Stations represent flexibility, aerobic, and muscular strength and endurance activities.

Balance is important in all aspects of fitness. Students get to experience that firsthand by mixing up their fitness routines with a roll of the dice.

Teaching Hints

▶ Review the health-related fitness areas: muscular strength and endurance, flexibility, and aerobic fitness.

▶ Remind students that these areas are important to maintaining a healthy lifestyle. Talk about how these activities will help them in their daily living.

▶ By performing all fitness areas in a workout they can continue to improve and keep their bodies in shape.

▶ Students will often use these areas during their daily living. Ask, "When would you use flexibility? Muscular strength and endurance? Aerobic fitness?"

Variations

▶ Design a timed-interval music recording consisting of seven to nine intervals of 30 seconds of music and 15 seconds of silence.

▶ Signs and dice can be color coded to reinforce the various components of fitness noted in the Physical Activity Pyramid.

- Aerobic fitness—red
- Muscular strength and endurance—purple
- Flexibility—blue

Inclusion Tip

Adjust exercises to meet the needs of individuals. Instead of jumping rope, a student in a wheelchair could turn a handle or place the rope on the floor and a student in a wheelchair or with low skill levels can roll or step back and forth over the rope. Alternatively, fold the rope in half so that both ends can be held in one hand to swing.

Home Extension

Pass out the At Work and at Play Handout. Have students look at their activities and see how the health-related fitness areas are present in their lives throughout the day. They can record their activities on the worksheet.

Assessment

▶ For lesson closure, have students show you one exercise that they did today that worked their abdominals.

▶ Ask them to point to a station that worked on strength.

▶ Ask them what their favorite aerobic activity today was.

▶ Ask students what three areas are needed to perform a total-body workout related to health-related fitness.

▶ Ask how these activities fit into their daily living.

MINI TRIATHLON

INTERMEDIATE

Pacing—Pacing in activities can help the body continue working for a longer time so that you can participate in activities longer. The goal of aerobic activities is to maintain vigorous activity for long periods, eventually working up to 15 to 20 minutes of activity each time.

Purpose

▶ Students will explain the changes that occur in the heart rate with an aerobic fitness activity.

▶ Student will identify the purpose of pacing in aerobic activities.

Relationship to National Standards

▶ Physical education standard 2: Demonstrates understanding of movement concepts, principles, strategies, and tactics as they apply to the learning and performance of physical activities.

▶ Physical education standard 4: Achieves and maintains a health-enhancing level of physical fitness.

Equipment

For each group of three you will need the following:

▶ Two cones to mark the start–finish line and turnaround point

▶ One football

▶ One soccer ball

▶ Stopwatch to count heart rate

▶ Heart rate monitors (optional) to take the pulse

Procedure

1. Divide the students into groups of three. The goal is not to be the first one finished but to perform continually at an even pace throughout the activity.

2. Each student will be doing three different events: jog, soccer dribble, and football throw.

3. Students record their resting heart rate before

Reproducibles

PACING YOUR MINI TRIATHLON RECORD SHEET

Your team name _____

Participant 1 _____
Resting heart rate before you begin _____ Beats per minute _____
Heart rate after activity _____ Beats per minute _____

Participant 2 _____
Resting heart rate before you begin _____ Beats per minute _____
Heart rate after activity _____ Beats per minute _____

Participant 3 _____
Resting heart rate before you begin _____ Beats per minute _____
Heart rate after activity _____ Beats per minute _____

Pacing Your Mini Triathlon Record Sheet, one per group.

AM I GIVING MY HEART A WORKOUT? CHART

Level 1	Too easy	• Not sweating • Heart beats at usual pace • Breathing normally
Level 2	Medium	• Begin to sweat lightly • Feel heart beating quickly • Hear yourself breathing
Level 3	Hard	• Sweating • Heart is beating fast • Breathing hard
Level 4	Very hard	• Sweating a lot • Heart is racing • Breathing very hard
Level 5	Too hard	• Sweating a great deal • Out of breath • Wobbly legs

Am I Giving My Heart a Workout? Chart.

beginning. They also record their heart rate at the finish, using the reproducible Pacing Your Mini Triathlon Record Sheet.

4. Person 1 lines up at the start with a soccer ball and a football behind her or him.

5. On the go signal, person 1 runs down to the turnaround point and returns to the start–finish line. You can determine the length, but half the length of a football field is recommended.

6. Person 1 dribbles the soccer ball with the feet down to the turnaround point and back to the beginning.

7. Person 1 then picks up the football, throws it toward the turnaround point, runs to the ball, picks it up, and throws it again until he or she has gone to the turnaround point and back.

8. The person takes her or his heart rate after crossing the start–finish line and records the beats per minute on the Pacing Your Mini Triathlon Record Sheet.

9. Persons 2 and 3 do the same sequence of activities. Before and after their turns they warm up and cool down while waiting.

10. When all students have finished, discuss how everyone's heart rate is different and why.

11. Ask students to describe the signs that the body uses to show that it is working hard. Use the Am I Giving My Heart a Workout? Chart to help guide the discussion. (Answer: sweating, red face, heart beating faster, breathing faster, tired muscles.)

12. Ask students to discuss how they paced themselves so that they could keep going without walking.

Teaching Hints

▶ Discuss that a triathlon is composed of combining three sports together into one competition. Usually it is bicycling, swimming, and running.

▶ Discuss pacing and target heart rate. By pacing through an activity an athlete conserves enough energy to continue to move through all three events without having to stop. This is why pacing is important. The pacing speed will be different for each person depending on what shape the person is in and how well the person understands what her or his body is capable of doing.

Using a mix of activities and sports helps keep exercise fresh and fun by preventing the mind and body to becoming too accustomed to just one activity, like running. Mini Triathlon gives students practice in pacing themselves throughout a variety of activities.

▶ Have the students record their resting heart rate and their heart rate at the end of the triathlon so that they can see the effects that exercise has on the heart.

▶ To find their pulse, they can use a stopwatch to count the number of beats that occur in six seconds and add a zero behind the number. They can then check the Target Heart Rate Chart to see whether they are in their target heart rate zone.

Sample Inclusion Tips

▶ Shorten the distance to the turnaround point.

▶ Use peer helpers.

Variations

▶ Pick three different sports and have students design what activity they can do with each sport to design a triathlon.

▶ Include all areas of health-related fitness in a triathlon.

Home Extension

Ask the students to create their own version of a triathlon and try it at home. Have students bring their event back to school to try in class for a warm-up activity.

Assessment

Ask students these questions:

▶ Why is pacing important?

▶ What happened to your heart rate from the beginning to the end? What do aerobic activities do for the body?

▶ Did you maintain a steady pace during all sections of the triathlon? Why or why not?

▶ Did you maintain your target heart rate or were you above it or below it? If you were above or below it, what could you do to move your heartbeat into the target zone?

INTERMEDIATE

Total fitness workout—As students participate in activities throughout the year they will be able to evaluate the benefits of a workout. Knowing the difference between health-related fitness and skill-related fitness can help students understand and value both.

Purpose

▶ Students will perform exercises in all fitness activities to get a total-body workout.

▶ Students will evaluate exercises and classify them as primarily developing health fitness or sport fitness.

Relationship to National Standards

▶ Physical education standard 4: Achieves and maintains a health-enhancing level of physical fitness.

▶ Health education standard 3: Students will demonstrate the ability to practice health-enhancing behaviors and reduce health risks.

Equipment

▶ Three to six volleyballs

▶ Three to six soccer balls

▶ Three to six stability balls

▶ Three to six basketballs

▶ Three to six jump ropes

▶ Six shuttle run blocks

▶ Mats for floor exercises and stretches

Procedure

1. Place students in groups of three. Give each group a Blackout Fitness Bingo Card. They are to complete ALL exercises.

2. Set up equipment around the gym for students to use when needed.

3. At the completion of the exercise students are to decide whether the activity developed skill- or health-related fitness and circle the answer on their Blackout Fitness Bingo Cards. After they finish, they should check their findings with you.

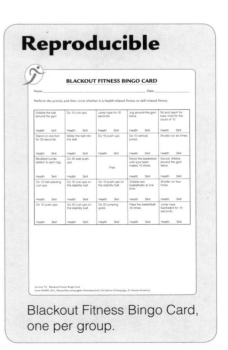

Blackout Fitness Bingo Card, one per group.

Teaching Hints

▶ Review with students the different components of health-related fitness and skill-related fitness.

- Health-related fitness deals with aerobic capacity, muscle strength and endurance, flexibility, and body composition.
- Skill-related fitness includes coordination, agility, reaction time, balance, power, and speed.

▶ Ask students to name an activity to develop each area.

▶ As students travel through the Blackout Fitness Bingo Card, check for understanding as they move around the gym.

Sample Inclusion Tip

Adjust exercises to meet the needs of students with special needs.

Variation

Have students design a Blackout Fitness Bingo Card of health- and skill-related fitness on a blank card.

Home Extension

Have students design their own Blackout Fitness Bingo Cards at home. They can use their cards with friends and family members and have them perform an exercise to get to fill a spot.

Assessment

▶ Go over the worksheet completed in class and correct papers.

▶ Have groups put their names on the worksheet used in class and evaluate their written work.

Students get a total-body workout while they compare health-related fitness to skill-related fitness during a sporty game of bingo.

Special Events

The previous chapters center on teaching health-related fitness concepts and principles through a variety of activities focused on components of health-related fitness. Standard 4 of the national standards for physical education focuses on achieving and maintaining a health-enhancing level of physical fitness; thus activities in class and outside of class are important to the development of a healthy active lifestyle. This chapter connects what students do in physical education class with their lives outside of class. Students are more likely to participate in physical activity if they have opportunities to develop interests that are personally meaningful to them. The activities included in this chapter provide students with fun and meaningful activities while celebrating holidays, traditions, and special health and physical education observances.

Some of these activities integrate classroom learning and use several of the multiple intelligence strategies that are used in quality physical education programs (Gardner, 1993). Multiple intelligence theory is concerned with the process of learning. Students learn in many different ways, and in fitness development, variety is the spice of life. What students do, they understand!

In keeping with the Physical Best program philosophy, the activities in this chapter teach fitness concepts through bodily–kinesthetic intelligence while integrating the remaining intelligences (musical, linguistic, intrapersonal, interpersonal, logical–mathematical, and spatial) into the lessons to increase opportunities for all students to succeed. Many health-related organizations keep updated lists of national health observances, which can generate additional fun and educational activity ideas for students. One such resource is the U.S. Department of Health and Human Services Healthfinder Web site. To

Figure 8.1 ABCs of Fitness, available on the CD-ROM.

access the National Health Observances calendar, go to www.healthfinder.gov. Many special events are also given in the NASPE Teacher's Toolbox at www.aahperd.org/naspe/publications/teaching-Tools/toolbox.

Besides the special events activities found in this chapter, you'll find a reproducible on the CD-ROM called the ABCs of Fitness (see figure 8.1). The alphabet is a building block for learning to read and write. Use the fitness ABCs as a building block in physical education class, too. Each letter of the alphabet corresponds with a concept included in the Physical Best and Fitnessgram programs. The alphabet can be used to reinforce the concepts and principles taught during the daily fitness development activity or at the end of the lesson as part of a closure activity. Week by week, let Physical Best help students reach their peak. See table 8.1 for a grid of activities in this chapter.

Table 8.1 Chapter 8 Activities Grid

Activity number	Activity title	Activity page	Concept	Primary	Intermediate	Month	Reproducibles (on CD-ROM)
8.1	World Fitness	228	Developing fitness areas		•	September	World Fitness Station Signs
8.2	Rake the Leaves	230	Benefits of fitness	•		November	Aerobic Fitness Health Benefits Poster
8.3	Family Fun Night Circuit	233	Benefits of activity and risk factors of inactivity	•	•	Any time of year	Letter Home to Guardians
							Family Fun Night Circuit Station Signs
							Risk Factor Cards
							Family Fun Night Circuit Questionnaire
8.4	Fitness Frenzy With Partners	236	Specificity of exercises		•	January	Fitness Frenzy With Partners Signs
							Fitness Frenzy With Partners Worksheet
8.5	Risk Factor Mania	238	Aerobic fitness		•	February	Heart Health Risk Factor Cards
							Am I Giving My Heart a Workout? Chart
8.6	Up and Down With Jump Ropes	242	Aerobic fitness and flexibility	•	•	February	Exercise Cards
8.7	Heart Smart Orienteering	244	Aerobic fitness and FITT		•	February	Orienteering Master Sheet
							Heart Smart Orienteering Questions Cards
							FITT Homework Assignment
8.8	March Into Fitness	247	FITT principles		•	March	March Into Fitness Station Signs
							Am I Giving My Heart a Workout? Chart
8.9	Exercise Your Rights Day	250	Schoolwide exercise	•	•	April	Exercise Your Rights Cards
							Health Benefits Signs
							Exercise Your Rights Letter to Guardians
8.10	Energize With Exercise	253	Cooperative learning	•	•	May	Energize With Exercise Routine
8.11	Marvelous Muscles for Summer	256	Specificity		•	May	Marvelous Muscles for Summer Station Signs
							Muscle Diagrams
8.12	Dash for Cash	258	Health-related fitness components	•	•	May or June	Dash for Cash Fitness Station Signs
8.13	Summer Fun–Summer Shape-Up Challenge	261	FITT principles	•	•	June, July, or August	Summer Fun–Summer Shape-Up Challenge Activity Sheet

INTERMEDIATE

Developing fitness areas—Including all health-related fitness areas in a workout can help your whole body.

Background

The International Day of Peace occurs annually on September 21. This annual event is dedicated to peace, or to the absence of war. It is classified as a temporary ceasefire in a combat zone and is observed by nations, political groups, military groups, and people. This day is a reminder of the human cost of war. A "peace bell" is rung at UN Headquarters. The peace bell, given as a gift by the Diet of Japan (Japan's bicameral legislature), is made from coins donated by children from all continents. On the side of the bell is written "Long live absolute world peace."

Purpose

To honor the International Day of Peace, share the previous information with students. Inform them that to celebrate this day they will travel around the room doing world fitness. Students will travel north, south, east, and west, naming an exercise to improve a specific muscle group.

Relationship to National Standards

- ▶ Physical education standard 4: Achieves and maintains a health-enhancing level of physical fitness.
- ▶ Physical education standard 5: Exhibits responsible personal and social behavior that respects self and others in a physical activity setting.
- ▶ Health education standard 3: Students will demonstrate the ability to practice health-enhancing behaviors and reduce health risks.

Equipment

- ▶ Six to eight jump ropes, one for each person at a station
- ▶ Five poly spots or floor tape to mark an X on the floor for the dot drill
- ▶ Four Frisbees to hold bingo numbers
- ▶ Bingo cards and numbers from a Bingo game (Check with a classroom teacher if you don't have one.)
- ▶ One foam ball or beanbag for each person at a station
- ▶ One towel for each person at a station
- ▶ One stretch band for each person at a station
- ▶ One scooter for each person at a station
- ▶ Mats for floor work

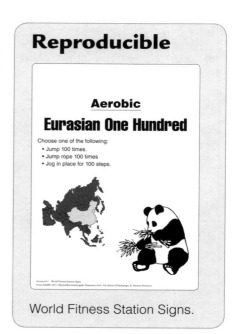

Reproducible

Aerobic
Eurasian One Hundred

Choose one of the following:
- Jump 100 times.
- Jump rope 100 times.
- Jog in place for 100 steps.

World Fitness Station Signs.

Procedure

1. Set up stations on the perimeter of the classroom. Correlate the continents in the north, south, east, and west directions.

2. Students travel around the world by fitness stations in groups of four.

3. As students go to each station, they should notice what muscles they are using. Stations include:

   - Eurasia—Aerobic fitness
   - North America—Aerobic fitness
   - Africa—Muscular strength
   - Australia—Muscular strength
   - Antarctica—Muscular strength
   - South America—Flexibility

World Fitness celebrates the International Day of Peace on September 21 through a set of continent-based activity stations.

Teaching Hints

▶ Begin with a map of the world in the room. Have students get orientated to where the continents are in the room in relation to north, south, east, and west. Have them say the names aloud.

▶ Begin the lesson by doing some of the exercises from each continent. People in each continent use various fitness areas to go through their daily lives, just as your students do.

▶ Each continent is working on a specific fitness area. Explain the exercise by using the World Fitness Station Signs on the wall.

▶ For the North American Dot Drill, use five poly spots or mark five Xs on the floor with tape where four Xs mark four corners of a square shape and the fifth X marks the middle of the square. Make sure that the Xs are not so far apart that a student cannot jump on outer corners of the square with both feet on different Xs.

Sample Inclusion Tip

Modify activities to meet the needs of students' ability levels. For example, have a student who uses a wheelchair turn one end of a jump rope for another student, use simulated rope turns with one or both arms, or fold the rope in half so that both handles are in one hand and turn the rope as if jumping.

Variations

▶ Do this activity in conjunction with the classroom teacher when the class is studying continents.

▶ Facts about each area or its associated countries can be integrated at the stations for a deeper cultural connection.

Home Extension

Ask students to share with their guardians why September 21 is important. Students can explain to their guardians how they celebrated with exercise and ask them to exercise with them in the evening. Have students report back to you about the types of activities they did.

Assessment

Name a specific health-related fitness area and have students give you an exercise to go along with the fitness area.

RAKE THE LEAVES

PRIMARY

Benefits of fitness—Through this activity students will be able to see the benefits of fitness, such as having strong bones, feeling better, reducing stress, enjoying more energy, having a stronger heart, and a better ability to learn.

Background

The changing of seasons brings about different weather. Fall is a good time to be outside and be active.

Purpose

▶ Students will be able to name the benefits of fitness.

▶ Students will think about daily chores or activities that use various health-related fitness components.

Relationship to National Standards

▶ Physical education standard 1: Demonstrates competency in motor skills and movement patterns needed to perform a variety of physical activities.

▶ Physical education standard 3: Participates regularly in physical activity.

▶ Physical education standard 4: Achieves and maintains a health-enhancing level of physical fitness.

Equipment

▶ 30 to 40 tennis balls with health benefits written on them: strong bones, feel better, reduces stress, more energy, strengthens heart, learn better

▶ Two barrels or milk crates for targets

Procedure

1. Students will be introduced to fall activities. Leaves start to drop from trees in fall, and they need to be raked up. Raking leaves is a form of exercise that can get the heart to beat faster, help strengthen muscles, and increase flexibility among other benefits. Discuss how various outdoor activities can enhance aerobic fitness as well as strength and flexibility. People can gain many benefits by being active and increasing their heart rate. Review the Aerobic Fitness Health Benefits Poster.

Reproducible

Aerobic Fitness Health Benefits

• Feel better
• Stronger muscles
• Healthy heart
• More energy
• Learn better
• Healthy body composition
• Healthy breathing
• Play harder

Aerobic Fitness Health Benefits Poster.

Students practice cleaning up "leaves" while they learn about health benefits that come from exercise.

2. Have students look at the tennis balls and read the words: strong bones, feel better, reduces stress, more energy, strengthens heart, learn better.

3. The tennis balls represent the leaves, and barrels represent the bag to put them in.

4. Students are to throw underhand to work on developing that skill. Review the proper form for underhand throws. With this activity, you are able to do two things at once—focus on the skill of underhand throwing and teach the health benefits of aerobic fitness. The goal is to get the tennis balls into the target while staying behind the throwing line.

5. Students may throw at either target, staying outside the throwing line. If you place the target in the center of the basketball lane, students are to stay behind the 3-point line to get balls in the target.

6. After all the balls are in the target, stop and talk about the benefits of fitness.

Teaching Hints

▶ Tennis balls can be obtained from various tennis groups in the community. Contact the high school tennis coach for old tennis balls.

▶ Talk to students about the benefits of fitness. Show them the words on the tennis balls.

▶ Tell them that they will need to know the benefits of fitness by the end of class, so they should be sure to look at the words before they throw. You might have students say the benefit aloud before throwing the balls in the target.

▶ Review the basic steps of an underhand throw.

Sample Inclusion Tips

▶ Have one student pick up two tennis balls and give one to a classmate who has difficulty bending over.

▶ Make the target closer to the student who is having difficulty throwing at the longer distance.

▶ Give some type of storage pouch to students so that they start with multiple balls and can throw independently.

Variations

▶ Repeat the activity using an overhand throw. This way you can focus on one throwing skill at a time and provide feedback to students.

▶ Play throughout the year with different themes, such as stuff the turkey or pick up your room.

▶ Use different locomotor movements to collect balls: skip, hop, crab walk.

▶ Keep track of how long it takes students to collect all the balls. Teach the concept of aerobic fitness and time. Refer to the aerobic chapter for more information in this area.

Home Extension

▶ Challenge students to find a physical activity outside and get some exercise. They can do an activity on their own, invite a friend over, or do something with their family, perhaps get a rake and clean up their yard or a neighbor's yard or pick up litter in the neighborhood. Students should report their challenge to you.

Assessment

▶ Check for understanding to see whether students can name the benefits of physical activity.

▶ Name a benefit of fitness. Have students give a thumb-up if the statement that you make is true and thumbs-down if the statement is false.

PRIMARY AND INTERMEDIATE

Benefits of activity and risk factors of inactivity—Parents and students go over the benefits of activity and risk factors that are involved with inactivity.

Background

Family Fun Nights are a great way to get students, teachers, and guardians together. This event can create a positive relationship around physical activity and exercise. Guardians and children become aware of the benefits of activity and the risk factors involved with inactivity. The gym is a place where students and guardians can share in activities and be encouraged to participate together outside of school.

Purpose

▶ Students will be able to demonstrate to guardians activities performed in class that benefit a healthy lifestyle.

▶ Students and guardians will be made aware of the risk factors of an unhealthy lifestyle.

Relationship to National Standards

▶ Physical education standard 4: Achieves and maintains a health-enhancing level of physical fitness.

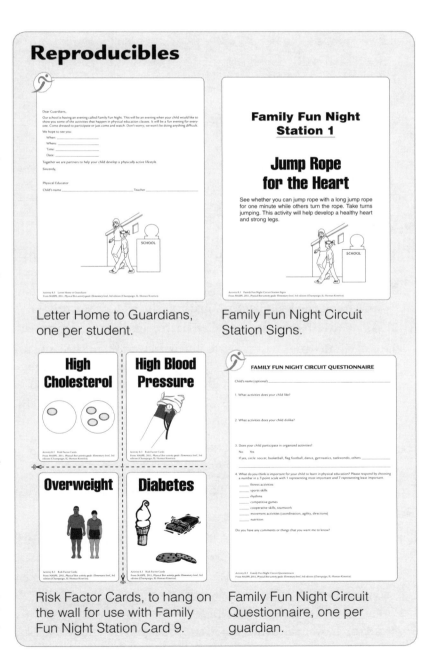

Reproducibles

Letter Home to Guardians, one per student.

Family Fun Night Circuit Station Signs.

Risk Factor Cards, to hang on the wall for use with Family Fun Night Station Card 9.

Family Fun Night Circuit Questionnaire, one per guardian.

▶ Health education standard 3: Students will demonstrate the ability to practice health-enhancing behaviors and reduce health risks.

▶ Health education standard 7: Students will demonstrate the ability to advocate for personal, family, and community health.

Equipment

The amount of equipment that you have at a station depends on the room that you are using and the number of people who are attending. It is recommended to have 5 to 10 pieces at each station.

▶ Stretch bands

▶ Stability balls

▶ Basketballs

▶ Soccer balls

▶ Jump ropes

▶ Beanbags

▶ One or two sit-and-reach boxes

▶ Hula hoop

▶ One or two rope fitness ladders on the floor (These can also be created by using tape on the floor.)

▶ Upbeat music and player

Procedure

1. Send to guardians a copy of Letter Home to Guardians inviting them to Family Fun Night. Select the best time of the year for your schedule and your school.

2. Set up 10 stations around the gym. Place a Family Fun Night Station Sign at each station and hang the Risk Factor Cards on the wall at station 9.

3. As guardians and students arrive, assign them to an open station.

4. Guardians and their child perform the action on the Family Fun Night Station Sign together and then move to the next station. Encourage the students to teach the guardians the activities and guide them through the movements. Play upbeat music in the background.

5. After they have completed all the stations, guardians will be invited to complete a questionnaire about the Family Fun Night activities.

Teaching Hint

Have students do the stations at school so that they will know what is expected at each station. Discuss with them that they are to do the stations and become the teacher to their guardians.

Sample Inclusion Tips

▶ Participants who are unable to jump can turn a jump rope. They can use the aid of another person if needed to turn the rope.

▶ Participants who have difficulties jumping off the ground can participate independently by stepping over a jump rope placed on the floor.

▶ Have participants in wheelchairs go into the middle of a long rope. Have the rope turned back and forth over the head. When the rope goes down, the participant puts the arms down. When the rope goes up, the arms go up. This action will symbolize the jump with the feet.

Variations

▶ Vary your activities to meet the space of your facility and the skills of your students.

▶ Ask students what they would like to teach their guardians on this evening. What do they do in physical education class that they would like to have their guardians try?

▶ Have a group dance that everyone can participate in. For example, give everyone two paper plates, add music, and do exercises with the plates: tap the two plates together, over the head, under a leg; turn in a circle; put plates under the feet and slide on the floor; and so on. Have your students help you create a routine before Family Fun Night.

▶ Plan this night with the help of the Parent Teachers Association.

Home Extension

Have students talk to guardians about developing an exercise plan for the family.

Assessment

▶ Have guardians fill out the Family Fun Night Questionnaire at the end of the evening.

▶ Ask students what the best part of the evening was.

© Brand X Pictures

Guardian involvement ensures that students keep active outside of school so they can gain the benefits of activity and to avoid the health risks of inactivity.

8.4 FITNESS FRENZY WITH PARTNERS

INTERMEDIATE

Specificity of exercises—Students need time to work on improving fitness and knowing what exercises help each fitness area.

Background

Students need to learn that doing activities with others can make a workout more enjoyable while improving their fitness level. January is a good time to begin a fitness routine because the beginning of the New Year marks the start of something new. Students can begin an exercise program and learn the importance of exercise.

Purpose

Students will name an exercise that correlates with a specific health-related fitness area.

Relationship to National Standards

▶ Physical education standard 3: Participates regularly in physical activity.

▶ Physical education standard 4: Achieves and maintains a health-enhancing level of physical fitness.

▶ Physical education standard 5: Exhibits responsible personal and social behavior that respects self and others in physical activity settings.

Equipment

▶ Eight jump ropes

▶ Four scooters

▶ Mats for floor work

▶ Light dumbbells

▶ Pedometers (optional) for counting steps

▶ Heart rate monitors (optional) for keeping track of heart rates

▶ Upbeat music and music player

Procedure

1. Students travel using various locomotor skills while the music is playing.

Reproducibles

Muscular Strength and Endurance Fitness Frenzy

- Do 10 push-up high fives by facing a partner in a push-up position and while holding yourself up do high fives by clapping one hand with your partner's and then the other.
- Do partner curl-ups by connecting your feet with a partner and touching fingertips when you curl up. How many more can you do over 20?
- With light dumbbells or some type of weights, do 12 arm curls, triceps presses, arm presses forward, and squats.
- Do a wall sit side-by-side with your partner. How long can you hold it?

Fitness Frenzy With Partners Signs.

FITNESS FRENZY WITH PARTNERS WORKSHEET

Partner names

Create a fitness workout at home. Write down how many exercises you and someone else did together. Exercises can be done by yourself, with a friend, or with a family member.

Muscular Strength and Endurance:

Flexibility:

Aerobic:

Was it more fun to exercise with a friend? _____ Why?

If you did not have a friend to exercise with, do you think it would have been more fun? _____ Why?

Fitness Frenzy With Partners Worksheet, one per student.

Learning about specificity in fitness activities is more fun with partners.

2. When the music stops students find their partners and perform one activity of their choice from the components of fitness listed on the Fitness Frenzy With Partners Signs.

3. Students must travel to a different sign before repeating a specific fitness area.

Teaching Hints

▶ Review with students the importance of daily physical activity.

▶ Talk to students about how they can get exercise into their lives during winter months. Working out with a friend can add fun to a workout. It is one way to beat the winter blues.

▶ Go over specificity and address the day's exercises with each area of health-related fitness.

Sample Inclusion Tip

By working in groups of three, students can help someone and still take turns to perform a task at their own ability level.

Variation

Have the class design the Fitness Frenzy With Partners Signs before they begin.

Home Extension

Have students take the Fitness Frenzy With Partners Worksheet home and create their own workouts in the health-related fitness areas.

Assessment

Ask students to perform a specific exercise and then have them name the area of fitness that it develops.

RISK FACTOR MANIA

INTERMEDIATE

Aerobic fitness—Aerobic fitness can help control some of the risk factors that lead to cardiovascular disease.

Background

February is heart month. Heart disease is the leading cause of death in the United States. Students can learn some preventive measure to keep the heart strong while getting an aerobic workout. Being physically active, especially aerobically active (moderate to vigorous intensity), can help prevent or control many of the risk factors for cardiovascular disease and other health problems. Risk factors are used to identify actions and health issues that may cause you more health problems such as heart disease and heart attacks.

Purpose

▶ Students will be able to identify several risk factors that negatively affect heart and body health.

▶ Students will understand that aerobic exercise can strengthen the heart and cardiovascular system and help control risk factors related to cardiovascular disease.

▶ Students will be able to identify whether they were working aerobically and be able to discuss how hard they were working during the activity.

Relationship to National Standards

▶ Physical education standard 2: Demonstrates understanding of movement concepts, principles, strategies, and tactics as they apply to the learning and performance of physical activities.

▶ Physical education standard 4: Achieves and maintains a health-enhancing level of physical fitness.

▶ Physical education standard 6: Values physical activity for health, enjoyment, challenge, self-expression, and/or social interaction.

▶ Health education standard 1: Students will comprehend concepts related to health promotion and disease prevention.

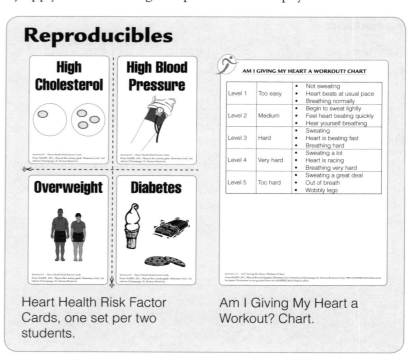

Heart Health Risk Factor Cards, one set per two students.

Am I Giving My Heart a Workout? Chart.

Equipment

▶ Foam balls (yellow for cholesterol if possible), one for each tagger (approximately one tagger for every eight students)

▶ Container to hold the Heart Health Risk Factor Cards

▶ Seven to twelve balls that can be dribbled

▶ Five poly spots

▶ Five cones

▶ Pedometers (optional) to keep track of steps

▶ Heart rate monitors (optional) to keep track of heart rates during the activity

Procedure

1. Place five Am I Giving My Heart a Workout? Charts around the gym for students to use during the activity. Put a cone under them so that students will know where to locate the charts.

2. The taggers should start with 5-10 Heart Health Risk Factor Cards already in hand. Place a container holding more Heart Health Risk Factor Cards in the middle of the gym so that the taggers have easy access to more cards when needed. Scatter five poly spots around the gym. These are safety zones where students cannot be tagged. Only one student may be on a single poly spot at a time. Place balls in a corner of the gym for tagged students to dribble around the room.

3. Discuss what is meant by aerobic activity and how a person can identify how hard she or he is working aerobically; use the Am I Giving My Heart a Workout? Chart.

4. Define intensity with regard to aerobic workouts. Intensity for aerobic fitness is how hard a person works the heart during physical activity.

5. Have students stand under a chart and decide the level at which they are currently working. Most students should be at a resting level because they have not begun moving to increase their heart rate.

6. Go over the Heart Health Risk Factor Cards, which represent the risk factors that people can control with a healthy diet and exercise.

7. Explain that the taggers will carry foam balls which represent cholesterol, a risk factor because it can clog a heart's arteries. If a tagger tags a student, the student is given a Risk Factor Card which they carry with them as they continue to play.

8. Tell students that each card they get takes them closer to having a heart problem. After a student has been tagged four times and collected four Heart Health Risk Factor Cards, she or he needs to read all of his or her Heart Health Risk Factor Cards and then return them to the container. The student should then exercise by dribbling a ball around the perimeter of the gym one time with the right hand and one time with the left hand.

9. Encourage students to remember the risk factors because at the end of class they will be asked to discuss them. Students should check the Am I Giving My Heart a Workout? Chart to see at what level they are working their hearts and then rejoin the activity.

10. Switch taggers after one minute or another suitable interval.

11. When changing taggers, ask all students to stand under the Am I Giving My Heart a Workout? Chart and determine their intensity level.

Teaching Hints

▶ State that February is heart month, a time when people should think about all the things that they can do to keep themselves healthy. For example, they can cut down on sweets and fats and get more exercise.

▶ Read the cards to students at the beginning and end of the lesson to help them learn the factors that they can control.

▶ Discuss that people cannot control some health risk factors, such as genetics, age, and gender.

▶ Focus on the fact that exercise can help make the heart stronger.

Risk Factor Mania uses a tag game to help students learn about the risk factors for cardiovascular disease.

▶ Emphasize that it is important to learn to work at the right intensity level. Use the Am I Giving My Heart a Workout? Chart to help with this goal.

▶ Students can be stopped at any time in the activity and asked to monitor their intensity signs from the chart. They can show you which level they are at by raising fingers to match the level number on the chart.

Sample Inclusion Tips

▶ Students walk when being chased by a person with mobility or visual impairments.

▶ Place the container high enough so that students with balance and mobility problems can easily pick up cards when they are a tagger.

▶ If necessary, have students dribble the ball only once around the gym, dribble in place, dribble for a certain number of times, or use two hands instead of one.

Variations

▶ Various skills can be used for the exercise. For example, students could stick handle a hockey puck, dribble a soccer ball, or toss and catch a ball.

▶ Add additional Heart Health Risk Factor Cards to the container.

▶ Put the names of different health risk factors on soft balls for taggers to use.

▶ Add factors that students can't control so that they can learn the difference.

▶ Create signs with healthy options to place on the poly spots such as eating fresh fruits and vegetables, getting enough fiber, drinking plenty of water, or eating healthy snacks so that students learn more ways to help control or prevent risk factors.

Home Extension

Ask students to perform at least one aerobic activity after school and determine their intensity level based on the Am I Giving My Heart a Workout? Chart.

Assessment

- ▶ Ask students which levels of the chart they should work at to ensure that the heart is getting a good but safe workout. (Answer: levels 2 through 4.)
- ▶ After the activity ask students to turn to a person next to them and share as many risk factors for heart disease as they remember.
- ▶ Ask students to define *risk factor* and tell how they can help control or prevent risk factors.

UP AND DOWN WITH JUMP ROPES

PRIMARY AND INTERMEDIATE

Aerobic fitness and flexibility—Aerobic fitness and flexibility are two of the health-related components to emphasize on most, if not all, days of the week. Aerobic means "with oxygen." Aerobic fitness occurs when your heart, lungs, and muscles work together over an extended period. Doing physical activity encourages your heart to beat harder, your lungs to breathe better, and your muscles to get more oxygen. It is recommended that children get at least 60 minutes of activity per day. Flexibility is the ability to bend, stretch, and twist the body. It is recommended that children get flexibility activity two to three days per week at minimum, but daily is preferred.

Background

February is heart month, a time for students to focus on the function of the heart and to add other health-related fitness areas to the workout. Aerobic fitness improves when the heart, lungs, and muscles all work together for an extended period. Flexibility is the ability to bend, twist, and stretch the body with ease through a full range of motion.

Purpose

- ▶ Students will be able to identify flexibility exercises.
- ▶ Students will be able to perform an aerobic activity.

Relationship to National Standards

- ▶ Physical education standard 3: Participates regularly in physical activity.
- ▶ Physical education standard 4: Achieves and maintains a health-enhancing level of physical fitness.
- ▶ Health education standard 2: Students will demonstrate the ability to practice health-enhancing behaviors and reduce health risks.

Equipment

- ▶ One jump rope for every two students
- ▶ Mats for floor work
- ▶ Pedometers (optional) to count the number of steps when jumping rope

Procedure

1. Have students walk or jog at least three laps around the gym before beginning.
2. Students work with a partner. One person is in the center of the gym with a jump rope, and the other person is against the wall.
3. Designate a stretching exercise from the Exercise Cards to be used. When the music begins, the student with

Reproducible

Modified Hurdle Stretch

Sit with one leg straight, the other leg bent, and the foot of the bent leg touching the thigh of the straight leg. With one hand on top of other and the arms straight, bend forward toward the foot to stretch out the hamstrings of the straight leg.

Activity 8.6   Exercise Cards
From NASPE, 2011, *Physical Best activity guide: Elementary level, 3rd edition* (Champaign, IL: Human Kinetics)

Reach for Toes While Sitting

Activity 8.6   Exercise Cards
From NASPE, 2011, *Physical Best activity guide: Elementary level, 3rd edition* (Champaign, IL: Human Kinetics)

Exercise Cards for the teacher to use.

the jump rope begins jumping and the partner performs the stretching exercise. After one minute, pause the music. Partners change places, and the activity continues.

Teaching Hints

▸ Talk to students about what areas of fitness they will be working on and why each is important.

▸ Explain that February is heart month. Focus on why the heart is important.

▸ Explain the importance of warming up the body before stretching.

Sample Inclusion Tips

▸ Students in wheelchairs can fold a jump rope in half and turn the rope to the side several times or do jumping jack motions with the arms to get the heart rate up.

▸ Stretching exercises can be changed to meet the needs of students.

Variations

Change activities of the nonjumping partner to muscular strength and endurance while the partner jumps rope.

Celebrate heart month with Up and Down With Jump Ropes, an aerobic and flexibility activity.

Home Extension

Encourage students to jump on their own or with a friend during recess or at home. If they don't have a rope of their own, they can borrow one from school.

Assessment

▸ Ask students what the class should do before beginning to stretch. (Answer: a full-body warm-up of five minutes or more.)

▸ Ask students to name a flexibility exercise.

▸ Name an exercise and an area of fitness and have students show a thumbs-up if the connection is correct or a thumbs-down if it is incorrect.

INTERMEDIATE

Aerobic fitness and FITT—Review of health and fitness concepts learned throughout the year.

Background

Promoting physical activity, developing cognitive knowledge, and participating in health-enhancing physical activity are three goals of the Physical Best program. The Heart Smart Orienteering activity is a fun way to bring closure to Healthy Heart Month (February) and to check to see whether students have developed an understanding of aerobic fitness concepts, the FITT principle, and the warning signs for a heart attack and stroke.

Purpose

By working together in a group, students can review health-related fitness information and concepts.

Relationship to National Standards

- ▶ Physical education standard 4: Achieves and maintains a health-enhancing level of fitness.
- ▶ Physical education standard 5: Exhibits responsible personal and social behavior that respects self and others in physical activity settings.
- ▶ Physical education standard 6: Values physical activity for health, enjoyment, challenge, self-expression, and social interaction.
- ▶ Health education standard 3: Student will demonstrate the ability to practice health-enhancing behaviors and reduce health risks.

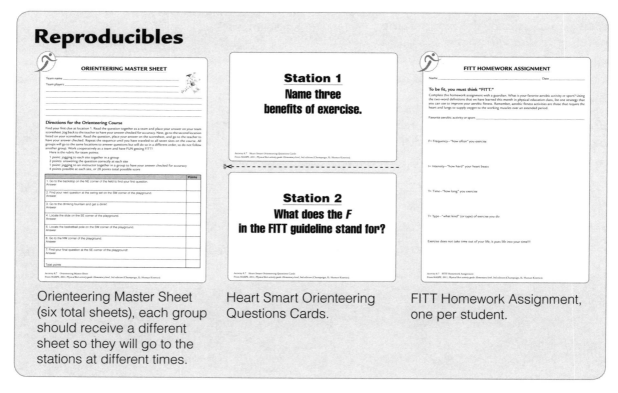

Reproducibles

Orienteering Master Sheet (six total sheets), each group should receive a different sheet so they will go to the stations at different times.

Heart Smart Orienteering Questions Cards.

FITT Homework Assignment, one per student.

Equipment

▸ Six to eight cones

▸ Pencils and clipboards for each group

▸ Fun, fast-paced continuous music and music player

▸ Physical activity equipment for groups who finish early

▸ Pedometers (optional) to count steps

Procedure

1. Students move from station to station and answer questions related to the key concepts that you have taught in your physical education program.

2. Create an Orienteering Master Sheet based on the number of stations needed and locations to be used. Alternatively, use the samples provided on the CD-ROM by changing each Orienteering Master Sheet to feature landmarks specific to your orienteering course and make copies for the students. Each Orienteering Master Sheet will have students moving from station to station but in a different order.

Orienteering is a fun and challenging way for students to review health and fitness concepts.

3. Make sure that students know directions (north, south, east, west) and where to find the key locations (basketball courts, backstop, small slide, drinking fountain, and so on) around your school or playground that you have included on your Orienteering Master Sheet.

4. Place the Heart Smart Orienteering Questions at each location.

5. Students work in groups of four to six or in squads. Designate a group leader.

6. Each group needs an Orienteering Master Sheet and a pencil.

7. Students begin by jogging together to the first location on their sheet. A Heart Smart Orienteering Question to answer will be at the location. Students agree on an answer, write it on their worksheet, and then return to you to receive their point total before moving on to the next location. The Orienteering Master Sheet lists the rubric for receiving points.

8. Have an aerobic activity planned for students to participate in when their group has completed the activity (individual, partner, or long jump ropes; jump bands; and so on).

Teaching Hints

▸ Orienteering combines walking, jogging, and map-reading skills. In this activity, we have used directions and playground markers as the checkpoints rather than a compass. If you have used compasses to teach orienteering with your intermediate students, change the sites and checkpoints to make the activity more challenging.

▸ Color coding or numbering each of the student Orienteering Worksheets will allow you to create a master answer sheet when students come to you to share their answers and receive their points.

▸ This activity lends itself to differentiation. Let students choose their own groups. Students like to work with friends or others who like to jog at the same pace as they do.

- ▶ Always include fun stations (getting a drink, sliding down the slide, and so on) to make the activity more enjoyable for the students.
- ▶ Change the markers (locations) on your orienteering sheets to match playground or indoor locations at your school.

Sample Inclusion Tip

- ▶ Students who are visually impaired can use a wand or baton and jog with a different student each time that the group travels to a new site.
- ▶ Students who are visually impaired become part of the group when using a jump rope that everyone holds on to.

Variation

Tie a jump rope in a knot to form a circle. Students will need to hold on to the rope while moving from station to station.

Home Extension

- ▶ Ask students to discuss the orienteering activity with friends and family. Encourage them to create an orienteering course with at least four locations and questions about fitness that their friends or family members must answer.
- ▶ Use the FITT Homework Assignment to apply concepts taught.

Assessment

This activity is itself an assessment. To check that all students worked together on the activity, ask a few of the Heart Smart Orienteering Questions as students line up to be dismissed for the day:

- ▶ Who can tell me what each of the letters in FITT stands for?
- ▶ What is one warning sign for a heart attack or stroke?
- ▶ Name three aerobic activities.

INTERMEDIATE

FITT principles—Frequency, intensity, time, and type are all used to develop health-related fitness. Finding the time needed to work out is sometimes difficult.

Background

This activity is a perfect one to use in spring around mid-March. Fitness assessments are usually done in April, so this activity is another way to prepare your students to do their best. By having the health-related fitness areas set up during a school day, teachers can bring classes to this area for a learning break where students will have a chance to exercise and work on health-related fitness areas.

Purpose

▶ Students will be able to perform health-related fitness assessments and work on their intensity level for each area.

▶ Students will know what assessment measures a specific area of fitness.

Relationship to National Standards

▶ Physical education standard 3: Participates regularly in physical activity.

▶ Physical education standard 4: Achieves and maintains a health-enhancing level of physical fitness.

▶ Health education standard 2: Students will demonstrate the ability to practice health-enhancing behaviors and reduce health risks.

Equipment

▶ Mats for floor work

▶ Sit-and-reach box

▶ Bar for bar hang or pull-ups

▶ Timer

▶ Six short paddles (e.g., ping-pong paddles) and six Wiffle balls

▶ Six basketballs

▶ Six volleyballs

▶ Stopwatch

▶ Pedometers (optional) to count steps

▶ Heart rate monitors (optional) to keep track of heart rate

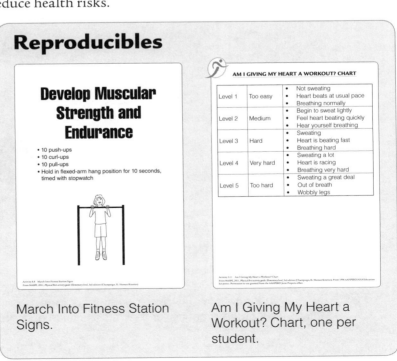

Reproducibles

March Into Fitness Station Signs.

Am I Giving My Heart a Workout? Chart, one per student.

Procedure

Before implementing this program be sure to include the principal and the classroom teacher. Safety issues of supervision, equipment setup and takedown, and scheduling need to be addressed before beginning. A sign-up sheet can be posted by the facility door for teachers to sign up for times when their students will be using the mini gym.

1. The six fitness stations can be set up for classroom teachers to schedule a time for their classes to take a fitness break. The stations can be placed outside, in a cafeteria, in a stage area, or at another place that isn't used during the day by other classes. Set up the equipment in the morning and put it away for storage as needed.

2. Students may be allowed personal time out from core classroom activities to work on fitness areas when adequate supervision is available. Provide a sign-up sheet to help classroom teachers schedule when they will use the mini gym.

3. The class can be divided into two groups. One group does the class lesson while the second group does the mini-gym activities. Groups change before the end of the class period. This approach could be used by a classroom teacher or a physical education teacher, depending on the lesson.

4. Students perform an activity at a station for one minute and then rotate to the next area. Set an egg timer set for one minute.

5. Each student should make it around the course at least twice.

March is a month of preparing for the physical fitness testing that usually comes in April. Help students prepare by setting up a circuit that classroom teachers can use any day of the week. This way, students get physical activity and get to practice for their fitness tests outside of PE class.

Teaching Hints

▶ Remind students that they are working on health-related fitness areas—the areas that they will want to be strong throughout their lives.

▶ Review the FITT principle and encourage them to try their best to improve their abilities.

Sample Inclusion Tips

▶ Be sure that a schedule of teachers or aides supervising the area is developed and given to all supervisors ahead of time. Remind supervisors the day before of the schedule and review their responsibilities with them. Make sure all understand that no activities will take place if supervision is not present.

▶ Use Velcro mitts and gloves for play by students with special needs.

▶ Use a partner for the basketball and volleyball activities who can help retrieve balls. Also use lighter-weight basketballs for shooting or a beach ball for hitting or catching.

▶ For pull-ups, use small hand weights or gloves with weights inside them.

Variation

If the class is divided into groups for games or activities, have one group work on the fitness stations.

Home Extension

Discuss with students the possibility of creating fitness stations at home where the family can all practice good fitness activities. Have students report back to class what they did.

Assessment

▶ Question students to see whether they know what area of health-related fitness each test measures.

▶ Have students use the Am I Giving My Heart a Workout? Chart for a self-evaluation of their workout.

EXERCISE YOUR RIGHTS DAY

PRIMARY AND INTERMEDIATE

Schoolwide exercise—The aim of this activity is to create a campaign with the students or the entire school to emphasize the importance of incorporating physical activity into the work environment. The campaign is called Exercise Your Rights Day.

Background

The Bill of Rights came into effect on December 15, 1791. This document lists the most important rights of the citizens of the United States. Among these are freedom of religion, freedom of speech, and freedom of the press. For more information search "Bill of Rights."

Purpose

▶ Students will recognize the importance of incorporating exercise into their daily routine.

▶ Students will know the health benefits of exercises.

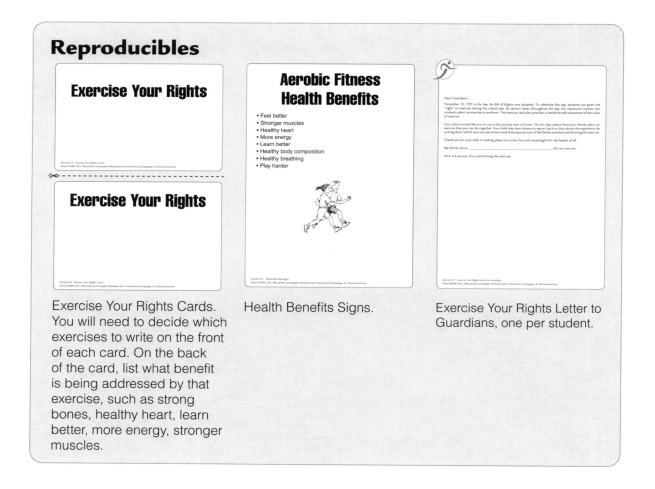

Reproducibles

Exercise Your Rights Cards. You will need to decide which exercises to write on the front of each card. On the back of the card, list what benefit is being addressed by that exercise, such as strong bones, healthy heart, learn better, more energy, stronger muscles.

Health Benefits Signs.

Exercise Your Rights Letter to Guardians, one per student.

Relationship to National Standards

▶ Physical education standard 3: Participates regularly in physical activity.

▶ Physical education standard 6: Values physical activity for health, enjoyment, challenge, self-expression, and/or social interaction.

▶ Health education standard 5: Students will demonstrate the ability to use interpersonal communications skills to enhance health and avoid or reduce health risks.

▶ Health education standard 7: Students will demonstrate the ability to advocate for personal, family, and community health.

Equipment

Each classroom teacher will work with their students to decide what activities to do, and they can work with you if they need equipment beyond what they have in their classrooms.

Procedure

1. Every classroom has five different Exercise Your Rights Cards.
2. The classroom teachers and classes decide what exercises they want to do during the class period.
3. The classroom teacher writes the exercises on the back of the cards. If the classroom teacher is having trouble doing this, you can provide guidance or prepare the cards.
4. At an appropriate time, the classroom teacher allows a student to draw a card. The whole class then performs the exercise given on the card.

All kids in school get a workout, practice making decisions, and experience freedom of choice in Exercise Your Rights.

Teaching Hints

▶ Give each classroom teacher a poster that will help him or her discuss with students the benefits of exercise.

▶ Classroom teachers should talk to the class at the beginning of the day about the poster and the benefits that it lists.

▶ Remind classroom teachers that exercises chosen need to be able to be performed in a classroom setting.

Sample Inclusion Tip

Include an exercise that someone with special needs can participate in easily.

Variations

▶ Have each class design a poster to help them remember the day and the health benefits.

▶ Make a list of exercises that students can pick from. This list can help the classroom teachers develop the exercise cards with students.

Home Extension

Have a letter ready to send home to guardians at the end of the day to explain the Exercise Your Rights Day activity.

Assessment

▶ Ask the classroom teachers how the day went for their classes.

▶ Ask the classroom teachers whether the students understood how exercise benefits the body.

PRIMARY AND INTERMEDIATE

Cooperative learning—Participation in a group fitness activity.

Background

ACES Day—ACES stands for All Children Exercising Simultaneously. Throughout the world, youth celebrate Project ACES Day every year on the first Wednesday of May. Many schools perform all-school continuous physical activity programs on ACES Day. Anyone can visit the ACES Web site (www.projectaces.com) for suggested activities, testimonials, and easy ways to develop an ACES Day event.

Everybody participates in a minimum of 15 minutes of exercise of some type. Many schools also try to perform the activity at 10:00 a.m., a time when they know that thousands of other youth in hundreds of other schools worldwide are also participating. If a school cannot have the event at 10:00 or on the designated ACES Day, the school and teachers are encouraged to pick a different day or time and have their own special ACES program. The goal is to develop a special fun fitness activity that can include as many teachers, staff, and students as possible.

This event can take place in classrooms, a gym, or outdoors—anywhere there is space to move. It is best to pick an area where several classes can participate together, such as in a gym, because the camaraderie adds to the experience.

Purpose

▶ Students will be able to recognize and use exercise routines as a way to enhance physical fitness.

▶ Students will understand the importance of participating in a moderate to vigorous physical activity with others to gain motivation to be physically active.

▶ Students will gain experience performing movement activities to music and with groups.

Relationship to National Standards

▶ Physical education standard 3: Participates regularly in physical activity.

▶ Health education standard 3: Students will demonstrate the ability to practice health-enhancing behaviors and reduce health risks.

Equipment

▶ Fast-moving music and a music player

▶ A microphone for the leader. The activity could also be broadcast over the public address (PA) system, or over the school television into the various classrooms.

Procedure

1. Briefly talk about the importance of physical fitness and group activities as ways to help people stay motivated.

Reproducible

Energize With Exercise Routine, one for each leader.

2. Discuss ACES Day and give background information about it. The Energize With Exercise Routine offers one activity that a class or an entire school can undertake to be active for 15 minutes.

3. Designate a time and place for the ACES event and encourage administrators, teachers, and staff to be involved in helping plan, advertise, and participate in the activity.

4. Designate a leader for the event who will call out the various movements in the routine and possibly demonstrate the various movements found in the 15-minute routine outlined in the reproducible. You can be the leader, as could a principal or a favorite staff member at the school. The leader may revise the routine to fit the needs of the participants.

5. Have the leader learn the movements in the routine so that she or he can give good and timely cues regarding transitions in the routine.

6. Have all participants spread out at least arm's length apart facing the leader. Or, if the routine is to be broadcast, have participants move to where they have the freedom to move a few steps in all directions.

7. When the music starts, the leader goes through each of the steps listed in the Energize With Exercise Routine in the order written and using the designated number of repetitions.

8. When the routine is completed, the leader can suggest that the participants high-five one another and pat themselves on the back for a job well done!

Teaching Hints

▶ Enforce safety during movement by making sure that there is enough room between participants, that all participants are wearing appropriate clothing and shoes, and that all can hear and see the leader.

ACES Day encourages all students to be active together and celebrate with activities such as exercise routines set to music.

▶ Be sure to invite all staff, administrators, and classroom teachers to be a part of the activity. The participation of classroom teachers and staff is especially motivating to students.

▶ Before starting, the leader should review the steps briefly so that all participants are familiar with the various movements and transitions. While the leader is teaching the steps, the second leader (see "Sample Inclusion Tip") could be performing the modifications for those who might need them.

Sample Inclusion Tip

Think ahead regarding students and staff who may need some steps to be adapted. Identify a second leader who will also stand in the front and will show various types of modifications at the appropriate times during the routine.

Home Extensions

▶ Encourage the students to tell their families about ACES Day and what the letters stand for.

▶ Suggest that students try doing the routine that they learned at school with their families, or that they go to the ACES Day Web site for more ideas.

Assessment

▶ Ask the students what ACES stands for, why they are part of an ACES Day Celebration, why it is important to exercise, and what motivates them to exercise.

▶ Ask the students what types of physical activity contribute to a healthy body.

▶ Ask the participants to name some of their favorite exercises that they remember doing in the routine.

MARVELOUS MUSCLES FOR SUMMER

INTERMEDIATE

Specificity—Specificity refers to the kind of activity that you do. When working on muscles, the muscles that you exercise are specific to the activity.

Background

Summer is a time for students to be active. By relating exercises to summer fun activities, students are able to see that health-related fitness is used all year. The areas of muscular strength and endurance, flexibility, and aerobic fitness are used daily and not just in school.

Purpose

Students will be able to list exercises or activities that develop specific muscle groups.

Relationship to National Standards

▶ Physical education standard 4: Achieves and maintains a health-enhancing level of physical fitness.

▶ Health education standard 3: Students will demonstrate the ability to practice health-enhancing behaviors and reduce health risks.

Equipment

▶ One carpet square for each pair of students at station 3

▶ One short rope for each pair of students at station 3

▶ Three long ropes

▶ Five cones

▶ One popper (see "Teaching Hints") for each student at station 1

▶ 15 beanbags

▶ One scarf for every three students at station 4

▶ Mats, as needed for floor exercises

▶ One stability ball for each student at station 6

▶ One or two scooters

▶ Pedometers (optional) to keep track of steps taken during all activities

Reproducibles

Popper Steps
Pop and Run for Fast Feet

Poppers are round rubber circles. When they are turned wrong side out, a few moments pass before they jump in the air. Put the popper inside out and place it on the ground. Do foot fire with your feet by stepping on one foot and then the other as fast as you can. See how many steps you can do before the popper pops. Don't burn your feet in the hot sand!

Marvelous Muscles for Summer Station Signs.

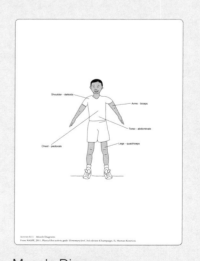

Muscle Diagrams.

Procedure

1. Explain and set up the six stations around the room.
2. Post the labeled Muscle Diagrams at each station in the gym so that students can look up which muscles they are using.
3. Have students determine what muscle group was used with the exercise at the end of each station. Students will be asked at the end of the circuit to give answers for the assessment.
4. Have students travel around to all six stations.

Teaching Hints

▶ Poppers are round rubber circles. When they are turned wrong side out, a few moments pass before they jump in the air.
▶ Review the definition of specificity. Explain that students will be putting this definition into practice today as they perform exercises that work specific muscle groups.

Students use specific muscles to get ready for summer fun. Marvelous Muscles for Summer helps students learn that good health and fitness are things to work on all year long, not just at school.

Sample Inclusion Tips

▶ Use two scooters to hold students who have balance difficulties.
▶ Students with mobility problems can substitute hands going up and down instead of doing foot fire with feet.

Variation

Have students create their own station ideas to improve muscular strength and endurance. Students should be able to explain why they chose that activity and how it relates to muscular strength and endurance. Additionally, have students look for activities or chores that they do at home and explain what muscles they are using during the activity.

Home Extension

Ask students to develop some kind of summer wave with their families. They can report back to the class what muscle group their exercise worked.

Assessment

Go over all the activities at each station and ask questions about the exercise and muscles used. Have students give a thumbs-up if a specific exercise works a certain muscle group and a thumbs-down if it doesn't.

▶ Abdominals—Push-Up Wave
▶ Triceps and biceps—Push-Up Wave
▶ Abdominals—Feed the Dolphins

DASH FOR CASH

PRIMARY AND INTERMEDIATE

Health-related fitness components—The health-related fitness components of muscular strength and endurance, flexibility, and aerobic fitness are used not only in activities but in school and everyday life. Knowing how to employ each of the components in a fitness routine is important for all-around health.

Background

May or June—End of the year celebration. The Physical Best program provides teachers and students with a variety of enjoyable fitness development activities while meeting school, school district, state, and national standards for physical education. After a full year of learning Physical Best education concepts, participating in health-related fitness assessment activities, and setting personal goals to maintain or improve fitness levels and healthy habits, students need a fun physical activity to celebrate their year of "moving to learn" and "learning to move." Dash for Cash integrates health-related fitness components and math skills in an action-packed activity.

Purpose

All students are active and make healthy and personally meaningful fitness choices while learning about the value of money and honesty.

Relationship to National Standards

- ▶ Physical education standard 3: Participates regularly in physical activity.
- ▶ Physical education standard 4: Achieves and maintains a health-enhancing level of fitness.

Equipment

- ▶ One box for the bank
- ▶ Copy and laminate 100 $1 bills. You cannot legally copy real $1 bills, so use play money to make your copies or buy some play money from a store.
- ▶ Three tumbling mats
- ▶ Six jump ropes
- ▶ Aerobic steps (or folded mats)
- ▶ Beanbags
- ▶ Fun, fast-paced music focusing on summer fun (any song by the Beach Boys) and music player
- ▶ Activity equipment for free-choice stations
- ▶ Pedometers (optional) to track the number of steps that students take while working on their fitness levels

Reproducible

Aerobic Fitness

Stay active for two minutes. Watch the clock!

- Develop a short jump rope routine. Try to put together 5 to 10 of the jump rope skills that you have learned this year in physical education class.
- Use the aerobic steps or a folded mat and keep stepping for two minutes. Add your arms to increase the intensity of your workout.

Activity 8.12 Dash for Cash Fitness Station Signs
From NASPE, 2011, *Physical Best activity guide: Elementary level*, 3rd edition (Champaign, IL: Human Kinetics)

Dash for Cash Fitness Station Signs.

Procedure

1. Place the Dash for Cash Fitness Station Signs and equipment around the activity area.

2. Students line up around the perimeter of the activity area on the boundary lines if available.

3. The banker (you) stands at one end of the activity area with money in the banker's box.

4. Students walk, jog, or run around the perimeter of the activity area at a pace that is good for them. Each time students complete one lap, they receive $1 from the banker.

5. After students complete three laps, they can choose either to keep moving or to pay the banker and go to one of the health-related fitness stations to exercise.

6. The object of the activity is for students to participate in all the health-related fitness stations before the allotted time is up. Participation at each station costs $3 (much like the monthly fee that adults pay to join a fitness club).

7. Students pay the banker each time they go to a new fitness station. Students can choose various strategies for participation. They can move aerobically and receive lots of money before spending it to participate in the fitness stations, or they can move, exercise, move, exercise, until they are finished.

8. If time remains after some students are done with the fitness stations, add a few free choice stations that might cost more money ($5) and let students choose a favorite motor skill or piece of equipment to work with (rock wall, juggling scarves, tennis skills, two-square, and so on).

Teaching Hints

▶ With slight modifications, this activity can be used with all elementary grades. Primary students need more time to complete the activity. They also need a different menu of exercises and activities to participate in based on their ability levels. You should be the banker with younger students to make sure that all students receive and spend the correct amount of money. When students are ready to participate in a fitness station, they will count the money back to you.

▶ Pairing up intermediate and primary classes is another way that younger students can participate in the activity. You would need to work out the schedule for this activity ahead of time with classroom teachers.

Dash for Cash combines health-related fitness concepts and math skills for an interdisciplinary activity.

▶ This activity teaches the life skill of honesty. After intermediate students have participated in the activity with your help, try it without a banker at the box. Building trust with students is a benefit to this modification. This approach also allows you to monitor the fitness stations better.

▶ Make some copies of larger bills ($5 and $10) and give those out to students as you see fit (developing a steady pace while moving, helping another student, working with a student with special needs, putting equipment away properly, and so forth).

▶ Talk about intensity with your students on day 2. Challenge students to work a little harder and make more money so that they have time to participate in one of the free choice stations.

▶ If you teach using skill themes, create motor-skill stations (catch, throw, strike, dribble, and so on) as part of your free choice stations.

▶ Dash for Cash would be a great activity for a family fitness night to promote National Physical Fitness and Sports Month. Create some free choice sport stations for families to participate in.

▶ You also can use Dash for Cash at the end of the year to promote lifelong and leisure (recreational) activities that students may want to participate in during the upcoming summer months. With this variation, each activity has a different dollar value depending on the intensity of the activity (bowling $3, rock wall $5, beach ball volleyball $6, tennis striking skills $7, and so on). Post signs at each station with the name of the activity, directions, and cost to play. You may also want to post a menu of activities at the bank so that students can read the activities and their cost each time they complete a lap.

Sample Inclusion Tips

▶ A student in a wheelchair could receive $2 per lap rather than $1 because it takes them longer to complete the task.

▶ Working with a peer helper will help keep students with a disability safe and more comfortable as they move around the perimeter of the activity area.

Home Extension

Have the students talk about the activity with their guardians and other family members and explain how they used their cash. Encourage the students to discuss with their families how various people do their exercise programs and whether they pay a certain amount of money to use fitness equipment and participate in fitness programs.

Assessment

▶ Have students name one aerobic, flexibility, and muscular strength and endurance activity that they performed.

▶ Ask students how they increased their intensity at one of the fitness stations.

SUMMER FUN–SUMMER SHAPE-UP CHALLENGE

PRIMARY AND INTERMEDIATE

FITT principles—The overload principle states that a body system (cardiorespiratory, muscular, or skeletal) must perform at a level beyond normal so that it can adapt and improve physiological function and fitness. Progression refers to *how* a person should increase overload. Proper progression involves a gradual increase in the level of exercise that is manipulated by increasing frequency, intensity, time, and type, or a combination of more than one of these components.

Background

Physical fitness is a journey, not a destination! The school year may have ended, but we want students to develop active, healthy lifestyles year round. They can join in the fun by participating in the Summer Fun–Summer Shape-Up Challenge with their families, friends, neighbors, or community.

Purpose

Students will chart exercise through the summer to help develop healthy active lifestyles year round.

Relationship to National Standards

▶ Physical education standard 3: Participates regularly in physical activity.

▶ Health education standard 3: Students will demonstrate the ability to practice health-enhancing behaviors and reduce health risks.

Equipment

None

Procedure

1. Use school letterhead or decorative summer-themed paper to create your Summer Fun–Summer Shape-Up Challenge.

2. Hand out the Summer Fun—Summer Shape-Up Challenge Activity Sheet to each class during the last week of school. Challenge students to try the activity for two months. Invite them to return their completed challenge sheets when the new school year begins.

Teaching Hint

▶ You can create a calendar to change the format of the challenge.

▶ You can develop a completely new set of activities for each month.

▶ Incorporate academic strategies (reading, writing, math) that your school has focused on during the year into the challenge activity.

Summer Fun–Summer Shape-Up Challenge Activity Sheet, one per student.

▶ Incorporate personal responsibility, life skills, or character education traits that your school has focused on during the year into the challenge activity (national standards for physical education 5 and 6).

Sample Inclusion Tip

Send a letter to guardians offering modifications for students with special needs (refer to the Tips for Inclusion sidebar in chapter 1). Give examples of activities that these children have accomplished in physical education class during the year.

Home Extension

This activity is a true home extension. Encourage your students to show the materials to their families and begin the fun! Remind them that you will discuss the results of their summer workouts during class when school starts again in the fall.

The Summer Fun–Summer Shape-Up Challenge encourages students to stay physically active all summer long with a take-home list of activity suggestions.

© Bold Stock/age fotostock

Assessment

▶ At the start of the new school year, discuss the summer challenge with returning students. Ask for feedback on participation and physical activities in which the students participated during the summer.

▶ Collect completed activity sheets and discuss observations about activities and their connection to classroom subject matter.

APPENDIX
NATIONAL OBSERVANCES RELATED TO PHYSICAL ACTIVITY

Many national and local observances are related to physical activity and nutrition. A few of these are listed here. Numerous Web sites describe these events in detail. You are encouraged to use a search engine and learn more about these and other useful resources that can enhance children's learning about health-related fitness and wellness.

FEBRUARY

American Heart Month
American Heart Association
www.heart.org

First Thursday
Girls and Women in Sports Day
Women's Sports Foundation
www.womenssportsfoundation.org

MARCH

National Nutrition Month
American Dietetic Association
www.eatright.org

APRIL

National Youth Sports Safety Month
National Youth Sports Safety Foundation
www.nyssf.org

April 7
World Health Day
American Association for World Health
www.thebody.com/content/art33029.html

First full week
National Public Health Week
American Public Health Association
www.apha.org

Third week
National Turn Off the TV Week
Center for Screen-Time Awareness
www.tvturnoff.org

MAY

National Physical Fitness and Sports Month
President's Council on Physical Fitness and Sports
www.fitness.gov
National Bike Month
League of American Bicyclists
www.bikeleague.org
National High Blood Pressure Education Month
National Heart, Lung, and Blood Institute
www.nhlbi.nih.gov

First week
National Physical Education and Sports Week
National Association for Sport and Physical Education
www.aahperd.org/naspe

First Wednesday
All Children Exercise Simultaneously Day (Project ACES)
Youth Fitness Coalition, Inc.
www.coordinatedfitnesssystems.com/yfc_page/hjsyfc.html

First Saturday

Parents and Children Exercise Simultaneously Day (PACES Day)
Youth Fitness Coalition, Inc.
www.coordinatedfitnesssystems.com/yfc_page/hjsyfc.html

Second week

American Running and Fitness Week
American Running and Fitness Association
www.americanrunning.org

Third Wednesday

National Employee Health and Fitness Day
National Association for Health and Fitness
www.physicalfitness.org

Fourth week

National Water Fitness Week
U.S. Water Fitness Association, Inc.
www.uswfa.com

JULY

National Recreation and Parks Month
National Recreation and Park Association
www.nrpa.org

Third week

National Youth Sports Week
National Recreation and Park Association
www.nrpa.org

SEPTEMBER

National Childhood Obesity Awareness Month
American Association for Physical Activity and Recreation
www.aahperd.org/aapar/news/newItems/obesity-awareness-month.cfm
Healthier Kids, Brighter Futures
www.healthierkidsbrighterfutures.org/

National Cholesterol Education Month
National Heart, Lung, and Blood Institute
www.nhlbi.nih.gov

Third week

National Turn Off the TV Week
Center for Screen-Time Awareness
www.tvturnoff.org

Last Sunday

Family Health and Fitness Day
Health Information Resource Center
www.fitnessday.com/family

OCTOBER

Family Health Month
American Academy of Family Physicians
www.aafp.org/online/en/home.html

Walk to School Month
National Center for Safe Routes to School
www.saferoutesinfo.org

First weekend

American Heart Walking Event
American Heart Association
www.heart.org

First Monday

Child Health Day
National Institute of Child Health and Human Development
www.nichd.nih.gov

Third Sunday

World Walking Day
Trim and Fitness International Sport Association (TAFISA), Frankfurt, Germany
www.tafisa.net

NOVEMBER

American Diabetes Month
American Diabetes Association
www.diabetes.org

REFERENCES AND RESOURCES

AAHPERD. 1999. *Physical Best activity guide elementary level.* Champaign, IL: Human Kinetics.

American Academy of Pediatrics (AAP) Committee on Sports Medicine and Fitness. 2001. "Policy Statement: Strength Training by Children and Adolescents." *Pediatrics* 107 (6): 1470-1472.

American College of Sports Medicine (ACSM). 2010. *ACSM's Guidelines for exercise testing and prescription* (7th ed.). Baltimore: Lippincott, Williams and Wilkins.

Bailey, B.C., Olson, J., Pepper, S.L., Porszaz, J., Barstow, T.J., & Cooper, D.M. 1995. The Level and Tempo of Children's Physical Activities: An Observational Study. *Medicine and science in sport and exercise* 27: 1033-1041.

Ballinger, D., Bishop, J., & Borsdorf, L. 2008. *Goal setting strategies for K–12 learners using Physical Best and FITNESS-GRAM resources.* Fort Worth, TX: AAHPERD National Convention.

Bar-Or, O. 1993. "Importance of Differences Between Children and Adults for Exercise Testing and Exercise Prescription." pp. 57-74 in *Exercise testing and exercise prescription for special cases,* 2nd edition, ed. J.S. Skinner. Philadelphia, PA: Lea and Febiger.

Bar-Or, O. 1994. "Childhood and Adolescent Physical Activity and Fitness and Adult Risk Profile." pp. 931-942 in *International proceedings and consensus statement,* ed. C. Bouchard, R.J. Shephard, and T. Stephens. Champaign, IL: Human Kinetics.

Bar-Or, O., & Malina, R.M. 1995. "Activity, Health and Fitness of Children and Adolescents." pp. 79-123 in *Child health, nutrition, and physical activity,* ed. L. WY. Cheung, J.B. Richmond. Champaign, IL: Human Kinetics.

Bass, R., Brown, D., Laurson, K., and Coleman, M. 2010. "Relationships Between Physical Fitness and Academic Achievement in Middle School Students." *Medicine and Science and Exercise 42*(5): 524.

Blair, S.N., Kohl, 3rd, H.W., Barlow, C.E., Paffenbarger, Jr., R.S., Gibbons, L.W., and Macera, C.A. 1995. "Changes in Physical Fitness and All-Cause Mortality: A Prospective Study of Healthy and Unhealthy Men." *JAMA* 273: 1093-1098.

Blanchard, Y. 1999. *Health-Related Fitness for Children and Adults with Cerebral Palsy. American College of Sports Medicine* current comment, August.

Bompa, T.O. 2000. *Total training for young champions.* Champaign, IL: Human Kinetics.

Boreham, C.A., Twisk, J., Savage, M., Cran, G.W., & Strain, J.J. 1997. "Physical Activity, Sports Participation, and Risk Factors in Adolescents." *Medicine and science in sport and exercise* 29: 788-793.

Boreham, C.A., Twisk, J., Murray, L., Savage, M., Strain, J.J., & Cran, G.W. 2001. "Fitness, Fatness, and Coronary Heart Disease Risk in Adolescents: The Northern Ireland Young Hearts Project." *Medicine and science in sport and exercise* 33: 270-274.

California Department of Education. 2002. www.cde.ca.gov/news/releases2002/re137.asp

Centers for Disease Control and Prevention (2004, September 17). *Morbidity and Mortality Weekly Report, 53*(36), 844–847.

The Cooper Institute. 2007. *FITNESSGRAM/ACTIVITY-GRAM test administration manual* (4th ed.), ed. Gregory Welk and Marilu D. Meredith. Champaign, IL: Human Kinetics.

The Cooper Institute. 2005. *FITNESSGRAM/ACTIVITY-GRAM test administration manual,* ed. Gregory J. Welk and Marilu D. Meredith. Champaign, IL: Human Kinetics.

The Cooper Institute. 2004. *FITNESSGRAM/ACTIVITY GRAM test administration manual* (3rd ed.), ed. Gregory J. Welk and Marilu D. Meredith. Champaign, IL: Human Kinetics.

Corbin, C.B. 2010. The New Physical Activity Pyramid for Kids (poster). Champaign, IL: Human Kinetics.

Corbin, C.B., & Lindsey, R. 2005. *Fitness for life* (5th ed.). Champaign, IL: Human Kinetics.

Corbin, C.B., & Pangrazi, R.P. 2002. Physical Activity for Children: How Much is Enough? In *FITNESSGRAM reference guide,* ed. G.J. Welk, R.J. Morrow, and H.B. Falls, 7. Dallas: The Cooper Institute.

Corbin, C., & Pangrazi, R. (1997). *Teaching strategies for improving youth fitness* (2nd ed.). Dallas, TX: Fitnessgram.

Cox, R.H. (2007). *Sport psychology: Concepts and applications* (6th ed.). Boston: McGraw-Hill.

Ernst, M.P., Corbin, C.B., Beighle, A., & Pangrazi, R.P. (2006). Appropriate and inappropriate uses of *FITNESS-GRAM*: A commentary. *Journal of Physical Activity and Health,* 3(Suppl. 2), S90–S100. Champaign, IL: Human Kinetics.

Faigenbaum, A.D., Kraemer, W.J., Cahill, B., Chandler, J., Dziados, J., Elfink, L.D., Forman, E. et al. 1996. Youth resistance training: Position statement paper and literature review. *Strength and conditioning* 18(6): 62-75.

Gardner, H. 1993. *Multiple intelligences: The theory in practice.* New York: Basic Books.

Graham, G., Holt/Hale, S., & Parker, M. 2010. *Children moving: A reflective approach to teaching physical education* (8th ed.). New York: McGraw-Hill.

Hass, C.J., Faigenbaum, M.S., & Franklin, B.A. 2001. Prescription of Resistance Training for Healthy Populations. *Sports medicine* 31(14): 953-964.

Hoeger, W.K., & Hoeger, S.A. 2011. *Lifetime physical fitness and wellness: A personalized program* (11th ed.). Belmont, CA: Wadsworth Cengage Learning.

Joint Commission on National Health Education Standards. 2007. *National health education standards: Achieving excellence* (2nd ed.). Atlanta, GA: American Cancer Society. Available: www.cdc.gov/healthy_youth/sher/standards/index.htm.

Joint Committee on National Health Education Standards. 1995. National health education standards. *Achieving health literacy.* Atlanta, GA: American Cancer Society.

Knudson, D.V., Magnusson, P., & McHugh, M. 2000. "Current Issues in Flexibility Fitness." pp. 1-8 in *The President's council on physical fitness and sports digest,* series 3, no. 10, ed. C. Corbin and B. Pangrazi. Washington, DC: Department of Health and Human Services.

Kraemer, W. J., & Fleck, S.J. 1993. *Strength training for young adults.* Champaign, IL: Human Kinetics.

Meeks, L., Hiect, P., & Page, R. 2007. *Comprehensive school health education* (5th ed.). Boston: McGraw-Hill.

National Association for Sport and Physical Education (NASPE). 2011. *Physical Best activity guide: Middle and high school levels* (3rd ed.). Champaign, IL: Human Kinetics.

National Association for Sport and Physical Education (NASPE). 2011. *Physical education for lifelong fitness: The Physical Best teacher's guide* (3rd ed.). Champaign, IL: Human Kinetics.

National Association for Sport and Physical Education (NASPE). 2010. *Active kids and academic performance.* Reston, VA: Author.

National Association for Sport and Physical Education (NASPE). 2004b. *Moving into the future: National standards for physical education* (2nd ed.). Reston, VA: Author.

National Association for Sport and Physical Education (NASPE). 2004a. *Physical activity for children: A statement of guidelines for children ages 5-12* (2nd ed.). Reston, VA: Author.

National Association for Sport and Physical Education (NASPE). 1999. *Physical Best activity guide: Elementary level* (2nd ed.). Champaign, IL: Human Kinetics.

National Association for Sport and Physical Education (NASPE). 1992. *Outcomes of quality physical education programs.* Reston, VA: Author.

National Dance Association (NDA). 1996. National standards for dance education: What every young American should *know and be able to do in dance.* Reston, VA: Author.

National Strength and Conditioning Association (NSCA). 1985. "Position Statement on Prepubescent Strength Training." *National strength and conditioning association journal* 7: 27-31.

Plowman, S.A., Sterling, C.L., Corbin, C.B., Meredith, M.D., Welk, G.J., & Morrow, J.R.

2006. The history of *FITNESSGRAM. Journal of physical activity and health,* 3(Suppl. 2), S5–S20. Champaign, IL: Human Kinetics.

Rowland, T.W. 1996. *Developmental exercise physiology.* Champaign, IL: Human Kinetics.

Sothenn, M.S., Loftin, M., Suskind, R.M., Udall, J.N., & Becker, U. 1999. "The Health Benefits of Physical Activity in Children and Adolescents: Implications for Chronic Disease Prevention." *European journal of pediatrics* 158: 271-274.

U.S. Department of Agriculture, Food and Nutrition Service. 2005. MyPyramid. www.mypyramid.gov.

U.S. Department of Health and Human Services (USDHHS). 1996. "Physical Activity and Health: A Report of the Surgeon General." U.S. Department of Health and Human Services, Centers for Disease Control and Prevention, National Center for Chronic Disease Prevention and Health Promotion. Atlanta: U.S. Department of Health and Human Services, Government Printing Office.

U.S. Department of Health and Human Services (USDHHS). 2008. *Physical activity guidelines for Americans: Active children and adolescents.* Available: www.health.gov/paguidelines/guidelines/chapter3.aspx.

Weiss, M. 2000. "Motivating Kids in Physical Activity," Research digest (President's Council on Physical Fitness and Sports), 3; 11, www. fitness.gov/digest900.pdf.

Welk, G. 1999. The youth physical activity promotion model: A conceptual bridge between theory and practice, *Quest,* 51, 5–23.

Werner, W., Hoeger, K., and Hoeger, S.A. 2011. *Lifetime physical fitness & wellness: A personalized program* (11th ed.). Belmont, CA: Wadsworth.

Wilson, G., McKay, H., Waddell, L., Notte, J., & Petit, M. 2000. The Health Benefits of a "Healthy Bones" Physical Education Curriculum. In *Physical and health education,* Autumn.

Winnick, J.P., & Short, F.X., eds. 1999. *The Brockport physical fitness training guide.* Champaign, IL: Human Kinetics.

Zwiren, L.D. 1988. "Exercise Prescription for Children." pp. 309-14 in *Resource Manual for guidelines for exercise testing and prescription,* ed. American College of Sports Medicine. Philadelphia: Lea and Febiger.

ABOUT THE AUTHOR

The National Association for Sport and Physical Education (NASPE), a nonprofit professional organization, is an association of the American Alliance for Health, Physical Education, Recreation and Dance. NASPE is dedicated to educating the general public about the importance of physical education for all young people. Through its members as well as corporate and public partnerships, NASPE develops and supports sport and physical activity programs that promote healthy behaviors and individual well-being. NASPE's 15,000 members include K-12 physical educators, college and university faculty, researchers, coaches, athletic directors, and trainers.

Physical Best is a comprehensive health-related fitness education program developed by physical educators for physical educators. Physical Best was designed to educate, challenge, and encourage all children in the knowledge, skills, and attitudes needed for a healthy and fit life. The program helps students move from dependence to independence and take responsibility for their own health and fitness. Physical Best educates all children regardless of athletic talent or physical and mental abilities or disabilities. This program is implemented through high-quality resources and professional development workshops for physical educators.

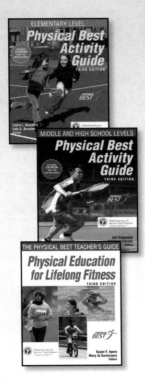

HOW TO USE THIS CD-ROM

You can use this CD-ROM on either a Windows-based PC or a Macintosh computer.

SYSTEM REQUIREMENTS

Windows

- ▶ IBM PC compatible with Pentium processor
- ▶ Windows 2000/XP/Vista/7
- ▶ Adobe Reader 8.0
- ▶ Microsoft Office PowerPoint 2003 or higher
- ▶ 4x CD-ROM drive

Macintosh

- ▶ Power Mac recommended
- ▶ System 10.4 or higher
- ▶ Adobe Reader
- ▶ Microsoft Office PowerPoint 2004 for MAC or higher
- ▶ 4x CD-ROM drive

USER INSTRUCTIONS

Windows

1. Insert the *Physical Best Activity Guide: Elementary Level, Third Edition* CD-ROM. (Note: The CD-ROM must be present in the drive at all times.)
2. Select the My Computer icon from the desktop.
3. Select the CD-ROM drive.
4. Open the file you wish to view. See the 00Start.pdf file for a list of the contents.

Macintosh

1. Insert the *Physical Best Activity Guide: Elementary Level, Third Edition* CD-ROM. (Note: The CD-ROM must be present in the drive at all times.)
2. Double-click the CD icon located on the desktop.
3. Open the file you wish to view. See the 00Start file for a list of the contents.

For customer support, contact Technical Support:

Phone: 217-351-5076 Monday through Friday (excluding holidays) between 7:00 a.m. and 7:00 p.m. (CST).

Fax: 217-351-2674

E-mail: support@hkusa.com